1 -

2

-8

16 NOV

THE CELL

COLIN FORBES

THE CELL

**SIMON &
SCHUSTER**

LONDON · SYDNEY · NEW YORK · TOKYO · SINGAPORE · TORONTO

First published in Great Britain by Simon & Schuster UK Ltd, 2002
An imprint of Simon & Schuster UK Ltd
A Viacom Company

1 3 5 7 9 10 8 6 4 2

Simon & Schuster UK Ltd
Africa House
64–78 Kingsway
London WC2B 6AH

www.simonsays.co.uk

Simon & Schuster Australia
Sydney

A CIP catalogue record for this book is available
from the British Library

Hardback ISBN 0-7432-3181-3
Trade Paperback ISBN 0-7432-3182-1

Typeset by Palimpsest Book Production Limited,
Polmont, Stirlingshire
Printed and bound in Great Britain by
The Bath Press, Bath

Author's Note

All the characters portrayed are creatures of the author's imagination and bear no relationship to any living person.

The same principle of pure invention applies to all the residences, villages, hotels, institutions and apartments in Great Britain and Italy.

Prologue

'It is now three weeks since Linda Warner, wife of the Minister for Home Security, disappeared overnight,' Superintendent Roy Buchanan told Tweed emphatically. 'Three weeks and not a clue as to what has happened to her.'

The senior detective from the Yard looked round Tweed's office at Park Crescent. He sat facing Tweed across from his desk. Gazing round he nodded to Paula Grey, Tweed's close assistant, seated at her own desk; at Bob Newman, ex-international news reporter. Behind him near the door a corner desk was occupied by Monica, Tweed's office assistant, a middle-aged woman with hair fastened back in a bun as she worked at her word-processor. It was the attractive Paula, in her thirties with long glossy black hair, who responded.

'Three weeks is a long time. Worrying. Has there been any kind of ransom note – assuming she was kidnapped?'

'No,' Buchanan told her. 'Which makes her disappearance even more worrying.'

'The news was splashed for a while in the papers,' Paula recalled, 'but now it's barely referred to.'

'Because the papers,' Newman explained, 'are full of rumours that, after September 11 last year in New York, Britain is now the System's next target.'

'Just how did she disappear?' Paula persisted.

'Victor Warner has two homes,' Buchanan reminded her. 'His penthouse in Belgravia and some place in the country

1

at Carpford. That's a weird village hidden away in the North Downs. Mrs Warner's Porsche was found on the wrong side of the road just beyond a curve. No signs of any attack. The engine switched off, key left in ignition. Mysterious.' He turned back to Tweed. 'I'd like you to drive down there with me to see for yourself.'

'Have you forgotten I'm Deputy Director of the SIS?'

'Of course not.' Buchanan paused. 'But you did break that Arbogast case* concerning five murders across two continents, to say nothing of the involvement of the Vice-President of the United States. And before you joined this outfit, you were the youngest homicide superintendent at the Yard. Arbogast proved you hadn't lost your touch.'

'Not possible. I have to concentrate on this job.'

Tweed was a man of uncertain age, of medium height, and wore horn-rim glasses. He was the man you passed in the street without noticing him, a characteristic he'd found invaluable in his profession. But recently he seemed to have grown younger, his fabled energy even more noticeable. His blue eyes were more lively, as were his gestures.

'As a favour to me,' Buchanan coaxed.

'I said no, Roy.' Tweed hammered his fist on his desktop. 'Also I've heard Warner has persuaded the Cabinet to give him full powers with no interference from any other service. He meant me . . .'

He paused as the door was thrown open, almost taken off its hinges. The Director, Howard, stormed into the office with sheets of paper in his hand. Six feet tall, he had developed a paunch from frequenting expensive restaurants and clubs.

He sagged into an armchair opposite Newman. Impeccably clad in a Savile Row blue bird's-eye suit, a crisp

* Author's previous novel, *The Vorpal Blade*.

2

white shirt, a speckled bow-tie, his voice was upper-crust. He was, Tweed felt, the ideal boss – he dealt with the senior civil servants in Whitehall, where he was popular, leaving Tweed free to run the Service in his own way.

'Triumph!' Howard boomed. 'Just returned from the PM. I persuaded him to cancel Warner's edict that only he can handle everything over here. Tweed, you can check out the mystery of Linda Warner's disappearance. PM's worried. Ugly rumours are circulating that Linda was too friendly with another key member of the Cabinet.'

'So,' Buchanan interjected with a smile, 'Tweed, you can come with me to Carpford, scene of Linda Warner's strange disappearance.'

'And,' Howard intervened, 'here is a copy of the authorization from the PM that we are completely independent of the Ministry of Security, that we continue to function as in the past.'

'He hasn't minced his words,' Tweed commented after scanning the document. 'But I'm still sticking to my decision not to investigate Linda Warner's disappearance. That's your problem, Roy, I don't think there's anything in these newspaper rumours that Britain is the next target of the System, as Victor Warner keeps calling it.'

'You did know Linda,' Paula coaxed. 'Maybe not well but she liked you.'

'I've made up my mind . . .'

The phone rang. Monica answered, placed her hand over the mouthpiece, pulled a wry face as she called out to Tweed.

'There's a Peregrine Palfry on the line. Warner's personal assistant. Insists on speaking to you.'

'That crawler. Probably bows to Warner every time he enters the room. All right, I'll speak to him for a minute . . . Tweed here.'

'Mr Tweed . . .' The voice was arrogant. 'I have been asked to inform you by the Minister . . .'

3

'Then put the the Minister on the line. I don't take calls from civil servants.'

'This is important, I would have you know . . .'

'Put the Minister on the line before I break the connection.'

There was a choking sound, a pause, voices whispering, then Warner himself came on the line. Not best pleased.

'Tweed, I'm a busy man . . .'

'That makes two of us. What is it?'

'Now listen carefully.' The tone was polite and determined. 'I have heard that you were considering investigating the strange disappearance of my wife. I absolutely forbid you to interfere with the investigation. It is in the hands of Superintendent Buchanan and Gareth Morgan, chief of Special Branch. Is that understood?'

'Absolutely.' Tweed, smiling, paused before continuing. 'I have to inform you there is a road-block to your request – my Service does not come under your jurisdiction. Thank you for calling. Goodbye . . .'

Tweed sat up straight, eyes blazing. He lifted his clenched fist, banged it on his desktop so ferociously Paula jumped. She was fascinated. Recently Tweed had undergone a change of personality. Normally calm, passive, he was now commanding, far more energetic.

'That does it,' he snapped. 'Warner telling me to keep off the grass. Obviously hasn't heard yet of the PM's edict. Roy,' he went on, speaking quickly. 'I don't want to start by driving with you to Carpford. Give me the address of Warner's pad in Belgravia. Also the name of his housekeeper.' He was standing up, hauling his overcoat off the stand, slipping quickly into it. 'Paula, you'd better come with me. You're good at spotting some detail about how people live that I might miss.'

'There's the address,' Buchanan said, hardly able to conceal his delight. 'Name of the housekeeper is Mrs Carson. I've seen her. Like talking to an iceberg. Got nothing out of her. Want me to come with you?'

'No!' Tweed gave Buchanan a friendly punch on the shoulder. 'Obviously you didn't ask the right questions. Now, Paula, I'll drive.' He handed her Buchanan's directions. 'You can navigate.'

'Maybe it would be best to phone first,' Paula suggested.

'No, it wouldn't. Catch the iceberg on the wrong foot. If icebergs have feet . . .'

Warner's London base was a penthouse on the fifth floor of a modern apartment block, fortunately hidden behind the grandeur of Belgrave Square, since its modernity was quite out of keeping with the square's stately buildings. Tweed used his SIS pass to shut up the aggressive porter. The elevator was luxurious, with gilded mirrors and red leather seats. It climbed silently and the doors slid back on the fifth floor to reveal wide corridors with deep-pile carpets.

'Warner owns the whole top floor,' Tweed remarked as they turned left, following Buchanan's instructions. 'Half of it he doesn't use. Just doesn't want other people near him, I presume.'

He stopped in front of a heavy oak door with a speakphone on the wall. Pressing the button he waited. A woman's harsh voice spoke.

'Who is it?' demanded the voice.

'Tweed, Deputy Director of the SIS.'

'Someone phoned to say you were coming. Who was it?'

'Superintendent Buchanan of the Yard.'

'Doesn't take any chances, does she?' Paula whispered.

They heard the three Banham locks being turned, the door opened and they faced a tall, forbidding woman, slim, with grey hair and well-dressed. She stared at Paula with her penetrating eyes.

'Who might this be?'

5

'It might be my personal assistant, Paula Grey. And it is,' Tweed said with a wry smile.

'I suppose you'd better come in. I must warn you I have very little time.'

'The interview will last as long as is necessary,' Tweed said, his expression grim.

They were led into a large living-room with white leather sofas and chairs scattered about. Tweed and Paula shared a sofa while Mrs Carson perched on a carved chair facing them, her lips pursed in her bony face.

'Now,' she announced, 'let us get on with it. I told you I was short of time.'

'I would have thought you'd be worried stiff about the disappearance of your mistress. It is over three weeks since she vanished without trace at Carpford.'

'The security forces are doing everything they can to solve ths mystery,' she snapped.

Her tone and manner were hostile. Paula decided she didn't like Tweed. She leaned forward and smiled as she spoke.

'Mrs Carson. A woman is more likely to give us the vital clue. Mr Tweed has told me – he knows her slightly – that Linda Warner is an avid reader. Always takes a book with her. Do you know what she was reading before she left?'

'Yes, I do. She was wading through Gibbon's *Decline and Fall of the Roman Empire*. Kept it by her bedside. Always took it with her when she was going somewhere – in case she had a few spare minutes.'

'Could I ask you to check whether this volume she was reading is now on her bedside table?'

'Yes, it is, with the marker in the page she had reached.'

'That suggests she anticipated a quick trip to Carpford, since she left the book behind. Would you agree?'

'Yes, I would.' Mrs Carson had relaxed, looking at Paula and ignoring Tweed all the time. 'She expected to be back in the evening.'

'Did she take any of her clothes with her?' Paula continued.

'No. Except for her sable. It is cold up at Carpford. I checked myself, carefully. The idiots from Special Branch never thought to ask that shrewd question.'

'Did she receive – or make – a phone-call before she left?'

'No. Another question they missed. Really, it is quite a relief to talk to someone who knows their job. Would you like something to drink? Tea? Coffee?'

'No, thank you. I've recently had breakfast. Did Mrs Warner give you any indication why she was going to Carpford?'

'All she said to me before she rushed off was she was going on an urgent mission.'

'On behalf of her husband?'

'That I can't tell you, although I assume that was the case. I do know Mr Warner was going to be back from the Ministry late in the evening. Some big meeting.'

'You must be worried about what has happened to her.'

As she continued her interrogation Paula was smiling all the time. Mrs Carson kept leaning towards her as she answered. Her original stiffness had disappeared.

'Miss Grey, I'm worried stiff. It is so unlike her. I did try to phone Carpford late in the the afternoon but no one answered the phone. I assumed she was on her way back.'

'Was she a sociable lady?'

'When it was required. Attending dinners with her husband. One by one her friends left the area. Mostly diplomats' wives who joined their husbands when they were posted overseas.'

'And did she spend much time up at their place in Carpford?'

'As little as possible. I gathered she didn't like the place. She once called it strange, whatever that meant.'

'When she went there I imagine it was with her husband. So she must have clothes up there.'

'No, she hasn't. She'd take what she needed and always she brought it back with her. Every item.'

Paula stood up, after checking her watch. 'Mrs Carson, you have been very generous with your time. We appreciate that. There is one delicate question which I don't expect you to answer, but we have to eliminate every possibility. How can I phrase this? Did she have any close men friends?'

'I'm a woman of the world. The Special Branch wretches did ask about that – more brutally. The answer is no, she did not. As her housekeeper I'm the one person who would know. If you think of anything else please contact me. You are the first person who has come here I feel will find her.'

'Thank you. We'll leave you in peace now – as much peace as is possible.'

'I didn't say one word,' Tweed commented as they got into their parked car. 'You did a wonderful job. I realized she didn't like me. What do you make of it now?'

'I find it sinister.'

'Before we go back, call Buchanan on that irritating mobile of yours. Tell him we are now ready to go with him down to Carpford whenever it suits him. Ask him to set up the scene they found – Linda Warner's car parked at a bend in the road.'

'What was Mrs Warner like? I never met her.'

'An exceptionally intelligent woman. Like her husband very patriotic. I'm baffled. I wish you hadn't used that word sinister.'

1

Arriving back at Park Crescent, they were surprised to see a black Saab parked outside the SIS entrance. Superintendent Buchanan was seated alone behind the wheel, tapping his fingers. Seeing them coming, he held up his hand. Tweed parked before driving into the Crescent. Buchanan drove out, parked behind them, jumped out of his car.

'We can leave for Carpford now,' he informed Tweed through his open window. 'After the lab people had checked Mrs Warner's car I had it sent back and parked in a garage near Abinger Hammer. It has now been taken up and is on the Downs, positioned in precisely the position it was found empty when she went missing. I'll lead the way. Ready?'

'We'd better get on with it,' Tweed agreed. 'Lead on Macduff . . .'

It was February, late morning and very cold under a brilliant blue sky as Buchanan headed on to the A3. Paula was glad she had worn her warm blue overcoat and kept on her gloves.

They were soon clear of the city traffic and racing down the A3 with open country on both sides. Both Buchanan and Tweed were fast-moving drivers, keeping just inside the speed limit. In less than an hour Buchanan was signalling them to turn off the main road up a slip road.

At the top he turned left and they were deep in the country. They sped up a steep hill, reached the top, plunged down a curving road with panoramic views across high rolling hills. Paula asked Tweed where they were.

'Entering the first sweep of the North Downs. I know this area. Carpford I've never seen, wouldn't know how to get there.'

'What do you know about Victor Warner's background?'

'Reputed to be clever. Did a stint with Naval Intelligence, joined Medfords Security as a director when he came into civvy street. Spotted by the PM before the present one. Gave Warner a safe seat so he became an MP. Climbed the ladder quickly. When the Ministry of Security was formed Warner was the obvious choice to take over as Minister.'

'Would I like him?'

'Don't think so. Dominant personality. Knows he's the cat's whiskers. But very able.'

'Why would he want another place way out here in the wilds?'

'You probably would, after hours of sitting in Cabinet sessions listening to a lot of hot air. Warner, like half-a-dozen others, is tipped as next Prime Minister.'

They had reached the bottom of the plunging hill, continuing along a main road with fields stretching away on either side. Not a lot of traffic. Buchanan was signalling again to be ready to turn right. They swung round an ancient inn of brick which protruded dangerously into the road.

'Abinger Hammer,' Tweed said. 'From here on I'm in no man's land. I think he's going up the Downs.'

They followed Buchanan round a steep turn-off on to a narrow climbing road which rose very steeply, swinging round sharp bends. Buchanan was using his horn as he approached one. The angle increased. It was colder still. Paula noticed traces of frost on the green slopes. A signpost to Holmbury St Mary which they drove past. Still climbing and now they saw a black dense forest ahead, a mix of evergreens and stark trees, leafless and like huge bristle brooms. Buchanan slowed down, turned slowly up a short road, part of a triangle, with another angle leading back to the road they had left. Jumping out, he ran back.

'So you know where you are, we are entering Black Wood.'

'Looks so welcoming,' Paula remarked cynically.

'Nothing about where we are going is welcoming,' Buchanan assured her. 'That "Road Closed" sign is to keep traffic away from the scene of the crime area, which is taped off.'

Buchanan ran back to his car, jumped inside, drove straight ahead up the steepest hill they'd negotiated yet. The road narrowed to a simple lane and they continued climbing. They were inside the dense wood now. Steep banks rose vertically on either side and they crawled. There was only just enough clearance to get through. Paula gazed up to the top of the steep bank on her side, saw Black Wood leaning over them.

'What if we meet something coming the other way?' she wondered.

'We'll have to hope we can squeeze into one of the setbacks they've carved out at intervals.'

'I feel like a rabbit in its burrow,' she remarked.

'This is Carp Lane. I noticed the sign at the entrance. Can't be far now,' Tweed said hopefully.

'Buchanan used the phrase scene of the crime. Disturbing. We don't know a crime has been committed yet.'

'Your imagination is running away with you. I'm sure he was referring to the police tapes they've put up wherever this abandoned car has been brought back to.'

'If you say so . . .'

The 'burrow' suddenly started dropping precipitously as they continued crawling. They emerged into daylight when Buchanan signalled a left turn. At a T-junction they turned left and began climbing again. At least we're out of that horrid wood, Paula thought. The rolling frosted slopes of a

11

high down swept away. The frost was heavy now, the colour of crème-de-menthe. Then the parked Porsche came into view and police tape barred their way. Several policemen in uniform stared at them curiously. Buchanan stopped his car, jumped out, addressed a policeman.

'Sergeant Abbott, if I remember. Sorry to put you to all this trouble.'

'If it helps find her, sir . . .'

Paula was the first to leave the car, followed by Tweed, as the policeman accompanied them. The Porsche, pointing homeward, was parked on the wrong side of the road, just this side of the bend. Paula, who had pulled on her latex gloves, walked to the car, peered inside.

'Sergeant Abbott,' she asked, 'is this exactly how it was found? The ignition key is still in place. Was it turned on?'

'No. It was exactly as you see it. You can get inside if you wish, even sit behind the wheel. The lab people have finished going over it thoroughly.'

'Did they find anything?'

'One or two red hairs were found against the back of the driver's seat. Compared with hair brought from her home in London they match. Nothing else in the way of fibres.'

Paula opened the driver's door, eased her way behind the wheel. She felt strange grasping the wheel. The previous hands in this position had presumably been Linda Warner's. She looked out at Buchanan, Tweed and Abbott standing outside.

'The only window down is the driver's. Is that the way you found it.'

'It is, Madame,' Abbott told her.

'She parked on the wrong side of the road. Any signs of another car coming up the hill which blocked her way?'

'I know what you're thinking,' Abbott said with a smile.

12

'That if it had been waiting there for a while it might have leaked oil. We checked. Not a drop.'

'Would it be possible,' Paula suggested, 'for me to back the car a short way round the bend – the way she would be coming?'

'No trouble. I'll stand at the bend and beckon you so there's no danger of another vehicle coming down and driving through the tape. Lunatics are everywhere.'

Paula switched on the engine, kept a close eye on Buchanan, beckoning her. Slowly she backed round the sharp corner where a limestone crag protruded dangerously. Stopping the car she tried to imagine she was Mrs Warner, who would know the road. She drove forward, crawling, realized why the car had been found on the wrong side of the road – it was the only way she could see safely round the bend. Pulling up at the exact point where the Porsche had been found, she sat, thinking.

'Something, someone stopped her.' She was talking to herself. 'She had her window down so she could hear if anything was coming.'

'Then,' suggested Buchanan, standing outside the window, 'a man with a gun aimed it through the window, ordered her to get out. One theory.'

'A man?' Paula queried. 'Or a woman.'

'Abbott,' Buchanan called out as Paula slowly left the car, 'get this vehicle out of the way. I want to take my associates up to Carpford.' He looked grimly towards Paula. 'You're in for a shock.'

'I don't like it,' Paula said to Tweed as they followed Buchanan beyond the bend and up another section of steep hill.

'You think she's been kidnapped then?'

'I just hope to God that's all it is . . .'

They drove over a crest and Buchanan pulled in on to the verge. A plateau stretched out before them. In the middle

13

was a large lake with a landing stage, a small yacht was moored and the light was fading as wisps of pale mist swirled in the distance.

'This is Carpford?' Paula asked. 'It's really weird.'

'Warned you were in for a shock. Look at the houses.'

Well spaced out and near the edge of the silent lake was the oddest collection of dwellings Paula had ever seen. The nearest to where they stood was a distance back from the lake, perched on a small hill. It had a massive tower at one corner with a mosaic-decorated roof rising high above the three floors below. Attached to it were lower floors with tall narrow windows. At the far end was a smaller tower with a peaked roof.

'What is it?' Paula said aloud. 'It's almost Italianate in architecture.'

'Victor Warner's hideaway,' Buchanan told her. 'Called Garda. Place is like a fortress. He's the only occupant who had his place built to his specification. All the others are rented.'

'Rented to who?' Tweed enquired.

'The New Age Development Corp. The rents are paid to a dubious lawyer in London. He sends the money on to the Banque de Bruxelles et Liège, a small bank in Belgium.'

'And it stays there?'

'We don't think so. But what happens to the money we have no idea. You know how difficult it is to get information from a Belgian bank. Much tighter even than the Swiss.'

'I might know someone who can track it,' Tweed remarked, staring round the lake.

Near the edge of the lake stood a dwelling reminding Paula of a concrete blockhouse. Cubes of massive concrete were piled on top of each other with circular windows carved out of the concrete. Tweed pointed.

'Who lives in that horror?'

'Drew Franklin, the most highly paid gossip columnist in Britain. An awkward so-and-so. Told me the police always got it wrong, that he'd only answer questions with his lawyer present.'

'And who has the pseudo-Cotswold cottage beyond?'

'Mrs Agatha Gobble. Believe it or not, that's a shop selling antiques. She'll talk if you approach her in the right way. Gets going and you can't stop her.'

'Gobble?' said Paula. 'You must be joking.'

'No. That's her name. Trouble is she's a bit muddled in the upper storey.'

'And,' Tweed persisted, 'what about that two-storey round wooden barn on the far side of the lake? First time I've seen a round barn.'

'It is a house,' Buchanan assured him. 'Occupied by Peregrine Palfry . . .'

'That's the name of Warner's assistant,' Paula interjected.

'The very same. Haven't been able to find him at home. In London he's always away from the Ministry – or so I'm told.'

'It's creepy,' Paula burst out. 'No one anywhere. A ghost village.'

'Not quite,' Tweed told her. 'A few minutes ago, over at the edge of Black Wood in the distance, a tall thin man wearing a long black overcoat was watching us through field-glasses. He chose his vantage point well – his coat hardly showed up against the wood. He's gone now. Vanished suddenly.'

'Let's go and talk to Mrs Gobble,' Paula said firmly. 'She might tell us something.'

'I'll wait here with the cars,' Buchanan decided. 'The lady doesn't like me.'

'What do you think of Carpford?' Tweed asked Paula as he strode off briskly.

'It's not of this world. The atmosphere is frightening.'

The Cotswold-style house was more welcoming when they

15

reached it. The windows were bubble glass so, peering in, Paula had trouble recognizing the array of small pieces of so-called antiques displayed behind the glass. She saw nothing she'd want to buy. When Tweed opened the door an ancient bell, hung above it on the inside, rattled away. A small plump woman in her sixties, a string of large blue beads round her neck, appeared behind the counter. Her mouth was clamped tightly before she spoke.

'I'm just closing.'

'Mrs Gobble?' Tweed said politely. 'A lady friend of mine recommended your shop to me. She said the way you presented your stock was a model of perfection.'

'Very good of her, I'm sure.'

'My name is Tweed. This is my assistant, Paula Grey. Here are my credentials.'

Mrs Gobble examined the folder, stared at them in surprise. She looked taken aback, handed Tweed his folder.

'Secret Service. Praise the Lord, someone is taking seriously what happened to poor Mrs Warner. I told police she had been murdered. They pooh-pooh me.'

'Tell us why you are convinced she was murdered. You saw something?'

'I know up here.' Mrs Gobble tapped her wide forehead. 'The rays of vision from above are always right.'

'You knew Mrs Warner then?'

'A lovely lady. Gave the village class. More than I can say about the rest of them. They're all batty. Mrs Warner bought a small landscape. Best in the shop. No attempt to 'aggle over price.'

Paula realized Mrs Gobble had been, up to this point, careful to 'talk proper', as she would probably put it. It was Tweed's manner of speech which had influenced her. She was wearing an apron decorated with strange symbols. Paula's reaction was to think of witchcraft.

'Well,' Paula remarked, 'it's very peaceful and quiet round here.'

16

'Until the motor-bikes arrive.' Mrs Gobble's mouth turned sour.

'Motor-bikes?' Tweed's tone sharpened. 'When do they come?'

'Every second day – or rather night – one zooms up 'ere at ten o'clock after dark. Makes me jump every time when it roars past and round the lake.'

'Any idea where it's going to?'

'Mr Margesson's place. Don't like 'im. He's strange. Big man with a beard, very unpleasant. Came in 'ere once, walked round, was going out without saying a word. I asked him why he'd come. Know what he said? "Just came to see what you're like." Then walked out.'

'He lives where?' Tweed persisted.

'Go over to the door. I'm switching out the light. Wait and I'll come over . . .'

She walked to the wall and pressed an old-fashioned switch. Standing by the door, they were plunged into darkness. Mrs Gobble joined them. She locked the door and pointed. A crescent-shaped moon gave enough illumination to see across the lake. A heavy cloud bank had settled over the village.

'See that funny round wooden house? Belongs to another unpleasant man, a Mr Palfry. To the left of his big tub, see the Georgian style 'ouse with a glare light?'

'Yes. Quite clearly,' Tweed told her.

'That's where the motor-cyclist delivers a big white envelope. He chats to Margesson for a moment, then he's off on his wretched bike back this way and off towards the main road.'

'Sounds like a courier,' Tweed remarked.

'Call 'im what you like, there's something funny about 'im. Told you 'e delivers a large white envelope to Margesson. At ten at night. I took some rubbish to the village bin one morning just after dawn it was. There in the bin was a large white envelope. Hadn't been opened.'

17

'You mean it was still sealed?' Paula asked.

'That's it. No one 'bout so I kept it inside the bin and opened it. Nothing inside. I asks you. Why deliver an empty envelope?'

'Someone probably forgot to put the contents inside,' Tweed said dismissively.

'How would Margesson know that if he never opened it?' Mrs Gobble snapped. 'Stay where you are while I switch on the light.'

She shuffled back to the wall, her carpet slippers making no sound. There was a whirring sound and electrically operated blinds closed over the windows. The light came on.

'I 'ad Jem come up from Foxfold to fit the blinds. Don't like the idea I could be watched after dark. By the man in the long black coat, whoever 'e may be.'

'What does he look like?' Tweed wondered.

'No idea. Appears after dark. Saw him when the moon was getting big.'

'Mrs Gobble,' Tweed began carefully, 'you saw a lot of detail right across the lake at ten o'clock in the night. You must have better eyesight than me.'

'That's my little secret.' Mrs Gobble chuckled. 'Come behind this screen and see what I've got 'idden.'

Close to the far window a three-sided tall screen stood, all its flaps opened. Looking behind it, they gazed at Mrs Gobble's 'treasure'. A high-powered telescope mounted on a tripod. Tweed bent down, peered through the lens. The glare light and Margesson's front door could be seen clearly. There was more to Mrs Gobble than he had realized.

He straightened up and she lowered the blind she had briefly raised.

'You have been very kind and helpful, Mrs Gobble. I think we will now go and pay Mr Margesson a visit. There are a number of lights on in his house.'

'Have a care. That man has strange powers. And don't fall into Carp Lake. Keep to the footpath all the way.'

18

'Has it carp in it?'

'Never seen any. It's very deep, that lake. I'll switch off the light when you've both got to the door . . .'

Tweed noticed she had three bolts as well as two Banham locks on the door as she opened it for them. They slipped outside and bitter cold hit them. The cloud was so low and dense it was like night. There was a heavy frost on the green round the lake.

'I think it might be a mistake not to interview Margesson,' Tweed remarked as Paula pulled up her scarf, closed the top button of her coat. 'I get a funny feeling about him.'

'I get a bloody funny feeling about the whole place,' Paula retorted.

2

Inside Tweed's office at Park Crescent Bob Newman sat reading the day's issue of the *Daily Nation*, London's big-selling 'serious' newspaper. While active as a foreign correspondent he had contributed major pieces to the paper – articles which had been syndicated to *Der Spiegel* in Germany, *Le Monde* in France and the *New York Times*. He looked up as Marler came into the office.

In his thirties, Marler was of medium height, slim, agile, good-looking and the best marksman in Western Europe. He was always smartly dressed and today he was clad in a grey two-piece suit, a crisp white shirt with a Chanel tie. After kissing Monica on one cheek he walked over to a corner, stood against the wall, took out a long cigarette, lit it and stared at Newman.

He saw a well-built man in his forties, fair-haired, strong nose and jaw. His eyes were blue, his personality formidable. He had never yet been mugged. Even tough rubbish took one look at him and decided to go looking for easier pickings.

'We have to go and see my informant, Eddie,' Marler told him.

'You always see your informants on your own. So what is different now? I'm sure Eddie isn't his real name.'

'It will do for now. First time Eddie has clammed up on me. Says he has news so dangerous he'll only talk direct to Tweed. Whom he's never met, of course. Fact that he knows Tweed's name shows he's the tops.'

'Tweed is somewhere deep in Surrey with Paula. No idea when he'll get back.'

'So our faithful guard on the front door, George, told me, so I'm not sure we can wait. I'm hoping he'll talk to you. Make with the feet.'

Newman was wearing jeans, and a heavy zip-up jacket hung from the back of his chair. He sighed, stood up and put on the jacket. His holstered .38 Smith & Wesson revolver was now perfectly concealed. He made a gesture of resignation to Monica and she saluted with a grin.

'Just so I know,' Newman said as they walked down the stairs from the first floor office, 'where are we going?'

'Deepest and darkest Soho.'

'Great. Haven't been there for ages. Can't wait.'

They parked Newman's car on the edge of Soho. Marler led the way and soon they were walking down a main street. Newman looked round in surprise.

'They've smartened the place up. It almost looks inviting.'

'Almost. It's all cosmetic.'

The narrow street was well lit. Crowds of youngsters were drifting along, wondering what to do next to raise some hell. Ahead of them on the pavement a burly man with a cap leant against a wall as he carefully lit a cigar. He had first glanced their way. Newman grasped Marler's arm to slow him down. They were close to the man, who had just taken a deep puff on his cigar. Newman stopped a foot away from him as the burly character blew out a smokescreen of foul smoke intended to catch Newman in the face. As the smoke cleared Newman stopped opposite him.

'Meant for me, mate?'

'You bet, sonny.'

Newman's clenched right fist slammed into his stomach. Cigar groaned horribly, bent forward, burning half of his cigar on the pavement. Newman pulled the cap down over his eyes and walked on.

'Welcome to Soho,' Marler quipped.

'Think he swallowed half of it. Hope he enjoyed the taste.'

'We turn down here.'

'Even more salubrious.'

This street was even narrower. Newman saw a greasy-faced man handing a small packet to his customer. Cocaine. Ahead of them a slanting neon sign which had once been straight had a name. *Belles.* Two young scruffy-looking blondes were standing by the door, watching them coming.

'Belles,' Marler said. 'He should be inside. We're punctual. Eddie doesn't like waiting.'

'We're better than what you'll find inside,' one of the blondes said, leering.

'So you say,' Newman snapped, following Marler inside.

A barrage of noise assailed them. A mix of voices and the voice of a skimpily clad black girl perched on a platform as she 'sang' into a microphone. Marler pushed his way between crowded tables to the back where a staircase led upstairs.

At a table tucked under the stairs sat a small shabbily dressed man with a broken nose, a scar on his left cheek. Marler grabbed the chair with its back to the wall, sat down as Newman moved one of the chairs so he faced the crowd.

'Eddie,' Marler introduced, 'meet Tweed's right-hand man. Bob Newman.'

'Why three bottles of beer?' Newman wanted to know.

'To keep people away from this table,' Eddie explained. 'Where is Tweed?'

'A hundred miles away. Newman will tell him what you have to pass on. You said it was urgent.'

'New York had September 11.' Eddie kept his voice down. He paused. 'London is next. This month. February.'

'Dates?'

23

'Tweed gets those. No one else.' Eddie sipped his beer as Newman watched him. Shabby clothes. Nutcracker face, his cheeks sunk. Could be any age. 'So when do I meet him?' Eddie persisted.

Newman turned away, studied the jostling crowd. A small man had entered, wearing a worn leather suit. What caught Newman's eye was the black turban he was wearing, the eyes scanning the place. Newman turned round.

'That newcomer,' he said, addressing Eddie. 'With a turban. What the hell is he?'

'Probably Taliban. Our stupid government has let a horde in through Dover. They don't wear the turban till they get up here.'

'Not al-Qa'eda?'

'Probably . . . He's come for the girl upstairs. Sorry for her. They don't know. Knew one who was maimed for life. Her attacker was only with her for five minutes.'

'What's the name of the girl upstairs?'

'Lily.'

'Excuse me.'

The man in the black turban was approaching the staircase. As Newman ran up it ahead of him Marler took one of the beer bottles, emptied the contents on to the floor, only adding to the rubbish.

At the top of the stairs Newman ran along a narrow corridor. One door had a crudely painted sign hanging from the door knob. He hammered on the door. Nothing. He hammered again and a seductive voice answered.

'Who the hell is it?'

'Now listen good. You've got a brutal Afghan customer on the way up. He'll cut you to pieces. Afterwards. Just for the fun of it. I'm Robert Newman, newspaper reporter. So for God's sake don't open the door. Lock it, bolt it, put a handle under the knob – the handle of a chair. And I'm damned well not joking . . .'

As he started back down the corridor he heard locks being

24

turned. He began descending the stairs. The Afghan was on his way up. Seen close up, Newman was appalled by the savage face, the death-like eyes. Newman stopped him.

'She's not for you. Get the hell out of here.'

The Afghan scuttled downstairs, close behind Newman.

Newman had sat down as Marler stood up. The Afghan was almost at their table. His right hand had slipped under his leather jacket. Newman had a glimpse of a vicious curved blade. Marler raised the heavy bottle with one hand, whipped off the turban with the other. The bottle hit the back of the Afghan's head with such force it broke in two. The Afghan sank to the floor, lay still.

'Tweed will be back by eleven,' Marler whispered to Eddie. 'Midnight at the latest. He's not coming to this cesspit.'

'You know Monk's Alley – off Covent Garden and King Street?'

'Yes.'

'Meet him inside the alley at midnight. You can come with him, but stay back.'

'Time we all went,' Marler warned.

'I'm gone,' said Eddie and he was out of Belles.

3

Tweed and Paula started out their walk to Margesson's villa by keeping to the path. Since it was paved with pebbles their footsteps made a lot of noise. Hoping to catch their objective by surprise, Tweed moved to his right, on to the grass, followed by Paula. It was not much of an improvement. The heavy frost was so hard their feet crunched the crystals.

'It's like Siberia up here,' Paula complained. 'Who would want to live here?'

'The people who do. What did you think of Mrs Gobble?'

'Far more going on inside her head than Buchanan realized. My guess is she didn't like him so she acted the simpleton. Cunning too – with her concealed telescope. Probably she knows even more than she told us.'

'Stop talking.'

They were over halfway round the large lake, approaching Palfry's 'tub', as Mrs Gobble had nicknamed it. An apt word, Paula thought. She looked to her left. The surface of the lake was very still and black, as if filled with tar. The silence was getting on her nerves, broken only by the crunch of their footsteps.

They came to a road and walked slowly past Palfry's house. No lights anywhere. Small windows on both floors and no sign of an entrance. The front door must be round the back. She looked at Margesson's dwellling and gasped as she saw it more clearly. All the brickwork and even the pillars flanking the front door were painted a light green.

'That's ridiculous,' she protested. 'A Georgian house painted green.'

'We'll find he's eccentric,' Tweed predicted, reaching for the bell-pull. 'And this thing is more suitable for an old cottage.'

There was a whirring sound and the heavy wooden door swung inward. Electrically operated. A massive figure stood in the doorway. At least six feet tall, he had broad shoulders and large hands. His chin was concealed behind a long black beard, matching the colour of the thick thatch on his big head. His forehead was wide and narrow, his brown eyes half hidden under heavy lids above a Roman nose and thick sensuous lips.

The strangest aspect was the long white robe he wore, which almost reached his ankles. The white collar stretched round his bull-like neck. His voice was soft, persuasive. Paula took an instant dislike to it.

'How may I serve you?' the huge figure enquired.

'I am Tweed, Deputy Director of the SIS.' He held open his identity folder. 'This is my personal assistant, Paula Grey. We are here to investigate the disappearance of Mrs Warner. She has been gone three weeks.'

'Please enter my humble home. I suggest we confer at the round table.'

They walked into a vast sitting-room as the door automatically closed behind them. Paula was not expecting this. The room was two storeys high with an arched ceiling. It reminded her of houses in the States which had similar living quarters called a cathedral room. The walls were painted white and decorated with framed English landscapes.

'Some wine?' Margesson suggested. 'A libation?'

They both refused as they sat on hard cushionless chairs with high backs. Paula tried to wriggle herself into a better position as their host arranged his robe and sat facing her. His peculiar eyes gazed straight at her as he spoke.

'There is no comfort in this dwelling. That is deliberate. We live in a world here where there is only softness, so we have a society which has collapsed. Into chaos.'

'Chaos?' Tweed queried sharply.

'There is no discipline, no morality, only the indulgence of pleasures, many of a dubious nature. Parents make no effort to control their offspring, so we breed a fresh generation which, if not controlled, will plunge us deeper into the pit of degradation.'

'Assuming that what you say is correct,' Tweed said agreeably, 'then what – if anything – could be done to reverse the trend?'

Paula, taken aback, glanced at him. Then she realized Tweed was subtly leading on their host. She assumed a solemn expression to match Tweed's.

'The present society must be wrenched free from its moorings, shaken to the core by the introduction of the most severe measures. For example, adultery is now regarded almost as a normal behaviour. If a woman is taken in adultery she has to be subjected to the most draconian punishment.'

'I should have asked earlier,' Tweed interjected. 'You are Mr Margesson?'

'Olaf Margesson at your service, sir.'

'Olaf? That isn't very English.'

'My ancestors long ago came from Finland.'

'Really?' Tweed paused. 'Yet your skin, if I may remark on it, has a brownish tinge. Not a colour anyone would inherit from Finland.'

Watching their host closely, Paula saw the eyes narrow even more, so they almost disappeared beneath the lids. She felt sure she had caught a flash of fury in those disturbing eyes.

'You mentioned a draconian punishment for women,'

29

she challenged him. 'What about men caught in adultery?'

'They would also receive a punishment to mark them out for the foul things they are. That is why I speak of discipline, of control. When a woman takes a man in marriage she must respect him in every way. As he must her. Can you argue against that?'

'Theoretically, no,' Tweed replied. 'I agree with the general idea, but not everyone is strong enough to resist temptation when it offers itself. You must . . .'

'*Temptation!*' Margesson's voice became a roar of fury, he raised both arms high, hands open like huge claws. His loose sleeves slipped down, exposing massive muscular arms. 'That is what it is all about,' he thundered. 'The refusal to give in to the lusts of the flesh, discipline. Self-discipline is the foundation of a strong society which will endure. The present one will not. It will drown in its own sea of naked self-indulgence. Not all America's atom bombs and aircraft carriers will protect it – or the West.'

'You express yourself with vigour,' remarked Tweed as he stood up to leave. 'I agree with a small amount of your view – but disagree with most of it. Now we must go.'

'Think deeply of all I have said in the darkness of the night, I beg of you.'

Margesson, standing, towered over Paula, who had also stood up. His whole personality had undergone a remarkable change. As he spoke these words to them both hands were stretched out, pleading.

Tweed made no reply as he walked towards the door with Paula by his side. With giant strides Margesson preceded them, pressed a button in the wall and the door swung open. Icy air flooded in. Once outside on the step Tweed turned, his manner polite.

'Thank you for your hospitality, Mr Margesson. Everyone has a right to his own views, providing they don't force others to adopt them.'

Margesson bowed low, one hand plucking at his dark

beard. It was a mannerism Paula had observed frequently while he was talking, as though he were plucking his thoughts from it.

'We'll go back the short way, along this side of the lake. The road's reasonable.'

'More than Margesson is.'

They met no one and Tweed was relieved when he saw Buchanan, arms banging round his overcoat, waiting for them. A mist had crept out of the forest and was advancing towards Carp Lake. It was almost a fog, and coils of it slid out over Carpford. When they looked back all the strange dwellings had vanished.

'Sorry to keep you so long, Roy,' Tweed apologized. 'We had two long interviews.'

'Goes with the territory. You left just in time. Caught up in that fog you could find yourself in the lake, which is deep.'

'How deep is it?'

'Thirty feet at least. Who did you see?'

'While you're both talking I must call Newman on my mobile,' Paula told them. 'He'll be worried by now.'

Tweed climbed into the back of the car while Buchanan got behind the wheel. The engine had been left ticking over so the interior was pleasantly warm. Beyond the windscreen the fog was drifting down towards them.

'Two interviews,' Tweed told Buchanan. 'Both weird, odd in different ways. One with Mrs Gobble, the other with Olaf Margesson . . .'

Abbreviating, he related the gist of the conversations and their impressions. Buchanan listened without speaking until Tweed had completed his resume. Then he turned round.

'I couldn't even get into Margesson's house. I suspect he was inside and just didn't open the door. I don't like the sound of him at all . . .'

Paula heard his comment as she clambered in beside

31

Tweed. She sighed ecstatically, taking off her gloves as she soaked up the heat.

'Bless you, Roy, for keeping the car warm. I could kiss you. Now, Park Crescent. Newman wants us back by eleven-thirty to meet someone. Didn't say who but, like me, he doesn't trust the security of both our mobiles.' She peered ahead as Buchanan began driving down the road. 'The Porsche has gone. Where is it?'

'Taken away on a transporter. And there's plenty of time for us to get back to town ages before eleven-thirty.'

'My tummy's rumbling,' Paula told him. 'I had no lunch and I'm desperate for food.'

'Then we'll turn off to Foxfold, a village down in the valley. There's a good hotel there, the Peacock. You can have a full meal and we'll still be back for Newman in good time.'

'I do not like Margesson,' Paula said vehemently. 'He's like some kind of priest, a mad one. I'm going to call him the Priest in future. Most poisonous.'

'Dangerous might be nearer the mark,' Tweed commented.

They had dropped to a much lower level after Buchanan had swung along a narrow lane to his left. As they entered Foxfold Paula realized it was a normal village, nestling in a deep gulch. There were street lights, and old brick-built houses and cottages stood well back from the road. High up on the gulch, overlooking the village, was a large house with a blaze of lights. Buchanan turned off the lane and climbed a steep drive leading to the perched house.

'That's the Peacock,' Buchanan said as he pulled up in front of a large window with leaded lights.

'Well,' Paula began, her mind darting about, 'at least we know that mysterious man with the black overcoat exists. Mrs Gobble has seen him prowling about in the night.'

'One thing I meant to ask you, Roy,' Tweed said as Buchanan switched off the engine, 'is do you know how it

32

was possible for Victor Warner to buy land and build that monstrosity. Everyone else has to pay rent to that dubious London lawyer.'

'He was smart. He had a surveyor check the area, found that developer, the New Age outfit, had overlooked it. Jumped in and bought it, then had his house built by workers imported from Milan in Italy. He's very rich. You know why?'

'No idea.'

'He keeps this quiet. His father owned a company which manufactured – of all things – a laxative. Victor inherited a huge fortune when his father departed this world. He likes to keep the source of his wealth quiet.'

'No wonder!' Paula chuckled. 'A laxative!'

They were about to enter the hotel when a Maserati sped up the drive, parked behind Buchanan. The driver jumped out of the car. Tall and slim, agile, he wore a long dark overcoat. Paula whispered to Tweed.

'It's him. The man you saw at the edge of the wood watching us in Carpford.'

'I don't believe it,' Tweed replied with astonishment. 'Of all people. This is my old friend from Belgium, ex-chief of their anti-terrorist squad. Jules Beaurain.'

As Tweed made introductions, Paula was struck by Beaurain's powerful personality, by his good looks, by his courtesy and command of English. He kissed her hand briefly and gave her a wonderful smile.

Six feet tall, in his late thirties or early forties, his hair was black, neatly brushed, his blue eyes piercing without any hint of anything but friendship. His face was long and beneath his strong nose were firm lips and a fine jaw. All his movements were swift.

'The brilliant Paula Grey,' he said, still smiling. 'When Tweed visited Brussels he praised your talents to the sky. So it gives me great pleasure to meet you. I had not expected someone quite so attractive. Don't know how you get any work done with this lady in your office.'

'That's right, pile it on,' Tweed replied with a mock grumble. 'We are just going in for dinner. Paula is starved. Can you join us?'

'I also have not eaten for years, so it seems. Certainly I should be honoured. And I trust the famous Superintendent Buchanan will be another guest.'

'How do you know he's a Superintendent?' Tweed enquired. 'I remember he was a Chief Inspector when we last met in Brussels.'

'I make it my business to know what is happening in so many different parts of the world. Does your friend realize my career, now ended, tallies not so far from his?'

'I do,' Buchanan said emphatically. 'Notorious would describe how we regard him at the Yard. But after commanding the anti-terrorist squad you returned to the police in the role of Commissioner.'

'This is fascinating,' Paula interjected, 'but I'm still in great need of food.'

'My apologies.' Beaurain took her by the arm and led the way into the hotel and the restaurant. 'Let me choose the table where we can talk openly. I am staying here at the moment.'

They sat down at a long table perched in a corner under the eaves of the ceiling. Before Tweed could open his mouth Beaurain, sitting next to Paula, was suggesting different wines from the list. He also recommended mushroom soup and lamp chops to follow.

'I, unlike my countrymen, prefer them *bien cuit.*'

'So do I,' said Paula. 'And the soup. My mouth's watering.'

She also ordered Chardonnay to drink and Beaurain nodded his approval. Everyone followed his choice and Paula began attacking the freshly-baked rolls. There were only two other couples, seated at tables well away from them.

'You will soon feel that life is worth living again after your grim experiences exploring Carpford. All the inhabitants are so peculiar. I doubt after leaving Mrs Gobble you enjoyed the encounter with Margesson. I doubt, also, that Mrs Gobble is all that she seems.'

'You,' Tweed accused, 'are the man with the field-glasses who watched from the edge of Black Wood.'

'The very same. I have been keeping an eye on what I suspect is a cleverly disguised base for some operation.'

'Incidentally,' Buchanan observed, 'I never once spotted you following us in that Maserati.'

'I should hope not. During my career I have had to follow some very dangerous villains without their knowing. It is not so difficult once you get the hang of it.'

'You just called Carpford a base,' Tweed observed quietly. 'A base for what? Run by whom?'

'I simply have no idea. We could discuss the notion when we next meet.'

'You remarked outside that your career has ended,' Tweed persisted. 'You have left Belgium for good?'

'I have. When I became Commissioner I soon realized that politicians were trying to control me. Since there is so much corruption over there I resigned.' He turned to Paula. 'You see, my father was Belgian but my mother was English. Also my wife was murdered. Before I left I tracked the killer down. I shot him dead.' He looked at her. 'I hope I do not shock you.'

'Not in the least. I'm sorry you had that experience.'

Paula found she was liking Beaurain. Seated alongside her, he had not once touched her as certain Frenchmen would have done at every opportunity. Buchanan twiddled the stem of his glass as he looked at Beaurain.

'What is your view on the disappearance of Mrs Warner?'

'Paula, excuse me, but I must answer frankly. I think she has been murdered. I hope there is not an even grimmer option.'

35

4

They separated when they left the Peacock. Buchanan was anxious to get back to the Yard. He had arranged for the sturdy Sergeant Abbott to drive Tweed's car back to Foxfold and it was waiting for them when they emerged into the icy night. Beaurain had said he was staying to 'continue my holiday'. He had promised to keep in touch with everyone.

'Funny sort of holiday,' Paula remarked as Tweed drove them down to the main road where they joined the route they had used coming down from London.

'I've never known Jules take a holiday,' Tweed told her. 'I think he's determined to unearth the secret of Carpford.'

'But is there a secret?'

'He seems to think so. Never known him to be wrong yet.'

The heavy meal, the warmth of the car, soon sent Paula to sleep. Her head sagged and she only woke as they were approaching Park Crescent. Tweed glanced at her.

'How did you know we'd arrived?'

'I sensed you were suddenly driving slowly. And we have a reception committee waiting for us,' she commented as they entered the Crescent.

Two cars were parked in front of the entrance to the SIS building. Newman was striding up and down, hands in the pockets of his overcoat. Characteristically, the calmer

Marler was seated behind the wheel of his car, smoking. Paula checked the time. 11.15 p.m.

'We're in good time,' she remarked.

'Doubt if Newman would agree with you,' Tweed replied as the rear door was flung open and Newman jumped inside. Paula told him to close the door since all the warmth was escaping.

'Now listen closely both of you,' Newman began, his tone unusually grim. 'One of Marler's top informants, Eddie – I doubt that's his real name – insists he has important information. The trouble is he'll only talk to you, Tweed. And we had a bit of an evening of it . . .'

He described tersely their experiences at Belles in Soho, including his confrontation with the Afghan. Paula was frowning as he came to the end of his story. She turned round in the car.

'Taliban? I think your imagination is running away with you.'

'You'd have said the same thing if I could have predicted the attack on the World Trade Center in New York.'

'But you didn't predict it.'

'When you two have finished arguing,' Tweed interjected, 'is there a deadline for this meeting with Eddie?'

'Yes, midnight at the latest. Tweed, you can travel in my car. Marler will follow in his own transport. Paula, I suggest you wait upstairs with Monica until we get back. Monk's Alley off Covent Garden is a dangerous lonely place at this hour.'

Tweed jumped out of his car, ran over to the front passenger seat in Newman's car. He waved to Marler. Before Newman could switch on the engine Paula had darted over and climbed in the rear seat behind Tweed. She didn't mince her words.

'Bob Newman, I'm a big girl now. Dangerous? What do you think it was like in that underground mine when I found out who was the murderer who had killed five people? So,

38

from now on . . .' she leaned forward and punched his shoulder '. . . no more lectures from you, thank you very much.'

Newman, uncertain, glanced at Tweed, who smiled.

'She's perfectly right. Let's get moving . . .'

London on a bitter night in February was deserted. There was hardly any other traffic and no pedestrians had ventured out. As they approached the labyrinth of small streets near Covent Garden Paula was checking her .32 Browning by feel. Satisfied, she unbuttoned her overcoat so she could reach the weapon swiftly.

Suddenly Marler overtook them, one hand waving Newman down through his open window. Engines were switched off and Marler jumped out and ran back to them. He spoke to Newman, who had lowered his window.

'You wait here while I check the situation. Eddie might be alarmed if three of us appear. Back in a tick . . .'

It was a long tick. Paula saw Marler move silently in his rubber-soled shoes, then disappear down to the right. Presumably he had reached Monk's Alley. She felt impatient but this was Marler's exercise.

There were no street lights at this point. Both Marler and Newman had turned off their headlights. Paula kept looking back, gazing out of the side windows, unable to sit still. Tweed, though, was motionless, but she could tell from the angle of his head that he was keeping an eye on the rear-view mirror.

'Maybe Eddie has changed his mind,' she remarked for something to say. She didn't like the heavy silence, the lack of anyone else about.

'Relax,' was Tweed's only reply.

'You're better at sitting still, waiting.'

'You're just as good if you're on your own.'

'I've got a funny feeling about this.'

39

'The atmosphere round here encourages funny feelings,' Newman reassured her.

'It's more than the atmosphere. Marler is taking too long coming back to us. Maybe we'd better explore.'

'Stay exactly where you are,' Tweed ordered.

'Well, here comes Marler, moving quickly,' Newman reported. 'Probably had to reassure Eddie that he really did have Tweed waiting here.'

Marler opened the front passenger door, looked swiftly at Tweed and Newman, then glanced at Paula. He spoke quietly, without his usual jaunty drawl.

'It's not good. In fact, it's pretty bad. Eddie is dead in the alley. Not a pretty sight. Paula, wait here, lock all the doors.'

'Now you're starting it,' Paula fumed.

She opened her door and was outside almost as quickly as Tweed and Newman. She was glad she was wearing sensible shoes – the street was cobbled, an ankle-breaker. She called out.

'Isn't anyone going to lock the car doors?'

'Sorry . . .'

Newman and Marler used their monitors to lock the cars. With Marler leading, they hurried down the street until he stopped at the entrance to a cobbled opening only wide enough for one person to walk down. Paula noticed the ancient plaque. *Monk's Alley*. The figure of a monk was engraved below the name. Marler had switched on his powerful torch, beamed it just inside.

Eddie's crumpled figure lay on the cobbles, his right arm outstretched, the fingers of the hand tightly clenched. Lying on his back, he was soaked with blood. Pools of blood were spreading over the cobbles. His eyes gazed up at the sky, lifeless. Paula thought she had never before seen so much blood.

'I reckon he was stabbed more than twenty times,' Marler informed them. 'My guess is someone went on stabbing well after he was dead. An atrocious assault. Whoever did it searched his clothes. Everything has gone. No indication of his identity. And his wallet was taken. I've checked him thoroughly. He was stripped.'

'You missed nothing?' Tweed queried.

'Excuse me,' Marler said indignantly.

'Mind if I just check? Hold your torch steady.'

'Suit yourself.'

Tweed crouched down. He looked for a long time, then he put latex gloves on his hands. Gently he prised open the fingers of the clenched hand. No sign of rigor mortis. This had happened fairly recently. Inside the palm was a screwed-up piece of paper. Paula was already holding a transparent evidence bag. Tweed dropped the screwed-up piece of paper inside. Then he carefully lifted the side of the body. A piece of dark cloth was protruding. He hauled out a long length of black cloth, crumpled as though it had at one time been folded.

'Jesus!' exclaimed Newman. 'Taliban. A turban.'

Paula had her mobile ready and Tweed agreed she should call Buchanan. He looked up quickly.

'Don't let him see that bit of paper . . .'

It was after one in the morning when they sat down in Tweed's office. Buchanan had arrived quickly with an ambulance. Marler gave him a brief resumé of events leading up to the hideous killing. Buchanan said he'd take a full statement later in the day.

Marler leant against a wall, lit a cigarette. When he spoke his voice was cold, as though suppressing strong emotion.

'Eddie was my best informant. He had contacts every-where – even in Italy. Milan, I think. The poor devil deserved a better fate.'

'I think hell has come to London,' Tweed said quietly as Paula handed him the evidence bag.

Wearing a fresh pair of latex gloves, Tweed carefully

began unrolling the tightly screwed piece of paper. Then he took a lot of trouble smoothing it out on his desk.

'Doesn't mean a thing to me,' he commented.

'It's drawn in charcoal,' Marler said, peering over Tweed's shoulder. 'Eddie used charcoal to write anything. Kept a stick of it in his top breast pocket. The killer took that too.'

'Some kind of symbol,' Paula said, peering over the other shoulder. 'Could be anything.'

'Yet Eddie,' Tweed pointed out, 'thought it was so important he screwed it up inside his hand even when he was being stabbed to death. And it tells us nothing.' He stared down at what Eddie had scrawled on the sheet of paper.

5

At 8 a.m. the next morning, bitterly cold with a bleak overcast, Tweed arrived at his office. He was surprised to see all his staff waiting. Newman, relaxing in an armchair; Marler in his usual stance, leaning against a wall; Paula seated at her corner desk; Pete Nield and Harry Butler.

The last two were very tough and experienced legmen. They often worked together, a formidable team. The contrast between the two men could not be more marked. Nield, as usual, was smartly dressed, his grey business suit perfectly fitting his lean frame. In his thirties, his brown hair was well brushed, his small moustache neatly trimmed. He had come to Tweed from Oxford University and spoke well so was able to mix in any society. He was quiet, thoughtful.

Harry Butler was clad in a worn pair of jeans, a creased shirt which had seen better days. More heavily built than Nield, he was a dangerous opponent in a street brawl, his happy hunting ground the East End. He merged into that type of area well. Muggers took one look at his wide shoulders, his ham-like fists, his dark glaring eyes, and kept well away.

'Why is everyone so early?' Tweed enquired, removing his camel-hair coat and sitting behind the antique desk bought for him by his staff. He was becoming fond of it.

'I phoned everyone when I got home,' Marler explained. 'To tell them about Eddie. They take a grim view.'

'If I ever meet that Afghan killer,' Harry said forcefully, 'I'll kick him between the legs, then stamp on his face so his wretched mother wouldn't recognize him. That for starters. We're going to have to play this one very rough.'

Unlike Nield, perched on an arm of Newman's chair, Harry was sitting on the floor, stocky legs crossed. Tweed noticed he was wearing boots with metal rims. The phone rang, Monica answered, looked at Tweed.

'There's a Peregrine Palfry on the line. Says the Minister, Victor Warner, wants to see you in his office.'

'Tell Palfry I'm very busy – and that if the Minister wants to see me will he do me the courtesy of calling himself.'

Monica kept repeating the same message, then broke the connection. She sighed.

'I think he's one of those,' she remarked. 'He's up in the clouds and tried to treat me like a serf. I think I got under his skin when I kept repeating exactly the same words.'

Paula was smiling at Tweed. 'The Minister of Security is going to love you.'

'It's a tactic,' Tweed told her. 'If he really does have a reason for seeing me he'll swallow his pride, call me back.'

'You really are a devil,' she said.

Within five minutes the phone was ringing again. Monica listened, clamped a hand over the speaker. She was grinning.

'It's him, his lordship. He sounded very upper-crust but he was polite to me . . .'

'Tweed here. Is there a problem?'

'My dear Tweed, I really would appreciate it if you could pop over here. Can't explain why over the phone. I also appreciate a man in your position must be overwhelmed at times, but this is rather urgent. What time would suit you?'

'Now? I can be there in thirty minutes.'

'Splendid! I really would be most grateful for your co-operation. I look forward very much to seeing you . . .'

'Smooth as silk,' Tweed told them as he put on his coat. 'Paula, I'd like you to come with me. Don't expect to like him. Very upper-crust, I've heard. A cog from the old boys' network.'

'Can't wait,' she told him.

'Wearing that coat you look like a member of Special Branch,' Paula teased Tweed as they arrived at the tall doors closed at the entrance to the Ministry of Security. 'Nowadays a camel-hair coat is their uniform.'

'I like the coat,' Tweed replied as he pressed the bell.

One massive door was opened almost at once and Peregrine Palfry stood there to greet them with a smile. He shook hands with both of them as he ushered them into a vast hall.

'It's very good of you to traipse all this way to see the Minister. Strictly between us I think he might have asked to visit you.'

Tweed was surprised at the firmness of his hand clasp. Paula was surprised by his warm welcome. His face was pale, his hair jet black. Clean-shaven, he would be in his thirties and he struck her as athletic. Not at all what she had expected.

Walking swiftly, he led them up a wide flight of stairs, along a hallway, and paused before a door. He pulled a face, as much as to say, 'Here we go!' He had knocked once when a voice beyond the door called out loudly.

'Enter!'

The office beyond was spacious and the Minister stood up from behind a long imposing antique desk. He strode round to greet them. Very tall and thin, he carried himself very erect and the thinness extended to his long face. On the bridge of a strong nose were perched a pair of gold-rimmed pince-nez, and his cold blue eyes scanned his visitors swiftly. His mouth was wide and again thin, his chin suggested a touch of aggression.

45

He was dressed in country clothes, a smart hunter's jacket and polo trousers tucked inside gleaming knee-length boots. Smiling, he ushered them to an enormously wide couch and sat next to Paula with Tweed beyond her.

'I am so sorry to drag you down here but I do have a Cabinet meeting soon. Pure waste of time. Bores me stiff listening to gabble-gabble. Now, what would you like to quench your thirst? Tea, coffee – maybe something a little stronger?'

Tweed refused anything and Paula followed suit. Warner looked over at the open door where Palfry stood waiting to bring refreshment, shook his head. Palfry dipped his head, withdrew, closing the door.

'Good chap, Perry,' Warner remarked. 'Member of MENSA – not that it impresses me. But he's so reliable and has the memory of an elephant.' He was addressing his remarks to Paula. 'I have heard of the legendary Paula Grey. Makes me wonder whether I should talk to her rather than you, Tweed.' He said it with a smile.

'If I am regarded anywhere as legendary it is exaggerated wildly,' she told him. 'Mr Tweed is the power.'

'Then I will talk to both of you.' He looked across at Tweed. 'I hope you will not take what I say as personal.'

'Depends what you say, Minister.'

Paula was startled. Minister? Then she realized Tweed was using softening up tactics, something be rarely did.

'It has come to my shell-like ear,' Warner began gravely, 'that you two have been poking about up at Carpford. I regard that as my private sanctuary.'

'Surely you are worried about the mysterious disappearance of your wife,' Tweed replied bluntly.

'I am worried sick. It is so unlike Linda to take off into the wild blue yonder. And the police are hopeless. That chap Buchanan simply says he has no news yet. After three weeks. I ask you.'

'Superintendent Buchanan is the cleverest and most

46

determined policeman in this country. The car your wife was driving, which was found abandoned, has been subjected to the most thorough lab search. No clues at all found inside it. Have you yet had any kind of message demanding a ransom? If you have you must tell me – even if the caller told you that was the last thing you must do.'

'No one has called.' Warner's voice had changed, was rasping. He was leaning against Paula to speak to Tweed and she caught a whiff of after-shave lotion. She knew he was quite unaware he was pressing against her as he continued vehemently. 'I have received no ransom demand. Dammit, man, if I had I would have told Buchanan. And, once again, why were you poking about down at Carpford?'

'Because, at Buchanan's urgent request, I've reverted for the moment to my old role of detective. You should be grateful.'

'Oh, I see.' He sat back. 'Someone told me you were once the star turn at the old Scotland Yard. Find anything? See any of the people up there?'

'Olaf Margesson for one. He's a fanatic on religion. Do you know him?'

'He's invited me over for the occasional glass of sherry. Don't understand your reference to religion. We talked mostly about cricket. Anyone else?'

'Mrs Gobble.'

'She's potty. Quite harmless though. So you got nowhere?'

'I didn't say that. There are rumours that al-Qa'eda has arrived over here . . .'

The effect of Tweed's words was electric. Warner jumped up from the couch, marched back to his desk, sat in the high chair behind it. Paula was astonished at the change in his personality. He looked choleric, his voice grim.

'Now listen to me, Tweed. I know you have in your outfit that foreign correspondent reporter, Robert Newman. If he tries to write about those rumours we'll put out a D notice,

47

stop him in his tracks. It's an absurd idea. I will tell you some criminal organization from abroad may be trying to establish some system in Britain with the drug cartel in Colombia. That's absolutely off the record. Muzzle that wild dog, Newman. Do you understand me?'

The couch they sat on faced the elevated desk. Paula was staring at Victor Warner's expression, hardly able to credit a man's face could undergo such a change. The long bony face was a picture of violent rage, mouth open, exposing teeth like those of a small shark.

'I gather,' Tweed said slowly, calmly, 'that you don't want Newman reporting the possible arrival of a drug cartel operating out of Colombia. Like me, I'm sure he hasn't heard a whiff of such an event. So he's hardly likely to write about it.'

'I was talking about this al-Qa'eda nonsense. For God's sake don't you realize the panic such an idiotic rumour would cause in London? After the World Trade Center atrocity in New York. Panic, *panic*, PANIC!'

'So there's not an atom of truth in those rumours?'

Warner threw both arms in the air. He looked up at the ceiling as though seeking salvation.

'Haven't you yet grasped it's all rubbish? Do I have to say all over again what I have already explained to you so absolutely clearly? Don't you think we would know if there was even the merest hint of truth in such a crazy idea? You really are sorely trying my patience.'

'And,' Tweed said, standing up, 'you are absolutely sure you have received no word from anyone since your wife vanished into thin air? Even a few words from the lady herself?'

'Nothing, as I have already told you once. Tweed, you really are an extraordinary fellow – you need everything repeated to you twice. I'm even beginning to doubt that you should hold the position you do.'

'But that decision . . .' Tweed smiled '. . . doesn't come

within your province, does it? I hope you soon receive better news about Linda.'

'Linda?'

'I met her at one or two parties. If I have any news I'll let you know.'

Tweed had reached the door with Paula by his side. When he spoke they both looked back. The Minister was standing now behind his desk, leaning forward, penetrating eyes observing them over his pince-nez. He was a striking-looking man, Paula thought.

'We will keep in touch,' Warner called out, smiling.

Tweed opened the door and Palfry was standing just out of sight by the wall. Above his head was a ventilator. He had obviously been listening. So much for security at the Ministry. Tweed closed the door and Palfry joined them as they walked towards the staircase, whispering.

'Miss Grey, if you ever find yourself in Carpford do come and have a cup of tea with me. Mine is the Round House.'

'Thank you, Mr Palfry. I'll be glad to do that if ever the opportunity arises.'

'The Minister gets like that sometimes,' Palfry continued. 'You should hear him in the House when he's lashing the Opposition.'

'I don't think I'd want to,' Tweed replied.

6

She was tall and slim, even seated in the armchair facing
Newman, who leant forward in his own chair, their knees
almost touching. Clad in a black trouser suit, her jacket
was tight enough to reveal her good figure. Her mane of
jet-black hair draped over her shoulders. Newman looked
up, interrupting his animated conversation with the visitor.
He was standing up and the striking girl joined him, inches
taller than Paula.

'George told me a lady had brushed past him and come
up after leaving a box of Fortnum & Mason chocolates on
his desk,' Tweed said gruffly.

'This is Eva Brand,' Newman said hastily. 'The niece of
Drew Franklin, the columnist.'

'Mr Tweed,' Eva Brand explained, her voice soft but
with an underlying stronger timbre, 'you were pointed out
to me by Drew at a party. He said you were the only man
who could save Britain one day in a time of great peril.'

'Did he?' Like Paula, Tweed was stripping off his coat.
'Anything he says – or writes – usually has a snide touch. I
expect he was mocking me.'

'No, he was very serious.' Paula was watching her warily.
Eva's large dark eyes seemed to look through her as she
assessed her. Eva extended her hand and Paula shook it,
noting the strength in her shapely fingers. Tweed also
accepted her handshake, but briefly, then went to sit behind
his desk, gesturing for her to sit down. The stranger crossed

her long legs, clasped her hands in her lap as Paula went to her corner desk.

'Mr Tweed, I'm sorry to gatecrash my way in but I've found that's the only way I can get quickly to a top person.'

'So you don't hesitate to push your way in anywhere you want to go,' Tweed remarked gently.

'No! Never! If it's important. And the reason I am here to see you is important.'

You're pushy, Paula was thinking. I'll bet you went to one of the best-known boarding schools – Eva had a cultured voice. Probably ended up as Head Girl. Paula also realized that with her personality and looks, whenever Eva entered a roomful of people conversation would briefly stop. The men would ogle her, the women would spit inwardly.

'Important to you or to me?' Tweed enquired, playing with his Cartier pen, another present from his staff.

'Important to you . . .'

'Does your uncle, Drew, know you've come here?' Tweed interjected.

'Heavens, no!' Eva lifted her hands in horror at the idea. 'He'd have a fit. So I shan't tell him.'

'Before you tell me what you think is so important I'd like to know a little more about you. Background, career, if any.'

She sat up very straight. Newman couldn't take his eyes off her. From behind her word processor on her desk Monica glanced across at Paula, raised her eyes to heaven.

'I was educated at Roedean, then Oxford. I know something about code-breaking – had a boyfriend who was in that area. I spent some time at Medfords Security Agency. That was a tough job – they asked me to get to know certain men, take them to bars and get them drunk so they'd talk. The trick was to get them chattering, providing secret information, then escape before the invitation to their flat.

I once used my knee to get away from a persistent character. Do you get the gist?'

'I think I do.' Tweed was smiling. 'A tough job, as you said.' He was careful not to look at Paula, who was gazing in astonishment. 'So why have you barged in here?'

'Barged in!' Eva laughed. 'I like that.' She assumed her serious expression. 'Every now and again I drive up to Carpford, an odd village way up in the North Downs. I clear up the mess Drew likes living in. Dusting and so on. I make occasional visits when I know my uncle is in London. Would you believe it – Drew never notices. Well, a week ago I was in his place alone at night and I heard a motor-cycle coming. It stopped outside. I had my pistol, loaded, in my hand in no time. A Browning . . .'

'A Browning?' Tweed enquired, concealing his surprise.

'Yes, a .32. Surely you of all people must know about the weapon. I'm a member of a shooting club near the Thames. To continue, I watched from behind a gap in the curtains – watched this motor-cyclist carry an envelope to Drew's door and push it through the letter box. Then he roared off.'

'What did he look like?'

'Couldn't tell. Wore all the leather gear and a big helmet which completely concealed his face. Now, the envelope. It had no name or address on the outside. So, cheekily, I used a method for opening it I learned at Medfords – so you can later seal it and no one can tell it has been opened. I'd seen what was inside when the motor-cyclist came back. I stood to the side of the door with my Browning. He pushed open the flap of the letter-box and called out through the opening.'

'Same chap?'

'As far as I could tell. Again his machine was a Harley-Davidson. He spoke slowly and had a thick foreign accent. I decided that if he tried to break in I'd shoot him in the leg,' she said calmly.

'Why in the leg?'

'Then he could be interrogated later. He called out, "I delivered envelope wrong house. Push it back." I kept very quiet and he repeated the same words three times, then he gave up, rode away on his bike. Here it is.'

She handed Tweed a sheet of paper. It was good-quality bond paper and drawn in pen was a skilful picture of a cathedral with a huge dome. Tweed looked at her.

'St Paul's Cathedral,' she said. 'Very accurate. Good as a photograph.'

'I agree. What do you make of it?'

'The next target. This time in Britain. St Paul's is the supreme symbol of Christianity – which the fundamentalist Muslims want to destroy.'

'You're reading an awful lot into one drawing.'

'Am I?' Eva lifted her hand to push back a thick lock of hair away from her left eye. She had made this gesture several times. 'After the World Trade Center catastrophe in New York I asked Drew, who knows the Arabs, whether they really would be capable of planning such an intricate operation. He said it didn't really seem likely. Left it at that. I began to think about it, studying all the info I could get.'

'You came to a conclusion?' Tweed enquired off-handedly.

'I damned well did. I know the States. First they'd need one of those copious air timetables giving all flights – so they could pick out long-distance flights carrying tons of petrol. They'd have to decide which flights would be best. Then they'd have to check security. Find out where it was slack. Then locate quiet flats to rent where there was a mix of nationalities, so the killers wouldn't stand out. They'd have to visit the Trade Center several times, study its structure, decide on the best place to hit both towers. Probably discover where the architectural plans were available so they could study the structure. And a whole lot more. I've been to Egypt, mixed with Arabs. They're not advanced enough to have planned September 11.'

'Who would be then?'

'My bet would be an American – or an Englishman.'

Eva was about to leave when Tweed asked her to wait a moment. He darted out of the office, ran upstairs to where he found Pete Nield and Harry Butler drinking coffee. He told them he wanted them to follow an Eva Brand who was waiting in his office. He described her vividly.

'I want to know where she goes, who she meets. You'll have to get cracking . . .'

Butler opened a cupboard, grabbed a beret and a cap which he shoved into his pockets. They wanted to take up positions outside before their quarry left. Tweed looked at Nield.

'Difficult for you to change appearance in that suit.'

'No it isn't,' Harry told him. 'He can turn it inside out and it's a boring grey colour. Seen him change in an alley. Timing? Thirty seconds. We're off . . .'

Like most of Tweed's staff they wore rubber-soled shoes, and without a sound slipped off down the stairs past the closed door of Tweed's office. Tweed slowly returned as the front door closed quietly. They would be in position well before his visitor left.

Whenever possible Tweed organized two people to shadow a target. The system worked well and made it very unlikely the target would have any idea he – or she – was being shadowed.

Eva was standing up, putting on her smart expensive grey coat. She smiled when he came in and checked her watch. Then she went close to him, kissed him on both cheeks.

'I have taken up too much of your time. Thank you so much for seeing me.'

'Didn't give me much choice, did you,' he replied with a warm smile. 'Do you want to give me your address and phone number?'

'Don't waste much time, do you?' she flashed back,

smiling wickedly. 'But Paula has all my details.' She looked back at Paula. 'You take care. See you tonight at the Ivy.'

Then she was gone. With her absence the buoyant temperature inside the office semed to have dropped. Even Monica seemed more subdued.

'What was all this business, Paula, about having dinner with her at the Ivy? You're developing expensive tastes,' Tweed remarked.

'It was Eva's idea,' Paula explained. 'She said it would be nice for just us two girls to go out and compare notes. I'm wondering whether she wants to interrogate me. I'll be careful. But, that apart, I like her. She's clever. That business about who planned the atrocity in New York.'

'For weeks I have been wondering exactly the same thing myself. For similar reasons. Oh, I arranged for Pete and Harry to follow her.'

'So you don't trust her?'

'It's just that. As you know, I never take people at face value. Also I thought it curious that she never mentioned the disappearance of Mrs Warner. It has to be the main topic at Carpford.'

The door opened and Marler strolled in. He leant against a wall and produced one of his long cigarettes.

'Who was that devastating gorgeous woman I saw leaving here? The one with a great mane of dark hair and very tall.'

'You've just missed out,' Paula teased him. 'That was Eva Brand and Tweed has just sent Pete and Harry to shadow her. Now, if you had been here . . .'

'I don't think I like you any more,' he commented.

Paula had a point. Had Marler been available, Tweed would probably have sent him after her. An expert tracker, he always worked on his own and none of the targets he had followed had ever been aware of his presence. He lit his cigarette.

'What was Glamour Puss doing here?'

The phone rang and Monica looked surprised. She called out to Tweed. 'You'll never guess who is waiting to see you downstairs.'

Tweed hammered a fist on his desk, part of his new physical vitality. 'I don't want to guess. I want to know who it is.'

'Jules Beaurain.'

Wearing a blue bird's-eye suit, Beaurain breezed in. Tweed introduced him to Newman and Marler. Holding a posy of fresh flowers, Beaurain then walked swiftly to Paula's desk, laid down the posy.

'For an exceptionally intelligent and beautiful lady. It's a Belgian custom.'

'Don't believe that last bit, Jules,' Paula replied. 'They're wonderful. I can't thank you enough.'

'Then don't try.'

He sat down in the armchair facing Newman, stared at him as though he was some strange species. 'You're the reporter. I've read all your articles. Sometimes they're very good,' he chaffed, smiling.

'They're always good,' retorted Newman, returning the smile.

'Enough of this chit-chat. What brings you haring back to London, Jules?' Tweed asked.

'To give you information about Carpford I don't think you have yet. I phoned Buchanan. There are two more people up there you don't know about. You know where Margesson's house is?'

'Yes.'

Tweed had taken a large sheet of cartridge paper from his bottom drawer. Monica had earlier rushed to pick up the posy from Paula's desk, now she returned with a vase of water with the flowers carefully arranged. She placed them on Paula's desk. Paula extracted a rose, trimmed it with scissors, then went over to Beaurain. She inserted

57

it in his lapel, using a safety pin to secure it. He looked up at her.

'With such appreciation next time I'll buy the whole shop.'

'Yes,' growled Tweed. He swivelled the sheet round. 'Have I got Carpford reasonably accurate?'

Paula leaned over Beaurain to study the drawing. She was amazed at how quickly Tweed had worked. Carp Lake was the centre piece. Around it he had drawn Garda, Warner's strange Italianate property; Drew Franklin's concrete blockhouse; Agatha Gobble's Cotswold cottage; Peregrine Palfry's round house and Margesson's Georgian horror.

'You missed your vocation,' Beaurain told him. 'You should have been an artist. Incredibly accurate. Now draw in two bungalows, well spaced apart, here, south of Margesson's house.'

Tweed drew two small oblongs where Beaurain's fingers had indicated. He looked up at Paula.

'I remember passing these before we met Buchanan again. I thought that, like every other dwelling, they were out of place.'

'In the first one lives a man called Billy Hogarth, like the painter. In the last one resides Martin Hogarth, the brother of Billy. They hate each other. Understandably.'

'What are they like then?'

'Billy is the black sheep. Half the time he's roaring drunk – when he's not driving off somewhere. Then he's sober. Bit of a thug. Ask him the time of the day and he's likely to throw a heavy clock at you.'

'And Martin?'

'English gentleman. Tall, in his fifties. Well-spoken. Good-looking. Polite. Master of chatting and telling you nothing.'

'And these two are brothers? Martin and Billy?'

'They are. And there's more to relationships up there

than you might think. Both Martin and Billy – wait for it – are cousins of Drew Franklin, the columnist.'

'They are?' Tweed was taken aback. 'Do they communicate with each other? I'd have thought it likely.'

'Not according to Martin when I asked that same question. His reply, mind you, was vague as usual. He said, "We all live out own lives. Haven't you heard that old saying – "the bloodiest battlefield is the family arena."'

'Doesn't tell us much.'

'Which seems to be Martin's way of conducting a conversation. He'll chat for ages, but give you no information at all.'

'Talking about relationships,' Paula began, 'maybe we ought to tell Jules about our strange visitor this morning. Eva Brand.'

Tweed then gave Beaurain a full report of everything Eva had said – including the fact that she was a niece of Drew Franklin. When he had concluded, Tweed took out of his top drawer the drawing in ink of the cathedral the motor-cyclist had delivered. Beaurain studied it for a moment, threw it back on Tweed's desk.

'St Paul's Cathedral.'

'Exactly,' Tweed replied. 'Could it be significant?'

'Decoy,' Beaurain said dismissively.

7

'Is that Ali?' asked the voice on the phone.

Spoken in English, it was impossible to tell whether the caller was a man or a woman. The use of a voice-distorter made the speaker impossible to identify.

'It is Ali from Finsbury,' the man inside the public phone-box replied.

'Abdullah speaking. Is the consignment on its way. All five of the transporters.'

'They are coming. On schedule. They arrive at their destination at eight o'clock tonight.'

'I will call again, using the other number you gave, at seven . . .'

Ali left the phone-box quickly. Located in a carefully chosen quiet area of London, it was rarely used, a fact confirmed by constant observation.

The transporters referred to were milk wagons, each driving south on a different road, the route they used every day at this time. Innocent enough cargoes, on this occasion they carried more than milk.

At the bottom of each load was a larger container, swathed thickly in waterproof cloth. There was also a thick cable wrapped round the container very securely. The end of the cable had a handle attached to a strong hook concealed just below the surface of the milk at the rear of the vehicle.

Later, arriving at a farm with a large barn, purchased weeks before, they would drive in. Once inside the barn the wagon would be opened, a gloved hand would feel for the handle, grasp it, hauling the metal container to the surface. Inside the barn it would be transferred to a small van with the words 'Fresh Fruit' inscribed on its outer bodywork. All five vans, refrigerated, had also been purchased weeks before. To bolster the supplier's confidence, a cheque on a London bank had been paid in advance. It was the supplier's understanding that a new company was entering the business of providing fruit to larger supermarkets at highly competitive prices.

The organizer of the operation, who used the name Abdullah, was confident that if the milk wagons were found, eventually, it would be too late. The spectacular and catastrophic attack would have occurred. Abdullah had no doubt the casualties would run into thousands, the dead casualties.

Inside each concealed container was a new weapon, the warhead armed with an explosive of devastating power.

8

When Beaurain left Park Crescent both Tweed and Paula escorted him downstairs. At the bottom he paused, spoke very quietly to them so George, the guard, could not hear what he was saying.

'Is there somewhere I could have a private word with both of you?'

'Visitors' room,' said Tweed, crossing the hall and opening a door into a barely furnished room. He closed the door as Beaurain looked round with a cynical smile.

'Don't make your visitors very comfortable, do you? Wooden table, hard-backed chairs, nothing to read.'

'There are visitors I feel I should see but don't want them to linger. What is it, Jules?'

'I want you to know that I'm flying to Brussels – there and back in a day. I have made an appointment to see the top Director of the Banque de Bruxelles et Liège. The place where you told me a dubious lawyer in London sends the rent money collected from Carpford. I want him to tell me where it is forwarded to – I'm convinced it doesn't just sit in Brussels.'

'But,' Paula objected, 'you did say Belgian banks are even more security-conscious than Swiss banks.'

'True,' said Beaurain. 'Clever girl. Luckily I know this man and I don't think he is aware I am no longer Commissioner of police. It was kept quiet, my resignation – maybe because I am popular with the people

63

for putting certain corrupt fat cats behind bars. I know certain illegalities the man I am going to see has engaged in. Blackmail is a powerful weapon.'

'You're wicked,' Paula said with a smile. 'One more thing. I was going to ask you if you know what lies behind that tall brick wall extending from Victor Warner's property. It's pure curiosity, I admit.'

'I imagine it's security,' Beaurain replied. 'Remember what his position is. As for behind it, the ground slopes down steeply and there's a lime pit and an old abandoned quarry.'

'How are you for time?' Tweed enquired.

'I must leave at once or I'll miss my flight. The bad news is I'll be back.'

He hugged Paula, shook Tweed's hand, opened the door and before they could leave the room he was gone.

'I'm going back to Carpford when I can,' Paula said as they climbed the stairs. 'I want to talk to those brothers – Billy and Martin. Something odd about them.'

'Then you won't go on your own. If I'm tied up, Newman can come with you.'

Newman looked up as they came in. He was grinning sardonically. He spoke to Paula.

'I think you've made a conquest. Jules has really taken a fancy to you.'

'Don't be so stupid,' she snapped. Sitting at her desk she glared at him. 'Instead of making foolish remarks you might as well help me. When I can I'm going back to Carpford. To see those two brothers, Martin and Billy. While I'm up there I'd also like to call on Drew Franklin, your favourite columnist. But when is he there?'

'My favourite creep,' Newman told her. 'He'll be there tomorrow evening. I know he likes to hide himself away when he's typing his column. You'd better watch it. He has a reputation for being a professional ladies' man.'

'That might help me to get him talking,' she teased Newman. 'You think I'm his type?'

64

'He'll either tell you to go to hell or flatter the life out of you. So you won't know whether you're coming or going.'

'In case you didn't realize it, I have had experience fending off numerous predatory males. I'll cope.'

'If I can, could I come with you? Unless you have Tweed by your side.'

'Thanks. I'll bear it in mind.'

'And,' Newman warned, 'those Hogarth brothers – strange name – don't sound like the sort you'd ask to dinner. Especially Billy.'

Tweed jumped up, began pacing as he gave orders to Monica. 'I've a load of work for you. I want dossiers compiling on all those people who live up at Carpford. Where they came from, their associates, as far as possible. Also a dossier on Victor Warner, the Minister. That will have to be dealt with delicately. Finally, one on Eva Brand. You've got her address, Paula.'

'Yes, she lives not far away from me in Fulham. Surely you don't suspect her of something?'

'I'm not trusting anyone. Eva came charging in here with her drawing of St Paul's. Can't imagine what that has to do with Warner's apparent interest in a Colombian drug cartel. Check her out. I'm also intrigued about the circle of relationships in that village. The Hogarths are brothers, but they're also cousins of Drew Franklin. On top of that Eva Brand is a niece of Franklin's. Too much coincidence. You know I don't believe in coincidences.' He extracted from a drawer his detailed plan of Carpford and its inhabitants, handed it to Paula. 'I'd like you to check that and show the position of Black Wood. I'm not sure how far away it was.'

'Pretty close. I'll draw it in for you.'

'Tweed,' Monica called out after answering the phone. 'I have Pete Nield on the line for you . . .'

'Pete, how are you getting on. Haven't lost her, have you?' he joked.

'As if we would. It's a bit odd. She first took a cab to the Ministry of Security. Was inside fifteen minutes. Then she comes out, catches another cab and goes into the maze of streets near Covent Garden. The cab waits while she walks out of sight of it and enters Monk's Alley, crouching to slip under the crime scene tape. She uses a torch – it's dark by now – and appears to be looking for something on the ground. When she comes out she's holding a Beretta automatic in her right hand which she slips inside her coat presumably so the cab driver waiting for her a distance back won't see it . . .'

'Hang on, Pete. How could you know it was a Beretta? You wouldn't be just behind her, I assume.'

'I used my monocular with the night glass lens attached to it. She gets inside the cab and it drops her at an address in Fulham . . .'

'Wait a second.' Tweed gestured for Monica to give him the slip of paper with Eva's address Paula had taken to her earlier. 'Now, what address?'

It was the same address Eva had written, plus her phone number, on the piece of paper she had handed to Paula before leaving.

'That's where she lives,' Tweed told Pete. 'What on earth is she up to now?'

'Getting ready to go out tonight would be my guess. The bathroom window is all steamed up.'

'Right. This is what you do. Stay there out of sight. I say that because I'm getting the impression she's pretty smart. She's having dinner with Paula at the Ivy. Follow her, then wait outside the restaurant. One of you had best grab some sandwiches and get that flask you always carry filled with tea. When she goes inside with Paula wait outside for them to come out. Something might happen.'

'Understood. We'll be ready for a fracas.'

Tweed began pacing up and down his office again, a sign

Paula recognized that the momentum was building up. He was about to issue another order when Marler strolled in, wearing a camel-hair coat as he went to lean against a wall. Tweed stared at the coat.

'In that garb you could be mistaken for Special Branch.'

'Which is the general idea. I've been talking to some of Mr Special Branch's informants. Way below the calibre of mine.'

'Well, get on with it,' Tweed snapped. 'Anything to report?'

'The mugs all tell the same tale. Rumours that top people from the Colombian cartel have arrived in London. They go vague when I ask where I can find them.'

'Warner has Colombia on the brain.'

'Agreed. But I also had a chat with a woman, Carla, who is my favourite informant. Wants to join our outfit, which is why she's working for me. She's clever. Well-educated, she can dress like a tart and talk the lingo so a Cockney would think she was from the East End.' He paused to light a cigarette while Tweed waited impatiently. 'Carla,' Marler continued, 'has heard a strong rumour that London is facing its own September 11 – a monstrous attack. She says the killers have slipped into the country, Saudis and a group from Algeria. No clue as to the form the attack will take or where or when, but soon.'

'You believe her?' Tweed pressed.

'Carla's never been wrong before. She was in that Soho joint, Belles, which we have reason to know. She has languages, including French and Arabic. She lingered at the bar not far from a table where three Arabs in white turbans were talking . . .'

'Not black turbans?' Tweed checked.

'I thought I spoke clearly. Black would suggest something else now. Maybe they weren't keen to advertise. She caught a few words. "The equipment is on its way. It has already left the farm." That was all she could hear.'

67

'You have a visitor,' Monica called out after talking on her phone. 'You'll be pleased. 'Waiting downstairs is Jasper Buller, chief of Special Branch, together with a partner.'

'Buller, the Bull, as his staff nickname him. A brute who terrifies everyone working for him. Should be fun.'

Tweed returned to his desk. He took off his jacket and rolled up his shirt sleeves. He glared at Monica as he was speaking.

'Tell Buller he can come up to see me on his own while his partner waits in the visitor's room. Actually, tell George, who won't stand any nonsense. If Buller doesn't like my suggestion he can go jump in the Thames.'

Newman got up from his chair and perched on Paula's desk. 'I met Buller recently. He's as thick as five planks.'

'He's on his way up,' Monica reported after a few minutes. 'On his own. I could hear him swearing at George who just kept repeating your instruction word for word.'

As Tweed expected, Buller was wearing a camel-hair coat when he stormed into the room. About five feet eight tall, he was very heavily built and had a large head. His hair was cut to a stubble and the face below it suggested aggression. Under thick brows the eyes were dark, hostile and flickered about, checking everyone in the room. In his forties, he had the broken nose of a prize-fighter, a tight-lipped mouth, a determined jaw and the air of a man who expected instant obedience.

'I won't stand for this,' he bellowed, 'shoving my partner in a bare room and locking the door on him.'

'Then try sitting down,' Tweed suggested amiably. 'It is normal to phone for an appointment first.'

'Blow that for a lark,' Buller growled and sagged into an armchair. 'You don't seem to know who you're talking to.'

'It is Jasper Buller, I presume,' Tweed said genially.

'It is the chief of Special Branch.' His tone was a snarl.

'Now, I need to know what you and that young lady . . .' He turned to look at Paula and his expression briefly became cordial as she stared back '. . . were doing ferreting around up at Carpford.'

'Why?' Tweed enquired. 'You think the place is populated with Colombian cartel barons?'

'Mr Tweed.' Buller leaned forward, lowering his voice to little more than a whisper. 'I would much appreciate it if we could talk in private. Please.'

Tweed called to Monica to ask if Howard's office was available. She told him it was, that Howard was not expected back for at least an hour.

Tweed stood up, went to the door, followed by Buller. He led the way upstairs to Howard's spacious office. He knew Howard was always careful to lock away any important documents when he was absent. They walked inside and sat down.

'I appreciate this,' Buller repeated. His whole manner had changed and he spoke politely with a warm smile. 'I think you should know that I visit the mosque in Finsbury, the one which is notorious.'

'I'm surprised they let you in.'

'Ah!' Buller smiled warmly again. 'I go dressed as an Arab. That is just between you and me. The Minister, Warner, has no idea I'm doing this. I know he wouldn't approve. He has Colombia and a drug cartel on the brain. I suspect that a number of Taliban have been smuggled into this country.'

'You have evidence of this infiltration?'

'Unfortunately, no. But I've seen several Arabs who have the appearance of having arrived very recently. In the end, it may come down to you and me. Not,' he added hastily, 'that I'm asking for cooperation. But I will attempt to keep you informed when I do have something solid. Now, I had better go.'

'Thank you for being so frank. Yes, do keep in touch . . .'

69

Tweed ran back down the stairs while Buller lumbered behind, heading for the exit. Tweed carefully closed his office door. He spoke rapidly to Marler, standing close to him.

'Buller is just leaving. He may separate from his partner. The man to follow is Buller – where he goes, anyone he contacts.'

'I'm on my way.' Marler grabbed his coat and was heading for the door. He called back over his shoulder. 'I have one of those small cameras, non-flash, which the boffins in the basement invented. Hold it in the palm of one hand.'

'Marler!' Tweed called out. 'Be careful. You could be walking into a cauldron . . .'

9

Inside the huge barn next to Oldhurst Farm in Berkshire the third milk wagon had eased it way inside. The English driver stepped down from his cab. He flexed his fingers, stiff with driving the large vehicle. He walked over to the leader he knew as Adam, who stood on a large sheet of canvas spread out over the floor.

'OK, mate. Another load of drugs delivered. What is it? Cocaine? And I'll take that two thousand quid you're holding in your paw.'

He was aware there were other men behind him but his eyes were on the fat wad of banknotes Adam was holding.

Adam was a small man, neatly dressed in English clothes. His skin was brownish, a tan from spending several months in the Seychelles. He spoke perfect English.

'By the mercy of Allah you have done well,' the little man said with a twisted smile.

'Allah!' The driver was appalled. 'You're a bunch of flaming Arabs. You . . .'

It was the last word he ever spoke, as a man behind him drove a wide-bladed knife into his back between the ribs. He twisted the knife, withdrew it, stabbed again and again as the driver, already dead, slumped on to the canvas.

No need to issue any orders. Several men with dark complexions stripped his clothes of all identification. They wrapped the corpse inside the canvas, rolling it up, then securing it with heavy chains. Three of them carried the

71

rolled canvas out of a back door and across a field. It was dumped into a large septic tank, sank to join the two other bodies of English drivers dumped earlier.

Inside the barn other Arabs dressed in English clothes had already unrolled another large sheet of canvas, ready for when the fourth English driver arrived with his milk wagon. 'Abdullah' had planned very carefully.

The neat little man, Adam, whose real name was Ali, now gave fresh orders. The milk wagon was opened and an exceptionally strong Arab was lowered inside on a rope ladder. Equipped with gloves, he felt round below the surface, located the hook, then the cable wrapped round the container resting at the bottom of the wagon. It took him all his strength to haul up the container, its wrappings dripping milk.

He hauled it over the side where other hands waited to grasp it and laid it on the ground. The bloodstained knife which had murdered the English driver was used to cut through the layers of wrapping, exposing a metal container. At this point Ali took over.

Unlocking a huge padlock, he lifted the lid. He warned his helpers in savage language to be careful. A curiously shaped weapon was gently laid on the floor. Perched on a strong-legged base was a huge shell-shaped object, the warhead already in position in its nose.

Ali repeated for the umpteenth time the instructions he had given earlier.

'It is harmless now. When it reaches its destination, with the weapons in their different positions, I will give the order to press the orange button. Then the weapon is active, but still harmless.' He pointed, at the button. 'At the moment when the stupendous attack is launched you press the red button.' He pointed to another button embedded in a shallow hole. 'Then London is devastated, praise be to Allah.'

None of the Arabs listening had any idea of the destination the weapons would be taken to. The master planner

72

had hired the drivers of the milk wagons by contacting men on the verge of release from prison for comparatively non-violent offences. They had been told they would, for the sum of two thousand pounds, have to drive certain vehicles transporting drugs.

They had also been told the original drivers of the milk wagons would be tied up when a truck, slewed across a quiet road, stopped them. What Ali had not told them was that the original drivers would have their throats slit, their bodies weighted and cast into convenient marshes en route. The master planner had also anticipated that in due course the companies owning the milk wagons would report their disappearance. But who would see anything sinister in the hijacking of five milk wagons?

Certainly not the police – or not until havoc had been created in London and thousands of bodies had been blown to bits.

10

It was two hours later and darkness had fallen. Earlier Monica and Paula had fetched lunches from a nearby deli for Tweed, Newman and themselves. When Newman had finished his meal Tweed had started pacing again. Paula watched him as he frowned. The momentum was building up again. He stopped by Newman, seated in an armchair.

'Bob, I want you to get moving. You know someone at the *Daily Nation*, someone you can trust?'

'I've several pals there. The most close-mouthed one is Ed Jenner, sub-editor. Why?'

'I want you to find out every little thing you can about Drew Franklin – where he lives in London, how much time he spends in his office at the paper, any rumours about new girlfriends. Every morsel.'

'That's easy,' Newman told him. 'And Franklin tucks himself away in a small office well away from Ed Jenner. See you all, some day . . .'

'Why has your attention switched to Franklin?' Paula asked when he had gone.

'Just a thought. I suspect he has great freedom of move-ment.'

Which tells me nothing, Paula thought. Tweed has got some bee in his bonnet.

Night had come later. Monica had been using the phone non-stop, scribbling on her pad as people told her things.

Tweed was studying his Carpford map again when Monica called across to him.

'I know you didn't ask me to check out Jasper Buller but I've done that among other people. Didn't think you'd mind.'

'Tell me.' Tweed was impressed. His staff knew him so well now they could guess what might be useful to him. 'Fire away . . .'

Before she could open her mouth Marler walked in with a vague smile. Paula knew he had succeeded in his mission to track Buller. He threw off his coat, lit a cigarette.

'I hit the bull's-eye, following Buller. No pun intended. I follow him to his pad in Pimlico. Then I wait, but not for long. The Bull can move. I've parked among other cars and what emerges from the flat? Buller, wearing Arab dress. Long flowing robe, the lot. He dives into a cab he must have phoned for. Where do you think we go to? The mosque in Finsbury. His cab waits round a corner. The Bull shuffles inside the mosque. Not there long. Probably kneels on the rolled-up carpet tucked under one arm, bows three times towards Mecca – that's a guess.'

'Oh, my God, who would have guessed it was Buller,' gasped Paula.

'Wait a little longer, my dear.' Marler squeezed her gently on the shoulder as he continued. 'Now we're off back in his cab to Pimlico. Pays the driver, disappears back into the flat. He's not there long. He comes out again, dives into another cab. This time he's clad in warm holiday clothes, carrying a suitcase. We set off again. Destination? Waterloo. Buller's heading for Eurostar when he swings round, catches me completely by surprise, talks straight at me. "Bit of a run-around for you, Marler. I want you to give a highly confidential message to Tweed. Tell him I'm on my way to meet a contact at Milan in Italy. I'm tracking the money route financing these hellish Taliban."'

'I'm staggered,' Paula commented.

'A bit more.' Marler took a folded sheet of paper from his pocket, handed it to Tweed. 'That's the name and address of his contact in Milan. He said you should have it in case he doesn't come back.'

'I don't like the sound of that,' Newman said grimly.

Tweed was reading the neatly written words on a sheet obviously torn from a notebook. *Mario Murano, Via Legessa 290, Milano.*

'This opens a new front,' Tweed said quietly. 'Italy.'

'Buller also said he might get the routes they were using, then he had to dash before missing his train. End of the story.'

'As long as it isn't the end of Buller,' Tweed remarked.

'I would never have dreamt all of this,' Paula burst out. 'I thought he was just a stupid bully.'

'Which tells you,' Tweed said half to himself, 'what a complex mixture people – men and women – are. That act of posing as the Bull is remarkable cover.'

'I bet his lordship, Victor Warner, hasn't a clue as to what Buller is really doing,' Paula reflected. 'And no one else inside his organization.'

'Oddly enough,' Tweed told Marler, 'Monica was compiling a dossier on Jasper Buller. On her own initiative.'

'Well,' Monica addressed him, 'I haven't dug up anything like what Marler has told us. Only his address in Pimlico, plus the fact his staff really hate him, and the intriguing fact that he often goes off on his own for hours – despite insisting that employees sent out on a mission must always travel in pairs. Nothing about secret trips to the Finsbury mosque. That's the notorious one.'

'I passed the short time he was inside taking photographs of everyone else who went in there,' Marler told them.

He produced his tiny camera, which not only produced negatives but also converted them into prints. Extracting a roll of prints, he dropped it on Paula's desk. She started separating them into individual prints with a pair of scissors, then took them over to Tweed.

'Don't suppose they'll amount to anything,' Marler warned.

Paula went behind Tweed's desk and leant over his shoulder. Tweed checked each print carefully. Just a bunch of Arabs in Muslim garb. Paula reached for one, examined it under the magnifying glass she had brought with her. She half-closed her eyes.

'This figure reminds me of someone. Damned if I know who.'

'Let me see,' Tweed requested.

The figure was leaving the mosque. Probably a woman. The figure carried a stick and appeared to have a limp. Crouched well forward, it was impossible to assess its height. The face was covered except for the eyes.

'Doesn't ring any bells,' Tweed decided. He beckoned to Marler, pointed a finger at the crouched figure. 'Did you by chance notice where this one went to?'

'Heavens no! I just snap-snap-snapped. Had to be careful. Finsbury isn't the safest area in town.'

'File them,' Tweed said pushing the photos towards Paula as she walked round the desk to head back for her own corner. 'Marler, you have achieved a minor miracle – finding out about the real Jasper Buller.'

'Where is everyone else?' Marler asked.

'I sent Newman to check up on Drew Franklin. Pete and Harry are following Eva Brand.'

'You can't suspect such a lovely creature.'

'She's a woman, not a creature,' Paula snapped.

'She's a niece of Drew Franklin,' Tweed remarked. 'Plus the Hogarth brothers, Billy and Martin, being cousins of Drew Franklin. We really don't know who knows who out at Carpford. So we're going to find out. Beaurain used the word base about the place.'

Paula had checked her watch. 'Heavens, I've got to go

78

to my flat and get ready for my dinner at the Ivy with Eva. That doesn't take five minutes.'

'How women compete with each other,' Newman remarked. He had just returned. Paula fled out of the room as he made his comment.

'You'd prefer them sloppy?' Tweed growled. 'It is one of their nice traits. I like it.'

The phone had rung while they were talking and Monica called out.

'That was a message from Jules Beaurain. He's landed back at Heathrow. Expects to be here in about an hour. Says he has important news, very important.'

Inside the barn at Oldhurst Farm the fifth and last milk wagon had arrived. The body of the English driver was already at the bottom of the septic tank. The weapon had been hauled up out of the wagon, was now transferred to the interior of a small white van bearing the legend *Flourishing Florist* on both sides of the vehicle. The three vans which had departed earlier bore a different legend, *Fresh Fruit.*

Ali, arms crossed, stood gazing with satisfaction inside the van where the weapon had been placed in position near the front of the vehicle. Its three strong legs rested on a metal plate which had holes drilled on four sides. Large metal screws were now in place, gripping the tripod tightly to the floor.

To any normal human being the device would have seemed sinister and menacing. The large shell, tipped with its warhead, perched on the brutal tripod holding it firmly in place, would have seemed horrific. Ali, on the other hand, was gloating as he visualized it leaving its platform when the red button was pressed. The special powerful explosive which, on hitting its target, would explode outwards and upwards to cause the maximum of havoc.

'Now fill the van with the camouflage,' he ordered in Arabic. 'Four of you get the job done.'

Huge bouquets of expensive flowers, including orchids, were piled up round the device, almost to the roof of the van. Large pots of flowers, secured inside boxes open at the top, were placed close together at the rear of the van. A number of very large pots, tipped backwards with wedges, were placed inside as the rear doors of the van were closed slowly.

'Abdullah' had hammered home this instruction to Ali. In the rare event that a van was stopped by a police car the driver would hand the keys to an officer, standing back.

When the officer opened a door an avalanche of heavy pots carrying plants would descend on him, possibly knocking him out. That would curb a patrol car's officers from probing any further into the van. Similar 'barricades' had been built up against the locked doors of the three 'florist's' vans.

Ali checked his watch. They were keeping to the timing. The master planner had insisted the vans, departing separately, should drive south so they would be caught up in the London rush hour. Hardly a time when police would be stopping vehicles and adding to the chaos. As with the planes which had flown into the World Trade Center in New York, everything had been thought of. London was doomed.

11

Paula, clad in a pale orange suit, glanced back through the rear window of the cab taking her to the Ivy. She couldn't rid herself of the feeling that she was being followed.

There were three cars behind her cab, but close behind the third car was a motor-cyclist. Black leather gear, a large helmet which concealed his face, the shape of his head. She'd thought she had heard a motor-cycle start up soon after the cab left her flat.

It was night, but the Strand was well illuminated. Street lights and shop windows glowing. They were close to the restaurant when she looked back again. The motor-cyclist was now behind her. She decided to pay the cabbie now, gave him a generous tip. As he pulled in to the kerb she threw open the door, jumped out, and ran to and inside the Ivy. The manager told her Miss Brand was already waiting at their table.

She followed him into the spacious restaurant. Already the place was almost full. Eva wore a close-fitting dress of gold with a high collar. She jumped up to kiss Paula and a bottle of Krug was nestling in an ice bucket.

'You look ravishing,' Paula said as she sat down. 'Gold suits you.'

'And your suit is so smart,' Eva replied with a wide smile. 'Now we've told each other how good we look let's have a toast.' She raised the glass the waiter had just filled. 'Here's to crime.'

81

'I prefer here's to the destruction of criminals.'

'Excuse me.' Eva chuckled. 'That was the toast we used to drink at Medfords, the security lot. Without crime we'd have been out of business. Mind if I smoke? Thanks.'

'I was really thinking of Mr Warner. A disappearance is in a way even more disturbing than a body. You wonder and wonder. Victor Warner conceals his emotions well but he must be going nearly crazy.'

'I agree.' Eva played with her cigarette in an ashtray. 'She was a nice lady. Like me she was a linguist.'

'You knew her then?' Paula asked.

'I met her at several parties. She loved England. Said she'd travelled but there was nowhere in the world like it.'

'What languages do you speak then?' Paula asked, looking up from the menu.

'Oh, French, Arabic, Spanish and Italian.'

'Arabic? That's impressive.'

'Medfords sent me once to Cairo after a man who'd absconded with a large sum of money. Now,' she said quickly, 'see anything that appeals?'

They ordered. Both avoided starters and Paula ordered the salmon fishcake. She had the impression Eva wished to get the conversation away from Arabs and Arabic. Determined that they would not just indulge in chit-chat, Paula changed the topic.

'What do you think has happened to Mrs Warner?'

'Who knows?' Eva waved an elegant hand. 'Kidnapped?'

'Then why no ransom note? I happen to know that is the case. After three long weeks.'

'It's a mystery others must solve. I heard your people are working hard on the case,' commented Eva.

'Among other things. So you're also fluent in Italian. I imagine you've been to Italy?'

'Rome, Florence and Verona. And Milan.'

'So when were you last in Milan?' Paula asked with a smile.

'If I didn't know you have perfect manners,' Eva began, her smile gone, her large dark eyes staring, 'I would get the impression you are interrogating me.'

'Now why would I do that?' Paula enquired with a smile. 'Is there some significance about Milan? Do tell.' She sipped her champagne. 'This is wonderful. I suppose you can get it in Milan,' she persisted. 'I've heard in Italy they push their own vintages.'

Eva, her expression neutral, buttered a piece of bread. She ate it before wiping her wide mouth.

'Italy does have some excellent wines. But of course, if you stayed at a top hotel you could get anything you fancied.'

She's evaded my question, Paula thought. Why? They began to chat about well-known people occupying tables a distance from them. Eva showed a malicious side to her humour.

'I do detest that fat pig over there. I avoid pop stars like the plague. Why have they become so important – self-important might be a better description. Making a fortune out of a ghastly row they call music. The fat pig has just looked at me and then obviously turned his head away. Maybe he can lip-read.' She chuckled. 'I do hope so.'

A skinny young man in a white suit who was not completely sober came to their table, grasped Eva's wrist below her full cuffs. His sensuous lips were open in an inviting smile, exposing bad teeth.

'Miss Eva Brand, if my eyes do not fool me. I'm Joe Yorkie, lead singer with the Busy Bees. Got a yacht in the Med. I could fly you down there.'

'If you don't remove your hand off me this plate of omelette is going to end up all down that silly white suit.' She took hold of the plate with both hands, began to lift it.

'Don't . . . thin . . . think you're my type.'

'Then fly down to the Med, dive off the deck and don't bother to come up again. Shove off, you nobody.'

Eva's tone was vicious. Paula stopped eating, convinced the omelette would end up on the suit if the drunk didn't get the message. He did, staggering a little on his way back to his table.

Eva smiled, as though nothing had happened. 'Now, what were we talking about?'

The rest of the meal passed pleasantly, with both women chatting about this and that. Paula was careful to keep away from any more controversial subjects. After coffee she checked her watch.

'Eva, it has been an evening for me to remember, but I have to leave. A business appointment,' she fibbed, 'at this hour. Such is life. And thank you again.'

'Do you mind if I wait?' Eva suggested with her wide smile. 'A friend is coming to have liqueurs with me. I still do the odd job for Medfords. Damned if I know why . . .'

Paula was collecting her coat in the lobby as the girl was about to help her on with her coat. Hands appeared behind her, grasped the coat.

'Allow me,' Peregrine Palfry said cheerfully. 'Don't forget we're having dinner some time. You really do look so devastating I could melt.'

'Thank you very much, Mr Palfry . . .'

'All my friends call me Perry. Please.'

Palfry, his smooth skin gleaming in the light, was wearing a dinner jacket. His greenish eyes held hers as he kissed her on both cheeks.

'Have a care,' he concluded.

Paula pretended to take time buttoning her coat, stepping back so she could see into the restaurant. Palfry bent down and hugged Eva, then sat down opposite her and began talking animatedly, waving his hands.

'That's weird,' Paula said to herself and walked out into the freezing night. They were waiting for her the moment

84

the door closed behind her and she stepped on to the pavement.

A short, heavily built man in working clothes, with a cap pulled well down over his swarthy face, grabbed her right forearm tightly. Since it was the right forearm Paula could not reach down for her Browning. Another even larger man with a bald head grasped her left arm.

'Got a limo to take you 'ome,' snarled the brute with the cap. 'Ups-a-daisy.'

Helpless, she knew her feet were about to be lifted off the pavement while she was carried to the limo. Harry Butler appeared out of nowhere, slammed a haymaker into the man with the cap.

'Shouldn't have done that, you piece of rubbish,' Harry rasped.

Her right arm was released and the grip on it had been so savage she could hardly move it. At the same moment, Pete Nield, also appearing out of nowhere, hit the bald-headed man with his stiffened right hand against the side of his neck, followed it up by a vicious punch into the kidneys. Blinking, but free, Paula stepped back.

This was only for starters. Harry's first punch had hit the attacker in the stomach and his target was bent forward, groaning. Harry jerked up his metal-rimmed boot between the man's legs. His target screamed, bent over the pavement. Harry rammed his head down on to the stone pavement. Paula heard something crack.

Pete now had a choke hold on Bald Head whose tongue was protruding from between his thick lips. While all this took place, Paula saw Newman running to the limo where a driver waited behind the wheel, his window up. Newman reached in through the open window with his left hand, pressed the button, closing the window. While it was partly open he tossed a smoke bomb inside. The driver stopped trying to release his seat-belt as acrid smoke filled the interior. He began to cough, spluttering, unable to leave his seat. Newman brushed his hands together, dived into his waiting car, drove it over to where Paula waited.

'Take you home, lady. Only a modest charge . . .'

She was already seated in the front passenger seat and he drove off as she fastened her seat belt. She looked back. Harry and Pete were still hammering at the two thugs who were now lying on the pavement. She had little doubt both of her attackers would be crippled for weeks.

'How come you were there? You saved my bacon, as they say.'

'Tweed's idea. He was nervous about that dinner at the Ivy, sent out Pete and Harry to wait for you. I decided to join the party.' He chuckled, 'Driver of that limo waiting to cart you off somewhere is having a smoke.'

'Sorry?'

'I chucked a smoke bomb inside his limo – after locking his door. Doubt if he'll smoke a cigarette for months. Now, how are you?'

'Shaken, but OK.'

'Park Crescent here we come.'

Arriving back at Tweed's office, they found him pacing, unable to keep still. He ran forward to hug Paula while Monica, noticing her ashen face, hurried out to make tea. Slipping out of her coat, Paula, in a state of shock, sagged into the chair behind her desk. Reaction had set in and she was trembling.

'What happened?' demanded Tweed.

Newman gave a brief but graphic report about the attack outside the Ivy. Monica returned with a cup and saucer, planted it in front of Paula.

'Sip that,' she ordered. 'It's sweetened tea. Know you don't like sugar but just get that inside you.' She watched over Paula as she grasped the cup in both hands, leaning over the saucer to take any spillage.

The door opened and Pete and Harry rushed in. Harry, who was especially fond of Paula, went over to her and laid a hand on her shoulder. She had stopped trembling and had finished her cup of tea. The colour had come back into her face. She sat up straight and looked round at the men in the room.

'I want to thank you all for saving me from what I imagine could have been a very unpleasant experience. What made you suspicious, Tweed?'

'Call it sixth sense.'

'I wonder why they wanted me,' she mused.

'My guess,' Tweed told her, 'was they were after information about how far we'd got in our investigation.'

'Investigation into what?'

'Could have been several factors. What interests me is how they knew you were at the Ivy. One answer is Eva Brand. Did she have a mobile?'

'She could have – in her handbag tucked by her chair. But she'd have to have worked fast. It was only minutes after leaving the table before I walked outside.'

'A brief call could have been made in seconds,' Tweed insisted. ' "She's on her way out now." '

'On the other hand I'm sure I was followed in the cab taking me there. By a motor-cyclist in black leather with a huge helmet.'

Marler, standing against a wall when Paula and Newman had arrived back, had remained silent. Now he spoke.

'My bet is on Eva Brand. What sort of conversation did you have with her over dinner?'

Paula recalled, word for word, what they had talked about. Tweed frowned at one point. Paula saw the frown and asked him what had struck him.

'Her reference to Milan, to speaking their language. Italy keeps looming into the picture . . .' He fingered the piece of paper with the address Marler had given him. 'Marler, tell us all about your experience with following Buller.'

They listened while Marler repeated the report he had given Tweed earlier. He left nothing out. Paula had heard it before but now she sat up very erect, waiting until Marler waved a hand, indicating he'd finished. Harry had sat cross-legged on the floor. He whistled.

'The Finsbury mosque. That's the one where those rats who belong to al-Qa'eda are supposed to be brainwashed and given their orders.'

'And,' Tweed emphasized, 'Milan keeps coming into the picture. First, Buller is on his way there. He's a bit like you, Paula – gets an idea and follows it up on his own. Now we have Eva Brand linked with Milan.' He checked his watch. 'Bob, get any information on Drew Franklin when you went to the *Daily Nation?*'

'Yes – and no. Met my pal, the copy-editor. Took him out to a pub. He said Franklin isn't liked by the rest of the staff, but they all admit his column is so brilliant and snide they know a lot of their readers turn to it first. Doesn't talk to anyone, gives the impression they are all members of a lower class, that intellectually he's way above them, and shows it. Has a London pad not far behind Eaton Square – I've got the address. Drives off up to Carpford to type his column. Goes to a lot of parties in London – I suppose he's picking up gossip. He goes abroad in January for six weeks. No one knows where to. He only misses handing over the text of his column for one week. Behind his back they nickname him Snooty. Not a lot, but he seems a bit of a mystery man.'

'Paula, time for you to go home, get a good night's sleep after the Ivy business. Beaurain is still trapped at Heathrow – Security at Heathrow got an anonymous call that there was a terrorist aboard his flight. Beaurain is marooned there until they've checked everyone. He'll be here later tonight so I'll wait.'

'So will I,' said Paula forcefully.

Half an hour later, Marler was looking out of the window

88

after pulling aside the curtain. Pete and Harry had earlier left to get something to eat. Marler whistled and grinned as he looked at Tweed.

'You're honoured. Prepare for a shock.'

'You'll never . . .' began Monica, who had answered the phone. She cut off the rest of her remark after a certain look from Tweed.

'You have a visitor,' she said quietly. 'Victor Warner, Minister of Security, wants to see you urgently.'

'We know by now what he is,' growled Tweed. 'Ask him up – by himself.'

'Arrived in a couple of black limos,' Marler reported. 'The second one is crammed with camel-hair coat types. They've jumped out, started parading round. Comedians . . .'

The door opened and Victor Warner, clad in a camel-hair coat – presumably to disguise his identity during the drive from Whitehall – dashed in, clutching a cardboard-backed envelope. He sat in the armchair facing Tweed.

'Thought it best to come over here. It's an emergency. We think we know the target – and who is behind all the rumours.'

'That would be a step forward.'

Tweed became silent as Warner extracted a photograph from the envelope. He slapped it down in front of Tweed. His expression was grim, his manner disturbed.

'What would you say that is?' demanded Warner.

'It is a photo of Canary Wharf, the main tower block. It is easy to identify.'

'Now look on the back,' Warner snapped.

Tweed turned it over. Scrawled in an illiterate but readable hand was one word. *Next?* Tweed raised his eyebrows, looked at Warner.

'Where did this come from?'

'Bit of luck. In my position you need a bit of luck. Learned that when I was with Medfords. A couple of policemen in that area saw a man taking photos of the building from different angles. They collared him, Buchanan phoned me, sent the pics over by courier. Chap taking the pictures is under arrest. A certain bigwig in the IRA. Released from prison a couple of months ago.'

Marler had glided over, appeared behind Tweed's back. Casually he picked up the photo and headed for the door. Warner swung round, furious.

'Where do you think you're taking that?'

'We have a chap on our staff who once worked at Canary Wharf,' Marler lied glibly. 'He can confirm positively that this is Canary Wharf.'

'Of course it is,' Warner roared. He stabbed a thick finger as he went on. 'And I forbid you to make any copies. Got it?'

Marler had gone. Tweed started doodling on a pad with his pen. He pursed his lips, then asked the question as though the answer wasn't important.

'What do you know about the track record of this IRA man, the bigwig?'

'Name is Tim O'Leary. Known to have been sent to the Mid-East at one time to try and get collaboration – arms – from groups out there. Speaks fluent Arabic. Believed to have spent three months out there, although the timing is vague.'

'And he was openly photographing Canary Wharf, despite the presence of two policemen?'

'Doubt if he'd noticed them. Probably thought if he took pics openly he wouldn't look suspicious. Bit of luck the police were there, spotted him.'

'So you think Canary Wharf is the next target of the Real IRA mob?'

'That and maybe St Paul's Cathedral at the same time. I have taken all precautions. Everyone who enters either building is thoroughly searched. More than that . . .' Warner was building up a head of steam. 'The RAF have fighters flying non-stop with orders to shoot down any airliner – even if crammed with passengers – if it enters the non-flying exclusion zone we've organized. We'll be ready for them if they come – on the ground or in the air. The PM has – albeit reluctantly – backed me.'

Marler had returned with the photograph, now inside a transparent evidence envelope, placed it on Tweed's desk. Warner glared at him, then spoke to Tweed.

'All this is confidential. I'd sooner he wasn't here. Nor that girl behind the word-processor.'

'Give us a few minutes alone,' Tweed said, thinking confidentiality was a bit late in the day. He pounced when Warner looked at Paula.

'Miss Grey stays. She knows as much as I do. If ever I was put out of action she'd take over command.'

Paula was astounded, even a little embarrassed. She had never before heard Tweed suggest elevating her to control of the entire organization. Warner nodded before continuing.

'So, I think, Mr Tweed, you'll agree I have everything under control. No need for you to concern yourself with this problem any more. And now, I had better love you and leave you,' he concluded, standing up.

'Thank you, Minister, for keeping me informed,' Tweed replied very quietly.

Paula walked to the door, opened it for Warner to leave. He hadn't even the courtesy to thank her. Tweed asked her to tell Monica and Marler. Newman, who had left without being asked to also came back.

A few minutes after Marler reported the two limos had left on their way back to Whitehall the phone rang yet once more. Monica reported that Jules Beaurain had just arrived. Tweed pulled a face.

'Now we know what has held up the poor devil so long. Warner's new security precautions at Heathrow. Tell him to come up now.'

91

Paula was expecting the Belgian to look exhausted after his long day, the irksomeness of hanging around forever at the airport. Instead, when he charged into the room he was bursting with energy and smiling broadly. He dumped the small case he had been carrying by the armchair, again sat opposite Newman.

He was wearing a neutral-coloured windcheater, corduroy slacks. Paula observed he was freshly shaven and guessed he'd tidied himself up inside the plane's toilet. Besides bubbling with energy he looked ready to start a new day. Don't know how you do it, she thought. He waved to her.

'I have news,' Tweed remarked, 'but I'm sure you have too.'

'Gentlemen first.'

Beaurain waved a hand in Tweed's direction. He settled himself into the armchair to listen. His eyes were fixed on Tweed's as he listened to the details of Warner's surprise visit. Tweed ended by shoving the evidence envelope across to the Belgian. He merely glanced at it, then pushed it back across the desk.

'Decoy.'

12

'*Decoy!*' Paula exclaimed. 'You used the same word when you were shown a drawing last time you were here.'

'Because I believe the only purpose is to lead Tweed in the wrong direction. They, whoever they may be, are conducting what the Americans call a campaign of disinformation. It is so obvious.'

'I agree,' Tweed interjected. 'I had the same reaction.'

'What's so obvious?' Paula demanded.

'Paula,' Beaurain explained, 'you have many talents and one of them is not stupidity. Consider the scenario at Canary Wharf. This Tim O'Leary – chosen because of his previous connections with the Real IRA – stands out in the open, snapping away with his camera. A one-time terrorist – you think he wasn't well aware of the presence of two policemen?'

'And,' Tweed added with a smile, 'Victor Warner has swallowed the bait hook, line and sinker.'

'Just the man to be Minister of Security,' the Belgian said drily.

'Paula,' Tweed suggested, 'I want Jules completely in the picture. Could you describe the attack outside the Ivy?'

She took a deep breath, began speaking rapidly. She was almost reliving the speed and brutality of the incident. Beaurain, his expression now grave, watched her intently. He nodded when she had finished, his tone grim.

'Now that I do find significant. They were obviously

93

going to kidnap you, interrogate you, maybe worse. I'll be thinking over everywhere you've been, who you have seen. With concentration on Carpford. You touched some-one's nerve.'

'You mean . . .'

'I mean whoever is behind all this is worried that you saw – or heard in conversation – something dangerous. So, play back in your mind everything. Incidentally, it is important we discover who knew you were at the Ivy. Maybe the motor-cyclist who followed you on your way there. But I would like to meet this glamorous lady, Eva Brand, when I can.'

'Oh, you'll enjoy that. She's so attractive,' she chaffed him.

'Paula,' Beaurain said with a cynical smile, 'in Belgium I met a number of fascinating ladies and listened while they chattered on and on. They ended up in prison, which is where I put them.'

'Jules, your trip to Brussels,' Tweed said impatiently. 'I am waiting for the details of your visit to that banker.'

'He collapsed very quickly – when I showed him certain documents which could put him behind bars. The money from Carpford, which mounts up to a considerable sum, does not stay in Belgium. It is immediately transmitted by wire to a certain individual in Milan I happen to know. A certain Mario Murano. Here is his address.'

Tweed masked his surprise as he read the sheet of paper Beaurain had given him. *Via Legasso 290.* He looked up and told Beaurain about Marler's encounter with Jasper Buller, new chief of Special Branch, at Waterloo before Buller boarded the Eurostar.

Beaurain leaned back in his seat and studied the ceiling. It was several minutes before he straightened up and spoke.

'I hope Buller can look after himself.'

'He probably can,' Tweed assured him. 'Why?'

'Mario Murano is a very dodgy . . . right word? Good . . .

94

customer. A battle-scarred con-man. He's in touch with the Mafia, who trust him. Then, for a fat fee, he reports to a top carabinieri officer – Italian police. When he has learned the hideaway of a top capo. But he also gives me info – again for a fat fee. One of these days he's going to trip himself up. Outcome? End of Mario.'

'Dangerous,' Tweed commented.

'I went to Paris from Brussels today,' Beaurain told them. 'I had to keep moving. I talked to your friend, Tweed, the chief of the DST – Direction de la Surveillance du Territoire – or French counter-espionage. He sent you a message. Not polite, I fear.'

'Tell me,' Tweed said with a smile. 'The old brigand is reliable.'

'He doesn't think the Brits, as he called them, are. He was fuming. They know key members of al-Qa'eda have moved over here recently. He sent the data to the Ministry of Security. They replied with thanks – and have done nothing. Not even arrested them. He thinks we are crazy.'

'He's right. I can hardly contact Warner and ask him what he thinks he is doing. You flew back from Paris then?'

'Caught the flight from Charles de Gaulle by the skin of my teeth. Then ran into the wall of security at Heathrow. I have decided to travel to Italy myself tomorrow, to see Mr Murano and ask him where the money from Brussels goes on to. Not just the rent. Someone code-named Brutus in Carpford sends huge sums. Anyone want to come with me?'

'Me!' Paula shot up her hand.

'You will permit?' Beaurain asked Tweed.

'She'll give me hell if I refuse.'

'That's settled.' Beaurain took out a notebook and wrote in it. Paula noticed he wrote as fast as he talked. He went over to her desk, gave her the sheet he'd torn from the notebook. 'My hotel, a small place near Victoria. My room number on the back. I'm registered as Mr Vance. We meet under the destination board at Waterloo at 4 p.m. tomorrow. Now, give me your Browning pistol. Thank you. I can smuggle this through with my own Beretta. Bring only one case, and plenty of warm clothes. I'll have the tickets. I'm off now!' He paused before opening the door. 'That nasty incident outside the Ivy. Don't overlook this man Palfry. He could have been waiting in the lobby until he saw you were leaving, dashed outside to signal those thugs, then back in to greet you. *Au revoir* . . .'

'Interesting what he told us about the information from Paris,' Tweed said half to himself. 'And they have an uncomplimentary version of the word London.'

'And I'm off to Italy,' Paula enthused. 'That will make an exciting change. I'll bet it's Milan.'

'Not too exciting, I hope,' Tweed replied with no enthusiasm at all.

13

Milano Centrale. The long-distance express glided to a halt. Beaurain, with Paula by his side, was already standing at the exit as the automatic doors opened. They stepped on to the platform, Paula gazed up at the vast cavern, curving above them like an arched cathedral.

'It's enormous.'

'It is,' Beaurain agreed as he grabbed her arm to hustle her along amid a vast crowd descending from another train. 'I want us out of here fast. We were followed all the way from Waterloo. That small smartly dressed man seated a few seats in front of us. Dark suit, carefully manicured hair which you called coiffeured. He used his mobile as we were coming in. I suspect someone unpleasant is waiting for us . . .'

It was late in the afternoon but still daylight. While on the express Beaurain had slipped something wrapped in thick glossy paper to her, suggesting she visited the toilet before unwrapping it.

Inside the toilet she had carefully unwrapped layer after layer of the paper, which felt strange to the touch. Inside she found her .32 Browning and three magazines. Earlier, from the same suitcase which had contained Paula's weapon, Beaurain had extracted a similar package, had visited the toilet. In a hip holster he now wore his favourite gun, a .38 Special Smith & Wesson with a shortened barrel, weighing only eighteen ounces.

When she had returned to her seat Paula had folded the odd-feeling paper and handed it to Beaurain. He had slipped it back inside his case, thanking her, remarking that it was very expensive.

As they approached the exit Paula looked to left and right. It appeared there were at least twenty platforms. Passing through the ticket barrier, they made their way across the crowded concourse to the exit, a long flight of very wide stone steps.

'Keep close to me,' Beaurain warned, his eyes everywhere.

As they descended towards a vast paved open space Paula gazed at the extraordinary edifice looming up higher than any of the other solid stone blocks situated round the space. A shaft of sunlight broke through the hazy clouds, beamed like a searchlight on the dominant edifice.

Immensely tall and slim, its sides were curved. They swung round at the end nearest to her, creating the impression of a gigantic cone. She sucked in her breath.

'That must be the world-famous Pirelli building. It really is an architectural masterpiece.'

'Yes, that's Pirelli . . .'

Beaurain sounded abstracted. He never stopped surveying the scene as though expecting trouble. No pedestrian coming towards them escaped his eagle eye, checked with a brief glance. They had left the steps and were walking towards Pirelli when Paula noticed a long black stretch limo parked by the kerb. As they reached the limo her attention was distracted by an Italian pushing a trolley towards them laden with fruit.

The rear door of the limo suddenly swung open, blocking Beaurain's way. At the same moment the Italian pushing the fruit trolley lost control. Fruit spilt all over the pavement.

'We have been expecting you, Signor Beaurain,' the expensively dressed businessman type seated inside the limo called out. 'We have made reservations at the Hassler . . .'

98

He stopped talking as Beaurain pointed his Smith & Wesson revolver at him. At the same moment the driver had dashed out of his seat, run round the front of the limo, holding a Glock pistol, a deadly weapon. He was aiming it at the Belgian's back when Paula rammed the muzzle of her Browning into his side.

'Drop that bloody gun,' she shouted. 'Or say goodbye now,' she snarled.

It was probably the ferocity in her voice which frightened the driver. He dropped the gun. She kicked it under the car. Beaurain leaned inside the car, struck the passenger savagely across the forehead. He slumped down in his seat.

'Let's go,' Beaurain whispered as he hit the driver such a blow on the jaw the man sagged to the pavement.

Bending down, he hoisted the unconscious driver up by the armpits, threw him into the back of the car, slammed the door shut.

'You're a major asset,' he said as he grasped Paula by the arm and hustled her out of the square. 'We can just catch that tram, I hope . . .'

They were inside as the automatic doors closed behind them and the almost empty tram began moving. With both their weapons already holstered, they sank into a couple of seats together.

Paula wiped her clammy hands on her trousers. She had removed her gloves when Beaurain had warned her as they left Centrale. Despite the bitter cold which hit them on leaving the express she'd taken that precaution in case she had to use her weapon. At least it was warm inside the trundling tram. She rubbed her hands together.

'You know something?' she remarked. 'No one took any notice of what happened. Maybe it's an everyday occurence in Milan. You know where we're going?'

'Yes. I know Milan well. This tram stops at a point near where we're going. Are you OK?'

'Never felt better,' she fibbed. 'Does our friend know we are coming?'

'You heard me calling someone on my mobile as we got near Milan. He knows the time that express arrives. And he's never been inside the Hassler in his life – equivalent to the Ritz in London.'

'Any idea who those two men were?'

'None at all. But I don't think they were interested in looking after our health . . .'

She peered out of the windows as the tram stopped. This street was lined on both sides with old four- and five-storey buildings. The ground floors were mostly small shops – bakeries, grocers, bookshops and the inevitable supermarket. The tram moved off again. Passengers had alighted, no one had come aboard. They were now the only travellers. Peering out, Paula watched women shrouded in headscarves, heads bent against the bitter wind, clutching plastic bags as they hurried along. The sun had vanished and it was getting dark.

'Next stop we get off,' Beaurain said. 'It's a bit of a walk but we can survey where we're going. Which is rather necessary after our reception at Centrale . . .'

When they got off after Beaurain had paid the fares Paula wrapped her woollen scarf round her head. Even so, the biting wind chilled her face. They walked along in silence as the tram passed them and Beaurain kept glancing back over his shoulder . . .

'Expecting more trouble?' Paula enquired.

'Someone may have used his mobile to warn we have arrived.'

'But both those thugs in the limo were knocked out,' she protested.

'You're forgetting the man on the express – Coiffeured Hair as you called him. He probably saw what happened and has again phoned ahead. There's the building, Murano's HQ and home.'

There were fewer shops, few pedestrians, but still plenty of traffic. Beaurain had nodded towards a strange building which jutted out into the street, narrowing it. Constructed of large blocks of grey stone, it had a weird eyebrow window on the first floor, an entrance below of two heavy wooden doors. Reaching it, Beaurain pressed the bell alongside a speakphone. Before he could say anything an accented voice spoke in English.

'See you come, my dear Jules. Push right-hand door, when it opens walk in and up the stairs. Door close automatically behind you . . .'

'It's very quiet round here,' Paula remarked.

'Too quiet,' Beaurain snapped.

Beaurain led the way across a small stone-paved entrance hall. He began to climb a spiral stone staircase in a corner, its sides solid stone. It curved all the way to the top, where someone opened a door. They entered a large stone-paved room with a low ceiling, so low Beaurain had to dip his head. He gestured to Paula, made an introduction to the sole occupant of the room.

Mario Murano was short and stocky. His hair was brown and short, his plump face wreathed in a welcoming smile. He reminded Paula of a teddy bear as he took her hand in both of his. He was garbed in a sleeveless leather jacket, leather trousers, suede shoes.

'You bring me a lovely present,' he gurgled. 'This beautiful young lady, who wears an air of competence, knows what she is doing. A professional. I sense it.'

His English was fluent and with barely a trace of Italian accent. Paula immediately felt at home in this strange room. She smiled back at him.

'You exaggerate, Signor Murano . . .'

'Mario! Please. I am Mario to my friends. I can tell you are already a good friend. Now, you find my home interesting, I can tell. Explore! Please do while I am pouring the wine.'

101

'Thank you, Mario. Yes, I do find your home interesting. It is so unusual . . .'

Her eyes had scanned the room swiftly. A quick scan to avoid giving offence. But Mario had noticed. She went over to the only window in the room, the eyebrow-shaped window she had noticed when they were walking along the street.

To examine it she had to crouch. Its base line was flush with the floor. At either end it curved upwards in an artistic arch. From the tip of the arch to the base it was no more than three feet high. She was looking down the street and pavement they had walked along. She stood up.

'So this is how you spotted that we were coming.'

'Yes, indeed.' Mario chuckled. 'Now come and join your friend, Jules, who has already made himself comfortable. But only when you have completed your exploration. I can tell it interests you, my rabbit's warren.'

Beaurain had quickly seated himself in one of the high-backed chairs with armrests. The chairs were covered with old and tasteful tapestry, placed round a heavy and large antique table. Paula continued her exploration, while Jules sat with an amused smile.

In three of the stone walls facing the window were alcoves which began at knee-height above the floor. She looked at several of the leather-bound books perched spine to spine. They covered a variety of subjects in different languages, including a number on espionage going back to the foundation of the British Secret Service in the time of Queen Elizabeth I.

'The wine is Chianti,' Mario told her. 'If you don't like it, the pot contains freshly made coffee. Also a carafe of water. Take your choice.'

'Your English is so perfect,' she remarked, sipping the wine.

'Ah! You see when I was young I spent three years in

102

London working in a fish and chip shop. They don't make such wonderful chips in Italy! Your health, my dear.'

'Mario, we are short of time,' Beaurain broke in with a hint of impatience. 'I need to know what happens to all the money sent to you by that scoundrelly Belgian banker.'

'I take a small commission and then transmit the bulk electronically to Aruba in the Dutch Antilles.'

'South America now,' Paula commented.

'That's tough,' Beaurain commented. 'Persuading a banker on that island is easier than breaking into Fort Knox, but not much easier.'

'From there it is transmitted to a secret destination,' Mario said with a smile. 'Aruba once made a mistake and I was sent a copy of the onward transmission. It then goes to a Canadian bank in the Bahamas. I have the details.'

'Fancy a trip to the Bahamas?' Beaurain asked Paula with a touch of mockery.

Mario was fiddling inside a fat wallet he had produced from his jacket. He extracted a sheet of folded paper, unfolded it, handed it to Beaurain. He chuckled again.

'There are people – nasty people – who would pay a fortune for that information.' He waved a hand. 'No, Jules, I do not want a penny.'

'Ed Pendleton,' Beaurain said, reading from the paper. 'I do know the gentleman. He's their top director.'

'You see!' Mario waved his arms excitedly as he looked at Paula. 'Jules knows the whole world. An amzing man.'

'He doesn't know the route used by al-Qa'eda to send their murderous killers to Britain,' she observed.

The whole atmosphere changed. Mario was silent. His face now had a grave, almost nervous expression. Paula had drunk her glass of wine and, smiling at Mario, she poured herself coffee from the elegant pot after removing its cover. She drank some cautiously, still smiling at Mario to cheer him up. The coffee was very strong.

103

'If the reply is going to put you in danger we don't want to hear it,' she said, careful not to look at Beaurain.

'Danger.' Mario repeated the word solemnly. 'I should warn you there is danger everywhere in Milan. You must be very careful . . .'

A phone started ringing. Mario picked up a mobile from a stool by his side. He began talking rapidly in Italian. His whole personality had changed. His rounded jaw tightened, his eyes were half-closed, his voice rasping. When he put the mobile back on the stool he looked grim.

'A problem?' Beaurain enquired quietly.

'I must apologize,' Mario said, turning to Paula, handing her a plate of biscuits. She picked one up, slipped it into her mouth. It tasted good. 'I have to go and meet someone,' Mario continued, standing up. 'It should not take long so you wait until I return.' He looked at Beaurain. 'In case I do not come back . . .' Paula's stomach nerves rattled, 'you have to go to Verona to meet the man who can tell you the route these evil men use to reach their base in Britain. He is Aldo Petacci. Shall I spell it? No, you have got it. Aldo will tell you. I do not know that information.' Picking up the mobile, he pressed numbers. Again he spoke in rapid Italian, the gist of which Paula, with her limited Italian, could not catch.

Beaurain looked across at Paula. His expression was as grim as Mario's. He eased himself back in his chair, his right hand slipping under his coat. She knew he was checking on his revolver. Mario put down the mobile.

'I have spoken to Aldo. He will meet both of you at Verona tomorrow evening at 6 p.m. exactly. Inside the amphitheatre. You know it, Jules?'

'I know Verona. And the amphitheatre.'

'It all sounds dramatic, but Aldo is like that. Secretive.' He stood up. He extracted a card from his wallet, handed it to Beaurain. 'Give Aldo this. It confirms you are who you are. One more thing. If I do not return within about

104

one hour . . .' Paula swallowed the third biscuit she had been eating to settle her stomach '. . . you leave here,' Mario continued, 'but not by the way you came in. You see that door over there? I will unlock it. You leave that way. It takes you down into a maze of alleys. Go quickly if you have to.'

'Can we help in any way?' suggested Paula.

'No! But thank you.' He went to the rear door, unlocked it. 'Watch your feet. There is a narrow staircase behind that door. I must go now.' He went over to Paula and hugged her. She nearly burst into tears. 'It has been such a pleasure to know you, to enjoy your company.'

At the door through which they had entered he turned back. He handed a folder to Beaurain. 'There are two return rail tickets to Verona. So you do not have to go to the ticket office at Centrale.'

'Do take care,' Paula called out.

'Thank you.' Mario smiled, became the same man he had been when they arrived. 'I go to my meeting in my Fiat. You probably saw it parked on the pavement when you arrived.'

The door closed on him as he left. Paula ran over to the eyebrow window, crouched down. It was dark but street lamps illuminated th area. There was no one about. All the shoppers had gone home.

'What are you doing?' Beaurain called out harshly.

'I can watch him leave.'

Beaurain joined her, bending very low. They did see Mario climb inside his Fiat, drive it off the pavement and down the street. He had only gone a short distance when men wearing balaclava helmets appeared from nowhere. They were holding automatic weapons. Uzis, Beaurain thought.

Mario had no chance. A hail of gunfire hammered into the Fiat. Mario stopped, threw open the front door, a gun in his hand. The gunfire increased in ferocity. Mario fell

105

forward, sprawled on the pavement under a street light. Paula could see the pavement turning red with his blood.

'Oh God!' she exclaimed, her voice a mix of fury and sorrow.

'They're coming this way,' Beaurain snapped. 'The rear door.' He grabbed Paula's arm. They ran to the door. They had just reached it when a fresh hail of gunfire hit the eyebrow window. The glass shattered. A large object was thrown through the defenceless window, landed on the floor. Beaurain had the door open, hauled Paula with him, slammed the door shut, a torch in his other hand lighting a very narrow winding stone staircase. There was a tremendous thump against the door Beaurain had closed behind them. The door shook, but held.

'What the hell was that?' Paula cried.

'They threw a big grenade – maybe a bomb – through the open window. And that door is three inches thick. We must move – but watch your footing.'

Gripping an iron rail, Paula followed him down the diabolical, twisting stone staircase. At the bottom Beaurain's torch shone on another heavy door, closed with a bar. He lifted the bar, peered out into a dimly lit alley, gun in hand as he'd switched off his torch, shoved it in a pocket.

It was very quiet and they had a choice of alleys. One to the right, another to their left, the third straight ahead. The latter was vaguely illuminated with side lights attached to the stone walls. The alleys were paved with old cobbles. No one anywhere.

'We must find a hotel for the night,' Beaurain decided, 'so follow me.'

He made his cautious way down the alley straight ahead and soon it curved round dangerous corners. Paula, gripping her Browning, kept glancing back. If the murderers of Mario found them here they'd have little chance of surviving.

14

Paula never forgot their creep through the sinister alleys. Like herself, Beaurain also wore rubber-soled shoes, so they made no sound as they advanced slowly like ghosts amid the long shadowed areas between infrequent lanterns hung from ancient stone walls.

They passed alcoves inside which heavy doors closed off the entrances. High up, at first floor level, square windows, showing no lights, were set well back. Every now and again even narrower passages led off the main alley. Beaurain continued straight ahead, pausing at every corner where the alley curved. He had Paula behind him, where he wanted her, would hold up a hand to stop her while he peered round a curve.

The cold was intense, like walking through a refrigerator. Frequently she took off her gloves to rub her frozen hands together. Much good that it did. Beaurain had paused once more as he checked what lay beyond a curve. He whispered.

'I think there's a hotel. I'll check it and you keep out of sight . . .'

A neon light over the entrance was flashing red on and off. He reached the entrance steps and a blonde girl smiled at him invitingly. A cheap fur hat was perched on her head at a jaunty angle and the fur coat she wore was short, exposing long slim legs.

'You're home, darling,' she said in Italian. 'Come on in and I'll warm you up . . .'

Beaurain shook his head, gestured for Paula to follow him along the alley. The blonde sniggered when she saw Paula, called out something in Italian to Beaurain.

'What did she say?' Paula asked him as they continued walking.

'Nothing you'd want to hear. Wrong sort of hotel . . .'

They emerged from the maze of alleys suddenly into a main street. Still, no one about. No traffic. Across the street a large building glowed with lights. *Albergo Pisa.* Inside the main entrance stood a doorman in a blue uniform, a gold cap. A Bugatti pulled up. A well-dressed couple hurried into the hotel and the car, with a chauffeur at the wheel, drove off.

'That's the place,' Beaurain said, taking Paula by her arm. 'Are you OK after all that?'

'I'm starving.'

After an excellent dinner with Beaurain Paula expected to fall into a deep sleep. Beaurain had booked two rooms and they had placed him in the next room to hers. Before she said good night to him at her bedroom door he had warned her.

'This should be safe, but we cannot assume that. If you are frightened by something bang on my wall. We can test it before I go to bed. Two hard knocks.'

When he had gone she had used her hairbrush to bang twice on the adjoining wall. Within seconds she heard his hard raps, acknowledging he had heard her. She climbed into bed, closed her eyes, opened them after only a few minutes. A vivid picture had entered her mind of Mario, smiling as he first greeted them. Taking a handkerchief from under the pillow she dabbed at her eyes, determined not to cry. She lay awake for a long time.

She was woken by rapping on the adjoining wall. Jumping out of bed, blinking, she threw on her dressing-gown, took the Browning from under her pillow, slipped it into her pocket. As she passed a wall mirror she paused briefly, dealt with her hair, then opened the door on the chain. Beaurain stood outside, wearing a smart blue English suit, a spotless white shirt and a matching blue tie. She was struck by his freshness.

'It's only ten in the morning,' she protested.

'I was up at seven o'clock,' he said with his engaging smile. 'You will want a good leisurely breakfast and then we have to take a taxi to the station – Centrale. Knowing Milan, the taxi will take ages to arrive.'

'Give me half an hour to shower, dress and pack.'

'I gather you didn't sleep well. Make it an hour. I checked and they serve breakfast all morning . . .'

She needed a fresh handkerchief and dived into the pocket of her coat hanging in the wardrobe. She felt something strange, took it out. One of Mario's biscuits she had slipped into the pocket before leaving his home. Her eyes began to water.

She dived into the shower. The water was just the right temperature. She stood under the shower, sobbing. Then she stiffened herself, held her face up to the shower for several minutes. Drying herself with a large towel, she peered again into the wall mirror. Thank God, her eyes were not puffy.

Three-quarters of an hour later she left her room, carrying her case, rapped on Beaurain's door. It was opened instantly and he stood with his coat over his arm, his case in one hand. He was smiling. He's always smiling at me, she thought.

The dining-room was large, well and tastefully furnished and had only two businessmen at one table. The head waiter tactfully guided them to a distant corner table where they would have privacy. Paula studied the menu and when the waiter came over she ordered polenta and coffee.

'Polenta!' Beaurain exclaimed when the waiter had gone. 'You'll never get through the huge helping they'll serve.'

109

'Oh yes, I will. I'm starved again. Probably put on a few pounds but I don't care.'

'What does it matter? You are as slim as a sylph.'

'Thank you, Jules. Now, I've been meaning to ask you. How does that protective paper wrapped round our hand guns work?'

'It was invented by a top chemist friend of mine at Louvain University. It is very special paper – I don't know exactly what it is. He soaks it in some chemical, dries it. It has the effect of rejecting any metal detector's attempt to spot metal. The Americans keep bidding up the price to get it but my friend refuses. He feels there is the risk it might fall into the hands of terrorists.'

'A second question. Who do you think murdered poor Mario?'

'My guess is the Mafia eventually discovered he was playing a double game.'

'I'm not so sure. They wore balaclava helmets but one of them – who stood in the background – had let his helmet slip up to his nose. It exposed a large jet black beard. That could suggest al-Qa'eda?'

'Possibly.' Beaurain paused as breakfast arrived. 'I was not going to mention this,' he went on when they were alone, 'but there was that vicious attack on you when you left the Ivy restaurant in London. I suspect you are the prime target. Maybe because during your investigations you talked to the wrong person. While we are in Italy you must never leave my side.'

'I won't.'

Paula was ladling large scoops of polenta, feeling better as it seeped into her system. In a few minutes she had cleaned her plate, then accepted a second helping. Also the very strong coffee helped. By the end of the meal she felt she was ready for anything.

Beaurain asked the waiter to order a taxi. When asked for their destination he simply replied, 'The Pirelli building.'

'When do you expect us to reach Verona?' Paula asked in a quiet voice.

'By late afternoon. I want to see the meeting place before dark. The express stops at two places before Verona. First Brescia, then a small port of Lake Garda called Descenzano.'

'You expect trouble?'

'I expect trouble all the time we are in Italy.'

'In Verona too?'

'Especially in Verona. I sense our enemy controls a vast organization. I'm beginning to think you are right. Our enemy may well be al-Qa'eda.'

15

The Venezia express emerged from under the giant canopy of Centrale into blazing sunlight. Looking out of the
window, Paula saw they were passing a zone of high-rise
apartment blocks. Washing strung on lines fluttered on the
balconies in a mild breeze. The usual boring exit from a
national capital.

'I'm glad to get out of Milan,' she said to Beaurain, who
sat beside her. 'It's all enormous stone blocks hemming in
the streets – like a vast prison.'

'There are better areas. The *gallerias* as they call them.
Full of very expensive shops and expensive ladies parading
through them. We missed that area. Well, at least the train
is picking up speed.'

'It goes all the way through to Venice?'

'All the way.'

Their first-class coach was almost empty and soon
they were racing through beautiful countryside. Cultivated
fields, flat as a billiard table, stretched away forever. Already
green shoots were projecting above the water-filled fields.
Paula pressed her face to the window, watching women
with bare legs tending the crop.

'Rice fields,' Beaurain told her. 'Those women really do
work. But we're in the Po Valley, the bread basket – and
wine basket – of Italy. The water comes from the river Po.'

A big male passenger in a business suit walked in as the
train swung round a bend. He lost his balance, crouched

down, bumped into Beaurain as he stood up. He lifted his dark wide-brimmed hat.

'Most apologies. So sorry.'

He walked on, gripping the tops of seats, then sat down several rows ahead of them. Beaurain glanced over the side of his seat. He nudged Paula, cleared his throat, his index finger on his lips when she looked at him. He cleared his throat again.

'We'll get off at Brescia,' he said.

She frowned, wondering what was going on, but kept quiet. He reached down to the side of his seat, got hold of something and jerked it loose, putting it into his pocket. Then he left his seat, strolled slowly up the aisle, stopped by the side of the seated passenger with the wide-brimmed hat. As the express thundered round another bend he seemed to lose his balance. His elbow hammered a hard blow into the jaw of the seated passenger. Such a hard blow the man drooped forward, unconscious.

He strolled back to Paula and sat down beside her. She gazed at him.

'What do you think you're doing?'

He took something from his pocket. When he opened the palm of his hand she saw a small round black device. The top was silver. She shook her head, baffled.

'When he lurched into me and crouched,' Beaurain explained, 'he attached this to the side of my seat. Listening device, with a magnetic base to hold it to the side of my seat. I noticed he had a concealed – almost – wire disappearing into his ear.'

'We can't get away from them,' she commented nervously.

'But now he thinks we're getting off at Brescia. He'll recover long before we get there. When we're coming into Brescia we'll get up, carry our bags, and wait in the exit space. He'll come and join us.'

'What do we do then?'

'It's what I'll do,' Beaurain said with a grim smile.

She looked out of the window. A misty glow was rising from the fields, creating a beautiful luminous glow of rainbow colours. She had never seen anything so hypnotic. This was the real Italy, a place she resolved to visit one day. It settled her nerves as she went on gazing. She would remember this luminous glow all her life.

The man Beaurain had hit with his elbow eventually recovered. Paula thought it significant that when he sat up straight he never once looked back.

As they approached Brescia the view from her window changed. In the distance hills were looming up above the mist. When Beaurain nudged her she picked up her case, followed him to the exit compartment. As they stood close to the automatic doors, which were closed, Wide Brimmed Hat appeared. She caught a glimpse of the right side of his jaw. It was swollen. He had taken a brutal punch. The train slowed, slid into the station, stopped. The doors opened. Steep steps led down to the platform.

Beaurain smiled, waved a hand, gesturing for Wide Brim to go first. The Italian waved his own hand, encouraging them to leave first. Still smiling, Beaurain repeated the same gesture. Wide Brim again waved his hand. Paula thought it was almost comic, then she noticed the useless wire disappearing into the Italian's right ear. Someone on the platform blew a whistle. The doors were about to close. Beaurain put a hand behind the Italian's back, pushed him forward. He tried to get his feet on the steps, failed, fell forward and sprawled on to the platform, face down. The doors closed, the express began moving.

'That can't have done him much good,' Paula remarked as they returned to their seats.

'I wasn't too concerned with his health.'

'You went to the toilet quite some time ago. To get rid of that listening device?'

'Smart lady. Yes. I lifted the lid, placed the device on the seat, crushed it with my foot, shoved the bits into the bowl and flushed the toilet. There will be someone else aboard. No matter.'

A kitchen man appeared, pushing a trolley. Paula chose a large ham roll, a cardboard cup of coffee. She munched it quickly. Beaurain stared at her.

'Hungry again? After all that polenta?'

'Got to keep up my strength. I don't think Verona will be very peaceful.'

'I'm sure it won't be . . .'

She looked out of the window. The hills seemed higher, closer. Soon they would be mountains. Beaurain leaned across her, pointed.

'They're much too far away for you to see them, but beyond those hills are the Dolomites. I have skied on them. I read in the paper, after going out from our hotel, that there is heavy snow. It will be cold in Verona.'

The express slowed, stopped suddenly in the middle of nowhere. Time passed. They were still not moving. Beaurain glanced at his watch, tut-tutted. Paula suddenly felt sleepy. She closed her eyes and fell asleep. She was woken when the express started moving again. Outside the sunlight was fading.

'Sorry,' she said, 'I had a short nap.'

'You have had a long nap. A whole hour. That means it will be dark when we arrive in Verona. We shall have to be very careful.'

'We'll be late for meeting Petacci in the amphitheatre?'

'No. But I wanted to check out the place in daylight. It can't be helped.'

'But it will be more dangerous.' She prodded him. 'I'm a big girl now. Won't it?'

'Yes, it will be much more dangerous.'

16

Late the previous evening in London Tweed had been checking his speed-up on the investigation. Monica was helping him as he read out the list. She was making sure he had missed no one.

'Pete Nield is watching the Ministry. Target, Victor Warner. Harry is with him. Target, Peregrine Palfry. When either leave the building. No news yet?'

'Both will call in a coded message when something happens,' she reminded him.

'Marler is out there somewhere, tracking Eva Brand. Again, nothing from him yet?'

'Not a dickey bird . . .'

'Newman is chasing after Martin Hogarth, the sober brother from Carpford Bob saw approach this building, then walk away . . .'

'Again zilch . . .' She picked up the phone, listened, looked at Tweed. 'There's a surprise visitor from Carpford. An Agatha Gobble. Runs a shop in Carpford? Right?'

'Right. The last person on earth I expected. Must have driven all the way here. I left her my card when I saw her in that peculiar village. Get her up here . . .'

Mrs Gobble was wearing a fur coat which had seen better days. She still had the blue beads round her neck. She plumped her substantial figure into an armchair when Tweed welcomed her, introduced Monica. When she took off her gloves he saw her hands were shaking. She accepted Monica's offer of tea.

'Very late for you to drive here,' Tweed said, smiling.

'Thought it safer to come after dark. Maybe nobody would see me then. Funny goin's on up at the village.'

'Relax. Take your time. Tell me what has disturbed you.'

'Frightened the hell out of me more likely. A lot goin' on up at the village and none of it good if you asks me. You were the only person I felt would listen. Two motor-cyclists have started making night calls on someone. Don't know who. They comes separately. One just after dark, t'other late on. They drives slowly round Carp Lake, keep stoppin' so I don't know who they delivers to. Saw one – funny foreigner.'

'How did you come to see him, Mrs Gobble?' Tweed asked very quietly.

She thanked Monica for the tea. Tweed waited while she drank the contents. Large swallow. Pause. Large swallow. Her round fleshy face was redder now, more normal.

'Gives me the shock of me life,' Mrs Gobble continued. 'I went out to empty trash and he comes round corner of lake on his bloody bike too fast. Keels over, sprawls on the ground, loses his helmet. Light from me 'ouse streamin' out and I sees 'im. Big black beard and fierce eyes. Gazes at me, then rams helmet back on before 'e gets up, lifts his machine, gets back in saddle and drives off towards Drew Franklin's place. I scuttled inside, closed door, chained and locked it. Didn't sleep that night. 'Orrible face.'

'Very strange, I agree. This was the second motor-cyclist?'

'Oh yes. We'd 'ad another earlier. Wish I'd never rented the shop.'

'How did that come about, Mrs Gobble? Your renting it.'

'Sees this ad in *The Times*. Single woman wanted to run small shop. Pleasant area in Surrey countryside. Rent reasonable. It gave a phone number. So I calls, goes to see this Mr Pecksniff.'

'What was the name?'

'Pecksniff. Like the Dickens character. I love Dickens. Can't say the same for the real Pecksniff. Here's his address. I gets there, he asks me a few questions, then says he's sure I'll do. Don't know why. Here's where he saw me. Mouldy place in the East End. Funny chap. I must go now.' She jumped up. 'Get back before dark.'

'It is dark now.' Tweed pointed out. 'We can find a decent place for you to sleep in London for the night.'

'I have a spare room at my flat,' Monica offered.

'I am going back to the village,' Mrs Gobble said firmly. 'I only sleep in one place – my own bed.'

'I'm going to my flat now,' Tweed said after their visitor had left. 'I may not be in tomorrow. I want to be quiet to think hard. Two motor-cyclists arriving at Carpford suggests the pace is hotting up. We may not have much time left. And so far we have a list of potential suspects and not one who stands out. I'm very worried. Don't phone me – except in case of an emergency.'

'Here are my biographies so far on the people you asked me to check out.'

She handed him a fat folder. He slipped it inside his briefcase, put on his coat, left the office.

Tweed was in his pyjamas, sitting up in bed. He was reading the last of the copious reports, a notebook by his side for him to scribble a thought. The phone rang. He checked the time. 6 a.m. and still dark outside.

'Monica here. So sorry to disturb you but you did did say call in an emergency.'

'What's happened?'

'Superintendent Buchanan has just been here. Roy told me Mrs Gobble has disappeared. Her car found abandoned on the road to Carpford.'

17

The Venezia express slid into Verona station, stopped, the automatic doors opened. Paula and Beaurain were already standing at the exit and descended on to the platform. The platform was deserted, it was night, the cold was raw and bitter.

'Wait a minute,' Beaurain said, and pretended to button up the top of his coat. He glanced to his left, to the far end of the express. Paula looked in the same direction. Two men in dark coats had alighted from the rear coach. Beaurain grunted.

'I said there would be more of them.'

'They could be businessmen returning home late.'

'Italian businessmen always carry a briefcase. They think it gives them an air of importance. Those two have no briefcases. We'll get out of here quickly, head straight for the amphitheatre.'

He was moving as he spoke, striding out with his long legs. Paula had to hurry to keep up. It was not long before she was gazing at the buildings of Verona in wonderment. Like travelling back into the Middle Ages. They were masterpieces of architecture, seen clearly by illumination from ancient streetlights and moonlight. There were superb arches, elegant rows of pillars on the ground floors. The colour was white or a muted ochre. She forgot why they were there as more and more magnificent ancient buildings came into view.

'They're Palladian, aren't they?' she asked.

'Yes and no. Palladio, the genius of architecture, worked mostly in Vicenza, often using brick and stucco. Here is a lot of stone. In a minute you'll see the amphitheatre.'

'Like the Colosseum in Rome?'

'No. That's a wreck. Verona's amphitheatre is intact, as it was when built ages ago. They even hold opera performances inside it in summer. There it is.'

Paula gasped, stood still. The high curving amphitheatre *was* intact. She could see that already. Slim windows towards the top. A massive symbol of another civilization. Beaurain ran across to the huge double doors, checked the padlock with his torch, ran back to her.

'It's still locked.'

'We're early?'

'Yes, by about an hour despite that long stop when the express sat in the middle of nowhere. We'll go into that bar. Warm you up – you must be frozen.'

As he pushed open the solid sheet of glass which was the door a wave of warmth greeted them. No other customers. The bar extended down the right-hand side with leather-topped stools. Restaurant tables were arranged in a large open space. A girl with black hair tied back came to serve them as they perched on stools.

'What can I get you folk?' she asked in an American drawl.

'Which part of the States are you from?' Beaurain asked with a smile.

'Kansas. Pop works in electronics in Milan. Couldn't put up with that city any longer, so I came here. He has the most enormous apartment here, like a palace. Now what can I get you?'

'I guess you're hungry again,' Beaurain said, looking at Paula with a smile. 'Coffee to drink?'

'Coffee for me. And are those macaroons?' Paula pointed to a plate inside a cooler.

122

'Try one. You don't like it we'll dump it.' She used tongs to extract one and place it on a plate. 'I'm Sandy.'

'I'm Jenny,' Paula said quickly. 'This is Peter.'

She crunched the macaroon or whatever it was, swallowed it as Sandy poured coffee for both of them. Paula asked for another macaroon. Sandy pointed to a table facing the door. 'Why don't you folks go and be comfortable. I'll bring it over.'

'Good idea,' Beaurain agreed.

He chose a chair facing the door which gave him a sidelong view of the entrance to the amphitheatre. Sandy came over with a tray. A plate full of macaroons, the coffee freshly poured. Sandy stood with a hand on her hip.

'You're British.' She laughed. 'You see, I got it right. I know you don't like to be called Brits. Can't blame you.'

Beaurain asked for the bill, explaining they might have to leave quickly. He included a generous tip. Sandy thanked him, then pulled a face as she picked up the Euro notes.

'This stuff is one reason I'll be glad when Pop takes me back to the States. Funny money. Dollars for me any time.'

'That was quick and smart of you,' Beaurain said quietly when the girl was back behind the counter. 'Making up false names.'

'I thought maybe when we've left someone will come in to interrogate her.'

'They probably will. Say we're friends to cover up their real motive . . .'

Paula had just consumed every macaroon on the plate, had a refill of coffee, when Beaurain checked his watch. Paula raised her eyebrows.

'I thought we were early.'

'We are, but someone I couldn't see very well has just unlocked the padlock on the doors to the amphitheatre. Do not assume it's Petacci.'

They said good night to Sandy and strolled to the doors,

now open. The man had vanished inside. Beaurain gestured for Paula to stay behind him. He entered slowly, peered round. Barely seen, a man stood in shadow beyond the entrance. Beaurain walked slowly up to him while Paula followed, glove off her right hand which gripped the Browning behind her back. Something wrong here.

'Mr Petacci?' Beaurain enquired.
　'Si.'
　'Mr Murano phoned you from Milan?'
　'Si.'
　'So what is Mr Murano's first name?'
　The shadowy figure shifted his stance. Shuffled his feet as though getting more comfortable. Both hands inside the pockets of his overcoat. Not a word of English so far. Silence. Beaurain had both hands down by his sides, neither wearing gloves.
　'Murano's first name?' he repeated.
　'First names do not matter in our circles.' Good English but with a faint trace of accent Paula couldn't identify. 'You have money,' the figure added.
　'You want something first?'
　'The money first, then I give you information.'
　Beaurain struck with the speed of a cobra. His fist hit the figure in the mouth. Then both hands grabbed his forearms, rammed him against the stone wall behind him. One hand whipped up, grasped his jaw, hammered it with force that made Paula flinch, so much force she heard the skull smash against the stone wall. All in seconds. The figure slumped down the wall. Beaurain bent down, hauled one hand out of the shadowy figure's pocket, produced the ugly sight of a Glock pistol when Paula switched on her torch, then off quickly. Beaurain checked the Glock by feel, shoved it in one of his own pockets. His eyes were accustomed to the dark now. He lifted the man by his armpits, rammed him inside one of the alcoves carved out of the rock, stood up.

124

'How did you know?' Paula asked.

'Didn't ask for that identification card Mario gave me. And they use first names a lot in Italy as a matter of course.'

'He was going to shoot us?'

'I think that was the general idea. The real Aldo Petacci has to be somewhere else inside this vast place.'

He was whispering but now he placed a finger to his lips. She had also heard the faint sound. Footsteps approaching the main entrance from outside, several pairs. Beaurain grasped her by the arm, guided her down a sloping ramp leading towards the arena, a huge oval shape below them. They hurried, soon reached the bottom. Still holding her arm, Beaurain guided her along the edge of the amphi-theatre, then pointed her up a flight of steps between a block of tiers of seats climbing high up.

'Don't think there aren't some of them here already,' he warned. 'Go up to the top – always take the high ground. I'll creep up the next flight . . .'

It was eerie. You could almost hear the silence. Amphi-theatre. Gladiatorial contests had been held here long ago – and now another one was building up.

She crouched down behind the wall below the tiers of seats, began to climb carefully. Once she glanced to her right, was appalled to realize that Beaurain, although crouched, was so tall his head was visible. She placed her rubber-soled shoes cautiously on each new step. There could be something on the flight which would make a noise.

Then her next tentative step felt a stone under it, small and round. Had she moved less cautiously the stone would have gone rolling down the flight behind her. In the dis-tance, further round the curved tiers, she heard the sound of something hard clattering down steps. Then whispers. There was a gang of them. She continued climbing.

The moonlight didn't penetrate the staircase but she had

good night sight and her eyes were now accustomed to the dark. She was approaching the top when she saw a figure above her, crouched with its back to her, holding some kind of machine pistol. He was staring to his right. He had spotted Beaurain, was waiting for the moment to shoot him down with a fusillade. She glanced to her right again. Beaurain was below her but his head was still so visible. Despite being shorter, she had made swifter progress up towards the top. Her legs began to ache. She ignored the pain.

The figure above her was moving now, elevating the barrel of his weapon, taking deliberate aim. She had earlier dispensed with gloves. She tensed, raised her Browning, gripped in both hand, fired. Once, twice, again. The figure stiffened, lost its balance, tumbled down the staircase towards her. The weapon clattered down after it.

She stopped the figure's fall with one hand, picked up the weapon with the other. Her Browning was holstered. The weapon was a Kalashnikov. She switched on her torch for a second. The weapon still had a full magazine. She checked the body quickly, again switching on her torch for a brief moment. Another magazine was protruding from a pocket. She grabbed it. The gunman was dead. Beaurain appeared at the top, ran down the few steps.

'You're too tall, Jules,' she snapped. 'He could see your head.'

'So I'm still alive because you spotted him. I'll take the Kalashnikov.'

'No you won't. I can use it . . .'

Recently she had spent her annual training session with tough Drake at the training mansion hidden away in the Surrey countryside. Drake had checked her on the Uzi, then trained her hard on a Kalashnikov.

'They may be coming for us along the top,' he said, his revolver in his hand.

They darted up. There was a wide terrace behind the

126

tier of seats at the top. Three men were running towards them. She aimed the Kalashnikov, fired a long burst. They all dropped, didn't move. A shot fired from lower down whipped past just above Paula's shoulder. Beaurain fired. The killer sank out of sight. More shots from different levels below. Beaurain swung his gun at different angles, firing each time. No more shots. He knew he had hit all four.

She heard feet clumping fast towards them from behind along the top terrace. Swinging round, she let loose another burst. The shock of her hail of bullets lifted the killer off his feet. He collapsed backwards, lay sprawled on the terrace, still as death.

One more attacker stood on a seat below them, took careful aim. Beaurain, his revolver refilled with fresh ammo, fired once. In the moonlight he saw blood spurt from the man's chest, then he sank out of sight.

'How many more?' Paula wondered as she slid in the second magazine.

'Listen . . .'

The amphitheatre, now filled with more blood probably than in the days of gladiatorial combat, was still, very silent. A voice called out, echoing round the amphithestre as though it spoke through a funnel created by holding up to hands to its face.

'Don't shoot. I am Aldo Petacci. Coming towards you along the top terrace. There are no more. I counted them coming in.'

He was lean-faced, cadaverous, as though he needed a good meal, a lot of food. Tall and thin, he wore a windcheater, came towards them with both arms raised well above his head. They could see him clearly in the torch beam Beaurain shone on him while Paula aimed her Kalashnikov.

He stopped. His hands were shaking. He walked up to them very slowly. Waited a good six feet away.

'I am Aldo Petacci,' he repeated. 'Have you something to show me?'

Beaurain produced from his wallet the card Mario had given him way back in Milan, which seemed a thousand miles, a year away. Petacci examined the card, looked at the back where Mario had drawn a strange symbol, then smiled.

'I have a water bottle,' he continued in English. 'If you are thirsty . . .'

'I am parched,' said Paula. She knew it was tension. She was surprised when Petacci extracted a clear handkerchief from his pocket, removed the screw cap from the water bottle slung over his shoulder, carefully wiped the neck before handing it to her. So hygienic. She took three swallows, handed it to Beaurain who also quenched his thirst.

'Mr Petacci,' Paula remarked, 'your English is perfect. You could be an Englishman.'

'I am.' The lean face broke into a smile. 'Mario told me a Jules Beaurain and friend would be coming. So I waited to see if you could survive inside this place. Had I realized you were British, like myself, I'd have come in to give a hand.'

'So Petacci is an assumed name?'

'One of many. My Italian is good enough to pass for one of them in this country.'

'You have information for us,' Beaurain said tersely.

'The route they use when they've come in from the East is via Milan. They board an express for Paris. Then they take a train to the coast of Britanny, end up in St Malo. Guides wait for them, put them aboard fishing vessels which cross the Channel. A few miles from the coast of Britain they transfer to dinghies when the sea's calm. They land at a remote beach somewhere near Hastings. More guides are waiting with cars to take them on.'

'Take them on to where?' Beaurain snapped.

'That he didn't know. But he knew the spectacular target is London.'

'They sound well organized. Mind telling me how you came by this priceless information? If it's true?'

Petacci smiled grimly. 'It is true. I persuaded an Afghan who spoken unnervingly good English.'

'Might I ask you how you persuaded an Afghan to tell you all this?'

'You may.' Petacci smiled. 'You just did. I used the one method which would make him talk. I threatened to cut off his beard. Without that he couldn't join his own people. They would know something had happened, stick a knife into him.'

'Have you any idea,' Beaurain persisted, 'how many of them have followed this route?'

'More than twenty. Their European base was Milan. Now it is somewhere in Britain. No idea where. But something very big is being planned. No point in telling Victor Warner, Minister for Home Security. Man's an idiot. Always gets it wrong . . .'

'What is your real name?' Beaurain persisted, still holding a wad of banknotes.

'Oh, for heaven's sake!' Paula protested.

Petacci smiled. 'Your Belgian friend is right to check me out. As far as he can.' He looked at Beaurain. 'George, Hugh, Alfred. Any name you like. None of them are right.'

'Don't answer me this question,' said Paula, 'and I will understand. But have you worked for some outfit in Britain?'

'Used to be with Special Branch. Since I'm a linguist they sent me over here to Europe. I made a lot of contacts. In those days I got fed up with Special Branch, a bunch of clods. So I decided to leave and go freelance over here. The money's much better.' He smiled again. 'But I do hear that since Buller took over as top dog they've cleaned up their act.'

129

'One more question,' Beaurain went on. Paula groaned to herself. 'Surely that Afghan you interrogated will tell his mob what he's told you.'

'Doubt it.' Petacci smiled again. 'After I'd bled him white I shot him in the head, dumped the corpse inside a deep ravine. And if you're returning to home which route are you using?'

'Same one we used to get out here,' Paula told him. 'By express from Milan to Paris, then Eurostar . . .'

'No!' Petacci was emphatic, still smiling. 'They will be waiting for you at Centrale. Take a train from here back to Milan. Slip out by the side exit, grab a cab, go to the airport. Fly back to Heathrow. It's late but there's been another hold-up, so flights are all leaving very late. I can drive you to Verona station.' He checked his watch. 'You should catch an express from Venice soon.'

'Thank you for your help,' Beaurain said, now gracious. 'He handed Petacci an envelope stuffed with notes. 'Your fee.'

Petacci riffled through the banknotes, took half, handed the rest back to the Belgian. 'I still love England. Half will keep the wolf from the door.' He looked at Paula. 'You'll be appalled when you see my car but I've installed a brand new souped-up engine. It goes like the wind. Which is the way you'd better go to get out of Italy alive. Beaurain, one question you didn't ask.'

'Which was?'

'Who are the people I've been talking about. Miss Grey – and yourself – have had a tough time. Thought I'd better keep that bit till last. They're al-Qa'eda.'

18

Late on the afternoon of the day when Beaurain and Paula were travelling aboard the express to Verona, in London Tweed was surprised to be visited by an unexpected guest. It was murky beyond the windows in his office, another typical February day. The only other two people with him were Marler, who had just arrived, and Monica, who seemed to live behind her word processor.

'A visitor for you downstairs,' Monica announced with a wry smile. 'Jasper Buller, that nice man from Special Branch.'

'He must have got back from Italy. Send him up.'

The bulky figure of Buller, wearing a raincoat – no camel-hair uniform this time – walked in. He smiled at Monica, then at Tweed as he sat down after removing the raincoat. His manner was so different from the Bull as his staff had nicknamed him Monica was taken aback.

'Would you like some coffee,' she suggested.

'A gallon of it would be welcome.' He swung round and again smiled.

Tweed studied him. Under his air of affability he thought he detected tension. Buller lit a cigarette after asking permission. He stared at Tweed over the flame of his lighter.

'The situation is probably desperate,' he said quietly.

'You found out something in Milan?'

'I did. London is the target. For the next al-Qa'eda spectacular. Atrocity would be a better word.'

'So Mario Murano came up trumps?'

'He did not.' He thanked Monica for the large cup of coffee she placed close to him on the desk. Tweed waited while he drank half the cup. 'No,' he continued, 'Murano was at pains to tell me nothing. Quite different from when I paid him a visit about something else six months ago. He was also very nervous. Couldn't wait to get rid of me.'

'Yet you come back with disturbing information.'

'That's right.' Buller emptied his cup and accepted Monica's offer of a refill. 'After leaving Murano,' he continued, 'I contacted another source. Ex-member of the carabinieri, which, as you know, is the police under army control. He had a high rank but couldn't stand the corruption. He resigned, set up his own investigation agency. One of his clever men infiltrated al-Qa'eda, second-in-command of their huge base in Milan. Got next to him, found he was bitter – his American wife had been inside the North Tower on September 11 when the plane hit it. He spilt his guts about the base moving to Britain since the next major target was London. The informant spoke English as well as Arabic. Shortly after telling his story his body ends up on a railway line. Police found it, dragged it clear minutes before the Rome express arrived. The autopsy showed the dead informant had swallowed a cyanide pill – probably just before he was tortured. Which makes the data he gave horribly reliable.'

'Poor devil,' Marler interjected.

'Are you passing this on to the Minister for Security?' asked Tweed.

'You must be joking,' Buller snapped. 'What use is he? He's absorbed in the idea that a Colombian drug cartel is the menace.'

'This is grimly convincing,' Tweed said reflectively.

'My next follow-up,' Buller went on, 'is to go up to that suspicious village, Carpford. I'll interview every one up there even if I have to drag them out of bed. There may be very little time left.'

'Go up when?'

'Tonight.'

Buller had drunk all the second cup of coffee. He stood up, put on his raincoat, gazed at Tweed. 'No time like the present.'

'You could be walking into something,' Tweed warned. 'So take Marler with you.'

'I know you're tops,' Buller said, looking at Marler. 'But on something like this I operate best on my own. No offence.'

'None taken,' Marler replied.

When Buller had left Tweed began pacing the office swiftly. His expression was grave. So was the tone of his voice when he spoke.

'I don't like this. Don't like it one bit.'

'You mean the awful news he brought us?' Monica suggested.

'That, of course. But also the idea of Buller driving up to Carpford by himself in the dark. Mind you, he can look after himself.'

'You hope,' Marler commented.

Within minutes Marler's mobile was ringing. He answered, then spoke to Tweed.

'It's Roy Buchanan. He's on his way here by car. Wants a word . . .'

'Yes Roy,' Tweed said after grasping the mobile. 'Before you get here I have news – if this wretched mobile is safe.'

'Yours or mine?' Buchanan snapped.

'I have to assume this one – belongs to Marler – is secure. It's a new model he pinched from somewhere.'

'Probably same as the new one I'm using. Latest news from Victor Warner's lot is he's convinced the Mafia is bringing in men to establish gambling casinos – which will

133

be distribution centres for hard drugs. In cooperation with the Colombia mob.'

'He should be sacked, the idiot. Are you near me?'

'Could be. In ten minutes.'

'Get over here then. There's a major new development I won't reveal over the phone.'

He handed the mobile back to Marler, began pacing again. Monica had the impression he couldn't sit still. From the look on his face his brain was churning full power.

'The major new development being Buller,' Marler remarked.

'Yes. But when I spent time at my flat yesterday I couldn't sleep. I was conducting a major exercise. Imagining myself as the man controlling al-Qa'eda. What would I go for to terrify London. One thing I decided was essential. Maximum number of casualties.'

Buchanan arrived about an hour later, which was much longer than Tweed had expected. He was also clad in a green oilskin. Tweed stared at him.

'Going fishing?'

'You could say that. Actually it keeps me warm, and outside it's an Arctic night. I'm furious with Warner. He's wasting so much manpower.'

'And how is he doing that? Not that I'm surprised.'

'He's still fixated on that drawing of St Paul's. He has heaven knows how many policemen at the entrance, checking everyone who wants to go into the place. On top of that he has a posse of detectives inside in plain clothes, pretending to be worshippers.'

'He's covering his backside – on the remote possibility the target is St Paul's.'

'That's only a part of it,' Buchanan fumed. 'He has more men at all entrances to Canary Wharf. You can imagine the reaction of the hundreds who work there. They're stopped and made to wait while they're searched and anything they happen to be carrying is examined. He even has marksmen at the top of the building complex. Anything to tell me?'

'Yes . . .' Tweed recalled everything Jasper Buller had told him. Buchanan frowned as he listened. He said nothing until Tweed had concluded his report.

'Well, if he thinks it's useless to inform Warner we can forget about our so-called Minister for Home Security. I don't like the idea of him driving up there on his own at night.'

'He refused to let Marler go with him.'

'Don't blame him,' Marler interjected. 'If I was in his position I'd have wanted to go on my own.'

'You'll have to excuse me now,' Buchanan said, heading for the door. 'I've got a job to do.' He turned round before he left. 'Al-Qa'eda. That sends shivers up my spine . . .'

Monica chewed the end of her pencil when they were alone. 'I noticed Buchanan was unusually secretive. Didn't give us a clue as to what job he was talking about.'

'I noticed that,' Tweed agreed. 'It's late, if anyone wants to go home. I'm staying.'

The phone rang. It was Beaurain. He sounded abrupt when he spoke to Tweed.

'I've arrived back from Italy with Paula. Now we're going to be here at Heathrow for God knows how long. Heavy security checks.'

'I'll wait for you however long it takes.'

He told Monica and Marler the gist of Beaurain's message. They said they'd wait too. The grim news came in just before Beaurain arrived with Paula.

'Roy here. Near Carpford. Buller has disappeared.'

'What do you mean? What about his car?'

'I checked with Special Branch HQ. A blue Ford. They gave me the plate number. Found parked by the side of a small inn on the main road before you turn off to Carpford. The key was in the ignition. No sign of

135

a struggle or blood inside the Ford. Buller has vanished without trace.'

'Isn't it time we dragged Carp Lake?'

'Which is exactly what we're doing now. Big team. Seven divers, whole lake lit up by flashlights – searchlights, I mean. One of the locals is kicking up.'

'Which one?'

'Drew Franklin. Says we'll kill the carp. I ask you. Lord knows what we're going to find before we're through. Three bodies?'

19

'Buchanan expects to find three bodies.'

Tweed was saying this when the door opened and Beaurain walked in with Paula. She had caught what Tweed had just said to Monica and Marler.

'What three bodies?' she wanted to know. 'Whose bodies?'

They both looked travel-stained. Tweed thought Paula looked fresher than the Belgian. As she sat behind her desk she stared at Tweed, her voice demanding.

'Whose bodies?' she repeated.

'I'm afraid Mrs Gobble has also vanished.'

Monica offered to get coffee and they both thanked her and agreed they needed it. Tweed sat back in his chair and continued talking. He spoke rapidly but it still took time to relate the arrival of Jasper Buller, what he had told about his trip to Italy, his determination to drive up to Carpford by himself. Then he recalled for them Buchanan's brief visit, what he had said, his anxiety about Buller driving up to Carpford on his own. He paused.

'A few minutes ago Buchanan phoned me from the Carpford area . . .' He concluded by reporting this gist of the superintendent's much later phone call, that Buller had disappeared, they were dragging Carp Lake.

'This is getting very grim,' Paula commented.

'And Buller reported that al-Qa'eda has moved its main base from Milan to somewhere over here,' Beaurain commented. 'Which links up with our experience.'

'Tell me,' Tweed said calmly.

He doodled as he listened, frequently glancing up at Beaurain. Nothing in his expression betrayed his reaction. When the Belgian had ended his story Tweed looked at Paula.

'Sounds as though you did pretty well during the battle of the amphitheatre.'

'I'd be dead if she hadn't been there,' Beaurain said.

'Oh, I guess we make a good team,' Paula responded casually.

'Describe this Petacci, who isn't really Petacci and who is English,' Tweed told Paula. He leaned forward, asked her for the man's likely age, height, colour of eyes, of hair.

She closed her eyes for a moment, visualizing him. Then she gave as detailed a description as she could.

'About fortyish, probably five feet eight, blue eyes, brown hair. No moustache.'

'It's Philip.' Tweed leant back in his chair. 'Left Special Branch several years ago. Good linguist so he went off trawling round the continent, made a living using contacts he'd picked up earlier to get information he could sell. But only to the West. Very patriotic.'

'His second name?' Paula asked. 'Philip who?'

'I'm not identifying him beyond what I've already said.'

'Reliable?' queried Beaurain.

'As reliable as you are.'

'Then his information about al-Qa'eda is to be trusted?'

'Absolutely. Combined with what Buller told me I think we can be sure their new base is somewhere over here – and that means they plan to make London our September 11. Not a comforting thought.'

'Maybe,' Beaurain suggested, 'we ought to explore Hastings and the area round it – where they come ashore.'

'Waste of time. Too late. They've landed at least twenty men. Similar number to the team which hit the World Trade Center in New York. So where are they hiding?'

'Up at Carpford?' Paula wondered.

'Unlikely. They could be driven there easily at night from Hastings, I agree. But where is the accommodation at Carpford to hide twenty men – maybe more? From what I know of the place it doesn't exist. It might just be the home of the mastermind, whoever he is.'

'What makes you so sure it is a "he"?' Marler drawled. 'Why not a woman? I've had a weird experience following Eva Brand.'

The idea stunned them. They sat silent, staring at Marler. He kept them in suspense as he took a cigarette from his gold cigarette case, didn't hurry lighting it, took a puff. He looked round, studying their expressions.

'Marler!' Tweed crashed his fist on his desk. 'Do get on with it. I have this horrible feeling the clock is ticking down to a catastrophe.'

'Yesterday evening she left her flat, took a cab to the Ivy, had dinner with the Right Honourable Peregrine Palfry . . .'

'I saw him meeting her when I was leaving,' Paula interjected. 'She told him about her experience.'

'Mind if I continue, my dear? Otherwise Tweed will slap you down. They spent two hours over dinner, seemed to know each other well. Then Eva, looking very serious, leaves in a cab she must have ordered. By now I'm back sitting in my car. I follow her. Back to her flat in Fulham. Once inside she turns on the light in the living-room, no curtains drawn. She unrolls a small prayer rug, kneels on it facing east, bows her head very slowly a number of times. Gets up, rolls the rug. tucks it under a sofa, showers – the bathroom window steamed up – then presumably goes to bed.'

'Are you sure of this?' Tweed asked, his tone disbelieving.

'You think I'd imagine a scene like that?'

'She's a ruddy Muslim fanatic,' Paula burst out.

'Hence,' Marler said gently, 'my question. What makes Tweed so sure the brain behind all this is a man?'

They were stunned again. Marler smoked his cigarette, looked at each in turn. Most people would be pleased with the idea of dropping a bombshell, reducing their audience to silence. Marler simply looked as though he'd been talking about the weather.

'Want to hear what she did next day?' Marler eventually enquired.

'Yes, we would,' Tweed said quietly.

'Gets up late – to avoid rush hour, I imagine. Has breakfast. Just croissants . . .'

'How on earth could you see that?' Paula demanded.

'Because, my dear, I'm using my monocular glass. She has good teeth. May I proceed? About ten she emerges, dressed in a windcheater, gets behind the wheel of her Saab after she's packed what she's carrying in the back . . .'

'What was she carrying?' rapped Tweed.

'I *was* coming to that. One very large Harrods carrier and a much smaller one which she puts in the car carefully. Briefly now, I follow her to Carpford. She parks the Saab out of sight behind Martin Hogarth's bungalow . . .'

'Not the boozy brother, Billy?' Paula queried.

'Who is reporting this sequence of events?' Marler gave her a look. 'Eva then reappears, carrying both carriers. The elegant Martin is waiting for her, opens the door, she goes inside. Spends a couple of hours there, then drives back to her Fulham flat. I wait nearby all day and half the evening. She doesn't come out again. So, here I am.'

'Mysterious,' commented Beaurain. 'I'd like to meet the lady.'

'You most certainly would.' Marler chuckled. 'I reckon she would dazzle you.'

'A good looker?'

'That's an understatement.'

'What Marler has told us brings Martin Hogarth into the picture,' Tweed broke in impatiently. 'We never thought about him . . .'

As though on cue, Newman walked in, followed by Harry and Pete. Newman's report on Hogarth was useless. He had tried to call on his target but the door was never answered. Even though Newman could hear movement inside the bungalow. He'd waited for hours but Martin had never appeared.

Harry's report was more positive. As always, he kept his narrative brief.

'Palfry stays in the Ministry until mid-evening, then takes a cab to the Ivy. I see Pete here watching the place.'

'I didn't see you,' Nield grumbled.

'You weren't supposed to. If you had seen me I'd be no good at my job, mate. By then Tweed had phoned me to watch the Ivy to guard Paula.' He looked at Nield. 'You certainly saw me then.'

'Bob,' Tweed said quickly, 'you were watching Victor Warner. What did you see?'

'Nothing. Never caught one glimpse of our brilliant Minister. All the time I was enduring the boredom of Whitehall Warner never appeared. I'm pretty sure he wasn't in the building. And that was a long absence.'

'Time I called on the lawyer, Pecksniff, who handles the finances for this invisible New Age company which developed Carpford.' Tweed was putting on his raincoat as he continued. 'You can come with me, Paula. I doubt we'll get anything out of him. A dubious lawyer.'

'I'd better come too,' Harry said. 'If he clams up I'll pay him one of my calls.'

Ali was waiting inside a phone-box in a remote village. He grabbed the phone on the second ring.

'Yes?'

141

'Who is that,' the strange voice talking through a distorter demanded.

'Ali.'

'Abdullah here. Is the equipment in place now?'

'Four milk vans carrying the bombs . . .'

'Idiot! I used the word equipment. You do the same. Well?'

'Four items of equipment are in place – inside the warehouse. They have to be transported to their ultimate destination. The fifth vehicle's engine wouldn't start. We're working on it. Another hour and . . .'

'You do realize you must not put it on the road until after dark. Get something right.'

'We are being very careful. All the team has arrived . . .'

Ali slammed down the phone and swore. Abdullah had broken the connection. As he walked out into the drizzle he again wondered was the voice that of a man or a woman? Impossible to tell.

Pecksniff & Co., Solicitors, were situated in Bermondsey down a narrow side street. Not the best part of Bermondsey, the old three-storey buildings had seen no renovation for years. Loose bricks, fallen from walls, littered the pavement. The windows had not seen a cleaner for ages. The miserable street was littered with rubbish. A dirty brass plate attached to the wall located the place. The *Peck* had been ripped away so the sign now read *sniff & Co, Solicit*.

'Not the best part of town,' Harry observed. 'Not even for the East End. Not safe either. Get mugged here for a box of matches.'

'We'll leave you to guard the car,' Tweed decided.

The moment Tweed and Paula left the car Harry locked the doors. Reaching down under his seat, he grasped a canister of mace gas, perched it on his lap.

Tweed pressed the bell beside the door with stained-glass windows in the upper half. 'Stained' described it well –

impossible to guess the original colours. No one came. He shoved his thumb into the bell and kept it there. When the door opened a strange apparition appeared.

Clad in a shabby black jacket which reached his knees, he wore an equally old-fashioned collar with the tips protruding. He was living up to his Dickensian-like name – even had an ancient gold watch chain draped across his waistcoat. Stooped, his hair was the colour of dirty mustard, his pinched face lined and his little eyes were cunning.

'We have an appointment,' Tweed said.

'I don't think so. I made no appointments.'

'I did.' Tweed held his SIS folder close to the face. 'Now let us in. This street smells.'

'I can only give you a few minutes . . .'

'You'll give us as long as it takes.'

Tweed was inside the poorly furnished office with Paula at his heels. The apparition closed and locked the door. Shuffling, he led them into another office which startled Paula. The furniture was expensive antiques with a large Regency desk. Unlike the outer office the room had been dusted, she noted. The solicitor sat down behind the desk in an antique high-backed chair. Paula caught a whiff of whisky.

'You are Mr Peck Sniff?' Tweed began.

'Pecksniff, if you please,' their host snapped.

'The New Age Development Company which built Carpford high up in the North Downs,' Tweed plunged on. 'You act for them.'

'Never heard of them.' Pecksniff's false teeth rattled.

'You handle collection of their rents – and other monies. The inhabitants have told us this. Stop lying.'

'I beg your pardon.'

Pecksniff straightened up, glared at Tweed. A picture of indignation and innocence. He clasped his bony fingers on his desk. The teeth rattled again.

'I must ask you both to leave.'

143

'You deny that you're connected with New Age?'

'Never heard of them.'

'Maybe,' Paula suggested nastily, 'another drop of Scotch would refresh your memory. We can always come back with a warrant and rip this dump to pieces.'

'I shall call a judge for an injunction.'

'Don't be silly,' Tweed told him mildly. 'You're probably in serious trouble.'

'The door is there.' Pecksniff had stood up. He pointed a quavering finger. 'This interview is concluded.'

'We tried to do it the easy way.' Tweed sighed as he stood up. 'We can find our own way out.'

They left the building. Harry unlocked the doors, slipped the Mace canister under his seat. Seated behind the driving seat, he turned round.

'Any luck? You've been very quick.'

'He won't talk.'

'Paula,' Harry suggested. 'While I'm away lock the doors. Get into this seat. I may be a while.'

Stepping out, he waited until Paula was behind the wheel, closed the door. Standing in front of the solicitor's door he stretched, widening his hefty shoulders. His thick thumb pressed the bell, held it pressed. He had his folder in his hand as the door opened. Swiftly he thrust it into Pecksniff's face, giving him little chance to examine it.

'Special Branch. I'm coming in . . .'

Harry pushed past Pecksniff, grabbed him by the arm, kicked the door shut behind him with his foot, hauled his captive into the inner office, used his foot again to kick the inner door shut, then pushed the solicitor towards the chair behind his desk.

'That looks like where you hold court.'

'I'm a solicitor . . .'

'Sit down.'

Harry pushed one of the hard chairs closer to the desk,

sat. Pecksniff, looking dazed, resumed his normal seat on his throne. He was looking more normal. Which would never do. Harry leaned both meaty forearms on the desk.

'That filing cabinet over there will have the papers. Get them out.'

'What papers?' A vague hint of indignation.

'The New Age development gang!'

'I have already told the man who came in before you . . .'

Harry half stood up. His right hand whipped out, grabbed Pecksniff by the wing collar, tightened it. He hauled him out of his tall chair so he was stretched half way across the desk, his own face close to the solicitor's. His voice was quiet and, like his expression, menacing.

'Now listen to me, Peckysniff. I have a short fuse. This ain't just about a property development. We'll have you for obstruction for starters. But there's more. You could go down as accomplice in two murders. So open the cabinet before I loses my temper.'

'Two murders . . .'

Pecksniff's voice was garbled, half-choking on Butler's grip. Butler sniffed again. Thought he'd caught the fumes of whisky when he'd entered. He relaxed his hold, jumped up, brought back a smeared glass from a side table, planted it in front of Pecksniff.

'Where's the bottle? Have a tot. Settle your nerves.'

Pecksniff, ashen-faced, tried to adjust his collar, then opened a drawer at the bottom of his desk, brought out a bottle of Johnnie Walker. He removed the top and was on the verge of drinking from the bottle when Harry stopped him.

'Don't do it like that. You'll choke. Pour it into the glass first. That's what the damned thing's for.'

A lot of rattling. Then the bottle was lifted from the drawer. Then the teeth. Harry, arms crossed, watched as Pecksniff poured a strong tot into the glass, held the shaking glass, looked at his visitor. Harry shook his head.

145

Earlier he had used a handkerchief to pick up the glass. No fingerprints.

Pecksniff drank the whisky in two swallows. He sighed. Pale colour was coming back into his face. He put the glass down next to the bottle where he could reach it. His voice was hoarse.

'Two murders?'

'Yes. Mrs Gobble at the shop in Carpford. The other one will make you think. Mrs Warner. Linda Warner. Wife of the Minister for Home Security. You could be in line for both – unless we get cooperation.'

Pecksniff sighed again. Standing up, staggering a little, he took a ring of keys from his pocket, made his way to the cabinet. Unlocking it, he stooped, hauled out a fat green folder, placed it on the desk.

'It's all in there. Records of money transmissions, monies concerning Carpford.'

'There are some very large amounts here,' Harry said after riffling through the sheets. 'One for £200,000. Another, quite recently, for £400,000. All this for rents? Come on.'

'He said they were for renovations at Carpford.'

'Who said that?'

'Gerald Hanover. The man who organized the creation of New Age, who supervised the building of the village. He also checked the credentials of the tenants. Except for one. He wanted an unmarried woman – or a widow – to take charge of the shop. She was to keep an eye on the other tenants. A simple soul, he said. I interviewed those who answered an ad in *The Times*. I thought Mrs Gobble fitted the bill. A simple soul. It did strike me as odd, but Hanover paid me generous fees.'

'What does this Hanover look like?'

'I have no idea. Always gave instructions on the phone.'

'What did he sound like?'

'Very odd. The voice was so distorted I couldn't decide whether it was a man or a woman. Victor Warner infuriated

146

Hanover when he slipped in and bought a large piece of land they'd overlooked. I didn't handle that transaction. I suppose Warner has some big solicitor in the City.'

The dam had broken. It had all come tumbling out because he was frightened. The whisky had probably helped.

'Ever try to trace Hanover?' Harry asked casually.

'Well . . . once. I used the two numbers which provide the number that calls you. Turned out it was a call-box in Berkeley Square. I rang a long time and a passer-by eventually answered, told me the number and where this phone-box was.'

'Nothing but the best for Mr Hanover. Berkeley Square. How was the money delivered to you?'

'By one of those big international transport firms who want a signature. That really is all I know about New Age.' He paused, his voice shook. 'I won't hear any more about those two murders, will I? I cooperated.'

'I can't promise, but I very much doubt it. Providing you never tell Mr Hanover about my visit. If you do we shall know.'

20

Tweed and Paula stepped inside the luxurious lift with its gilded mirrors and red leather seats. He had decided Victor Warner must be working away from the Ministry and inside his flat in Belgravia. As the elevator ascended, Paula glanced round.

'Some people live in style.'

'He has money,' Tweed told her.

'I know. From some brand of laxative.'

Mrs Carson, the forbidding grey-haired housekeeper, opened the apartment door. She was polite but distant.

'Good afternoon, Mr Tweed. I didn't know you were expected.'

'I'm not. This is an emergency . . .'

The Minister looked up from a desk in the palatial living-room, hastily scooped up a pile of papers, put them inside a Cabinet red box, closed it. He stood up, tall, agile and bad-tempered. His hawk-like face was grim, his eyes glittered behind the pince-nez, his voice was crisply upper crust.

'People call for an appointment before they come barging in without notice.'

'Yes, I know. I recall your summons via him.'

He pointed to Palfry, seated on a sofa when they arrived. He had now stood up with an unctuous smile. The small neat man tried to pour oil on the troubled waters.

'Either of you . . .' he gave Paula a beaming smile 'could have contacted me but I sense an urgency about you. Is there a problem?'

'Of course there is. I imagine you both know a very major attack is expected on London soon. Or doesn't that bother you?' he suggested, staring straight at the Minister.

'Please do sit down, make yourselves comfortable,' Palfry said quickly, ushering them to a sofa facing Warner's chair sideways on. 'We are all on the same side.'

'Most reassuring,' Tweed responded in an unconvinced tone.

As they sat on the sofa Warner was still standing, glaring. With obvious reluctance he swung his chair round to face them, slowly sat down. Even seated he appeared tall, lean.

'Have you ever heard of Gerald Hanover?' Tweed snapped.

'Who?' Warner polished his pince-nez, perched them back on the bridge of his prominent nose.

'Gerald Hanover,' Tweed repeated.

'Can't say that I have. Who is he?'

'Oh, probably the key piece in this deadly game of chess we are playing with the invisible enemy . . . So far that's all we know.' He paused. 'Could be a man or a woman . . .'

The door opened and Eva Brand walked in, carrying a tray with tea for three. Paula stared as Eva placed the tray where they could reach it. She blew a kiss at Paula. Again Palfry spoke up quickly, smiling amiably.

'This is Eva Brand. I think you know her, Miss Grey. Eva, her companion is Tweed of the SIS.'

'Happy to meet you,' Eva said, as though she had never met Tweed in his office. 'How do you like your tea? It's Earl Grey. I hope that is acceptable.'

'It is most acceptable and very kind of you,' said Paula, who had taken over Palfry's role of covering for her host. Tweed was sitting in grim silence.

'Eva,' Palfry went on explaining, 'is a close friend of mine. An exceptionally intelligent lady.'

'Does a bit of work for us,' growled Warner, annoyed at others taking over the conversation. 'Nothing secret, of course.'

'Then that may make some of what I have to say awkward,' Tweed snapped.

'Don't worry, my dear chap,' Warner said, smiling acidly. 'Miss Brand was with Medfords Security. She is the epitome of discretion.'

'I suppose you've heard,' Tweed plunged forward, 'that the head of Special Branch, Jasper Buller, has disappeared. In very similar circumstances to those of your wife – and Mrs Gobble.'

'It's distressing, disturbing.' Warner gazed at the ceiling.

'It's more than that. It could be mass murder,' Tweed went on brutally. 'And it centres on that weird village, Carpford. We need to tear the place to pieces.'

'Already happening,' Warner said harshly. 'I've been to Carpford – I have a home there – and Buchanan has dragged Carp Lake. His team worked with searchlights through the night . . .'

'And found what?'

'No need to be so aggressive, Tweed. We have to keep our heads. He discovered nothing – except tadpoles. And that with a very large team of divers. I told Buchanan he had to clear the place up before they left . . .'

'And how did he respond to that?'

'Said he had already ordered his men to do just that. So, a complete waste of time.'

'News is beginning to get into the papers,' Tweed stormed. 'That there is a major threat to London. And Buller's disappearance, linked to the other two, will appear in the *Daily Nation* tomorrow. Newman has written a large article on these sinister events.'

'We could put a D notice on that,' warned the Minister.

'What on earth for? The public must be warned. It's not a state secret.'

'I just hope . . .' Warner paused to clean his pince-nez, a trick Paula suspected he used to emphasize what was coming next. He replaced the pince-nez, smiled unpleasantly.

151

'. . . As I was saying, I hope Newman hasn't gone wild and produced something that will panic London!'

'He hasn't mentioned where the danger is coming from. If that is what is unnerving you.'

'Nothing wrong with my nerves.' Again the twisted smile. 'I do know we have to be on our guard against the Real IRA.'

'We're going.' Tweed stood up with a face like thunder. 'I don't think we have anything more to say to each other.' He paused near the door, Paula by his side, his tone gentle. 'I just hope you will soon hear better news about your wife.'

'Thank you. Most kind of you.'

Eva had joined them. 'I'll see them out,' she called back.

She closed the door and Mrs Carson, tight-lipped, appeared. Eva smiled at her. 'I'm showing our visitors out. I know you have so much to do.'

Mrs Carson glared, not pleased at what she considered was her position being usurped. Without a word she walked away, slammed a door behind her.

'She's a bit touchy,' Eva said with a smile. 'Since Victor isn't often here she feels she has control here.' They had stepped into the lift. Eva spoke rapidly as it descended. 'Mr Tweed, could I come to see you again at Park Crescent? I'd phone first, of course.'

'Come at any time, please do.' Tweed was now his amiable self. 'We can have lunch or dinner, if you like.'

'I would like.' She gave him a flashing smile.

'You were pretty tough,' Paula observed as Tweed got behind the wheel of the car and Paula sat beside him.

'He gives a good impression that he hasn't a clue. What did you think?' he asked as he manoeuvred into heavy traffic.

'Totally clueless.'

★   ★   ★

Rush hour. The traffic was dense. At times they were crawling, at others stationary for minutes, then there was movement. At Hyde Park Corner it became gridlock. It was dark now and cars' headlights glared everywhere. They were stationary.

'London is packed solid with people,' Paula commented.

'What did you say?'

'That London is packed solid with people. Ah, we're moving again.'

They were halfway round the Duke of Wellington's statue and then stopped once more. A car was drawn up alongside Paula. She glanced at the driver alone behind the wheel, a brown-faced man, youngish with short hair. He caught her glance, leaned out of his window and tapped on hers with his left hand. She lowered her window, her Browning already in her hand. As the traffic started moving his right hand appeared. The Glock pistol it held was aimed point blank at Tweed. She fired once. Her bullet hit his right hand. Blood appeared, he dropped the Glock.

'*Move!*' Paula shouted.

Traffic behind the gunman's car was honking as it stayed where it was. Tweed swung his wheel, saw a gap, raced down Buckingham Palace Road. Paula looked back. The gunman's car was still stationary. The honking of cars behind him rose to a crescendo, then faded as Tweed continued driving fast.

'He was going to kill you,' Paula gasped.

'Saw it all out of the corner of my eye. You were so very quick. A significant event. Someone with a mobile must have been watching Warner's house, reported we were leaving.'

'Or someone inside the house. He looked Egyptian.'

153

21

Everyone was assembled in the first-floor office when Tweed and Paula walked in. Newman was seated in an armchair while Pete Nield perched on one of the arms. Harry Butler sat cross-legged on the floor while Marler leaned against a wall. Beaurain relaxed in the other armchair, waved to Paula who walked over to her desk, puzzled as to why the team was all present. Tweed seemed to read her mind as, after hanging up his raincoat, he sat behind his desk, his expression grim as he leaned forward.

'You were all asked to be here so we can see where we are. The key element is we now know the enemy is al-Qa'eda. We have three confirmations of this dangerous development. Marler's top informant, Carla, told him this. In Milan, Jasper Buller's link with the ex-carabinieri officer told him the same thing. In Verona, Philip, a man I know to be totally reliable, now masquerading as Petacci, told Jules the same thing. Three entirely different sources.' He slapped his hand hard on the desk. 'I now feel there is no doubt any more. The powerful cell which was located in Milan is now on our doorstep. Why? Obviously to launch a September 11 attack on London . . .'

'Hadn't you better tell them about the attempt to kill you?' suggested Paula.

'Thanks to you they didn't succeed . . .' He briefly explained the incident at Hyde Park Corner. Newman reacted instantly.

'From now on you don't go anywhere without an armed guard.'

'We'll see about that . . .'

'No!' Newman was fierce. 'We won't see. That's how we'll proceed . . .'

'If you'll just let me continue. Al-Qa'eda is the menace, a formidable one. So what don't we know? Just about damn-all.' The hand slapped the desk again. 'We don't know the target in London, we don't know where the cell is located, we don't know who the mastermind is . . .'

'What about Carpford?' Nield interjected.

'If I may continue. At Carpford there isn't, so far as I know, sufficient space to hide between twenty and thirty brainwashed killers . . .'

'We could check that out,' Newman interjected. 'Today I bumped into a friend of mine who runs Airsight. An outfit with light aircraft equipped with high-power cameras. Used by estate agents to get an aerial view of an area with rich properties. He's also used confidentially by the MoD . . .'

'Then get him to fly over Carpford tomorrow and take a lot of shots. Weather forecast is very good.'

'No can do tomorrow. He was on his way to Eurostar for a two-day trip to Paris . . .'

'Then book him for the day after he gets back, for Heaven's sake. From now on I want calculated *action!*' Tweed stared round, making sure he had everyone's close attention. 'Now, the other night I stayed up imagining I was the mastermind. How would I do the job? What would I aim for? Maximum casualties – scores? No. Hundreds or thousands of dead bodies. A spectacular. But don't anyone mention St Paul's or Canary Wharf. Do that and I'll throw the book at them . . .'

'Smoke and mirrors, as the Americans say,' Beaurain spoke for the first time. 'Decoys, as I said. To divert our attention from the real target.'

'So we don't know anything,' Paula remarked.

'Actually we do.' Tweed's mood became relaxed. 'There are some strange relaionships we've discovered. Martin and Billy Hogarth, up at Carpford, are brothers, who apparently hate each other. They are cousins of Drew Franklin, a man we really know nothing about. Then there is Eva Brand, niece of Drew Franklin. A ring is beginning to form. Eva is also a companion of Peregrine Palfry. Furthermore we find she knows Victor Warner well enough to be welcome in his house. The ring widens . . .'

'May I tell you something?' Monica suggested quietly.

'By all means.' Tweed smiled. 'Go ahead.'

'The dossier I've drawn up on her confirms what she told us when she appeared here out of the blue. Educated at Roedean, went on to Oxford, studied languages – French, Spanish and Arabic. While there her mother was killed in a car crash on the M25. You see, this is new data. Left Oxford and then there is a strange two-year gap. Talked to her closest girlfriend and she had no idea where Eva was during those two years. Reappeared in London, joined Medfords, which we know from what she said . . .'

'What about her father?'

'The second info gap. Nobody seems to know who he was, what he did. A girlfriend at Medfords told me she never talked about him. I ran out of contacts.'

'A mystery lady,' Tweed commented. 'Missing for two years and no trace of a father. What about money?'

'I was coming to that. When her mother died she left Eva half a million pounds. The mother came from a rich family.'

'Hence her liking for good restaurants . . .'

He stopped speaking as the phone rang. Monica answered, gave the phone to Tweed.

'It's Eva Brand on the phone . . .'

'Tweed here. I'm looking forward to our dinner together tomorrow night.'

157

'That's why I'm phoning,' the soft voice replied. 'Could I ask for a great favour? Could we dine tonight at seven? I do hope I'm not being a nuisance. Something cropped up for tomorrow – a friend from abroad.'

'That would be quite convenient. But instead of the Ivy I'd like you to join me at Santini's. Do you know it? It has a terrace extending out over the Thames.'

'Super! I haven't been there for ages. I could meet you there. Same time suit you?'

'Seven at Santini's. Take care . . .'

He told the others of the change in his arrangements. His expression hardened. 'While I'm having dinner with Eva you will all be very active. We need positive information about the main players in this drama. I no longer mind if the people you'll be tracking know they're being followed. It will put pressure on them. Under pressure people crack – or make a mistake. Newman, you wait outside the *Daily Nation* offices. Your target is Drew Franklin. You said he works late. Take one of those advanced non-flash cameras, photograph anyone he meets.'

'He could recognize me.'

'So much the better. Pressure. Marler, go down to Whitehall. Follow Peregrine Palfry. Same instructions as I gave Newman. Harry, you track Pecksniff. First phone him, ask him which estate agent handled the property transactions at Carpford. Then go and park near his office until he emerges. The same instructions I've already given. Pete, you go and park near Buller's place in Pimlico. Marler can give you the address.'

'But,' Paula objected, 'Buller has disappeared, his car found abandoned on the way to Carpford.'

'And,' Tweed told her, 'what would be the way to pretend to vanish? To leave your car where Buller's was found. By arangement someone else picks him up, returns him to Pimlico.'

'I suppose so,' she replied. 'Two things bother me a lot

– the two missing years in Eva's life. The impossibility of finding anything out about her father.'

'So, as I'm dining with her tonight, maybe I can solve the mysteries . . .'

'You also mentioned earlier the possibility of a ring being located at Carpford – presumably a ring controlling the al-Qa'eda cell. Could all of them at Carpford be in it?'

'An intriguing theory.'

'One thing you've overlooked,' said Beaurain. 'You'll be driving across London alone to get to Santini's. Already there's been one attempt to kill you. You'll be leaving here about 6.30 p.m. I imagine? Good. I'll call a girlfriend and take her out to dinner. At Santini's. I'll be close behind you during the drive there.'

'If you insist.'

'I do.'

Ali, who passed under the name of Adam, was inside the public phone-box when it began ringing. He glanced round. A deserted side street in London.

'Who is this?' he asked in English.

'Your name?' the distorted voice demanded.

'Ali here.'

'Abdullah speaking. I sense that Tweed is becoming dangerous. What went wrong?'

'Mehmet came close to shooting him at Hyde Park Corner. But the girl travelling with Tweed shot Mehmet before he could fire. Her bullet smashed Mehmet's hand. The police arrived. Mehmet is now being treated at St Thomas's Hospital.'

'Then send someone there, disguised as a doctor, to kill him. You should have thought of that yourself. Shut up! I haven't finished. Get someone else to kill Tweed immediately. Is the equipment in place now?'

'Up to a point. It has to be transferred to its ultimate site. Don't push me on that. London is crawling with the police.

159

You must leave it to me. The last small van with what it was carrying has arrived.'

'Kill Tweed. Make it look like an accident . . .'

Once again Abdullah broke the connection without warning. Ali, who spoke such perfect English he might have been an Englishman, swore, in good old-fashioned Anglo-Saxon.

The monster truck of the type supermarkets use to transport supplies was parked at the edge of Park Crescent nearest to Euston. A red triangle a short distance from its rear warned drivers to steer clear. The truck was hauled by a cab attached to the main vehicle. The driver wore a floppy cap pulled well down, an old leather jacket and a pair of worn denims. He was watching the entrance to SIS HQ.

He had earlier studied a photograph taken of Tweed. It had cost Abdullah a small fortune to obtain the print from a sleazy man who specialized in taking pictures of important people. Most of his income came from private detectives – hired to watch a man or a woman suspected by their partner of playing the field.

The driver had a small pair of night binoculars looped round his neck. The binoculars were hidden inside the leather jacket. Whenever anyone left the building he checked them with his binoculars. Several men had already left but no one who looked like Tweed.

As he had expected, a patrol car had pulled up because he was a nuisance to other traffic. He had waited until one of the officers got out of the car and asked what was the problem.

'A little trouble, Officer, with engine. Fixed now. Will drive away in minutes.'

'See that you do.'

The officer was tired. So he failed to notice that the typically dressed driver spoke English with a faint accent. Minutes later Tweed emerged, climbed behind the wheel

160

of his car. The driver climbed swiftly back up into his cab, revved up the engine, drove forward slowly. He increased speed as Tweed headed towards Baker Street. With the weight of his juggernaut he would crush Tweed's car flat. The body would be unrecognizable.

22

Harry Butler was the last to leave on the mission Tweed had given him – to watch Pecksniff's office. Tweed was amused as he listened to Harry phoning the solicitor.

'That's Pecksniff, isn't it?'

'Yes. Who is this?'

'I called on you. We had a nice little chat about Carpford. Remember me?'

'Yes. Unfortunately. What is it now? I still have a lot of work to get through.'

'Mr Pecksniff, one question I overlooked. I'm sure you won't mind answering. If you feel inhibited I can always pop down now in the car . . .'

'What is the question?' The voice quavered.

'You said you never handled the transaction for Victor Warner's purchase of that chunk of land New Age overlooked. But what about the legal junk when you rent a place? Who dealt with that?'

'I did, of course. No outside agent was involved.'

'See you . . .'

Before he put down the phone Harry thought he heard a choking protest. He grinned, told Tweed what Pecksniff had said.

'Something not right about that village,' Tweed remarked as he put on his raincoat. 'I'm off now for dinner with Eva . . .'

Outside, he paused under the nearby street lamp to pull

up the collar. Getting into his car he drove to the end of the Crescent, noticed there was very little traffic as he turned left towards Baker Street. It was bitterly cold. He guessed most commuters had left for home early.

In his rear-view mirror he noticed a juggernaut coming up behind him. Too big for the roads, he thought. One of the really big jobs with a cab hauling its immense load. He'd seen them take half a minute to negotiate a sharp bend, holding up all the traffic behind them. He wondered how many tons the leviathan weighed. Too many.

The lumbering giant had picked up speed, was almost on his tail. A situation he always disliked. If he had to make an emergency stop, would the brute pull up in time? He doubted it. He drove faster to get away from it. The juggernaut driver also increased speed. Idiot! Tweed pressed his foot down.

Inside his Audi with the souped-up engine, Beaurain sat with his girlfriend, Sally, parked in the shadows of Park Crescent. He had only known her for a month and already decided she was high on good looks and low on intellect. He knew he'd soon be bored with her.

The advantage was she had a cultured voice and smart – if not daring – in dress sense. She would fit in at Santini's. She fiddled in her evening handbag, produced a cigarette case, perched a cigarette in her mouth.

'Don't light that, please,' he requested mildly.

'Oh, I see. I'm stuck with one of those non-smoking fanatics.'

'Actually, no. I do smoke. But never in a car. Smoke can get in a driver's eyes at just the wrong moment.'

'Well, let's get moving. I'm hungry.'

'So am I. We don't want to be first in the restaurant. You won't be able to make a grand entrance,' he said with a wry smile.

'I suppose you've got a point, Jules.'

Earlier Beaurain had noticed the juggernaut parked with its cab protruding. He had also noticed the binoculars used by the driver whenever anyone left the SIS entrance. Then Tweed came out, got into his car, drove off. Beaurain started his own engine and Sally, who had been tapping her varnished fingers on her bag, let out a sigh of relief.

'At long last.'

Beaurain timed it so the Audi emerged from the Crescent just as the juggernaut drove past towards Baker Street. He sat on its tail. At a curve he saw that Tweed had increased his speed. The juggernaut driver did the same thing. The lumbering brute was almost touching Tweed's boot. Tweed went faster. The juggernaut driver revved up like mad.

Beaurain knew now he was going to ram Tweed. He dropped back. Ahead was a junction, no other traffic. To the left reared a new office building site, festooned with scaffolding rising high up. No workmen – they had all gone home. Beaurain started overtaking the juggernaut, honking his horn non-stop. The driver glared down. For a moment there was a wide gap as Tweed pressed his foot down again. The driver revved up to high speed.

Beaurain was ahead of him. He signalled left, cut in front of the juggernaut, missing him by inches. The driver panicked, swung his wheel to the left to avoid hitting the wrong target. Then he screamed.

The massive building site was rushing towards him. His hands slipped on the wheel, covered with the sweat of fear. The cab had been jerked round too suddenly. Behind it the huge load pushed it forward. It slammed at speed into the maze of scaffolding, rushed on, crashing into a huge concrete wall. The cab concertina's, was squashed into less than half its normal size, stopped. Deathly silence.

'What happened?' Sally asked in her dumb voice.

'Truck skidded,' Beaurain said calmly, driving on. 'I saw the driver climbing down out of his cab,' he lied.

23

'I've decided to drive up to Carpford,' Paula announced.

'Tweed wouldn't sanction that,' Monica burst out, appalled. 'It's dark. There's no one left to come with you. That is just about the most dangerous thing you could do.'

'He sanctioned my going to Italy.' Paula was feeling restless. As she spoke she slipped on her wool-lined windcheater. She was also clad in warm jeans. She put on her knee-length boots as she went on talking. 'The evening is a perfect time to interview people, to catch them off guard.'

'Beaurain was with you when you went to Italy,' Monica protested.

'True. But Jules isn't available, is he?'

She unlocked a drawer, took out her Beretta 6.35mm automatic. Empty, it weighed only ten ounces and was about four-and-a-half inches long. She checked to make sure it was unloaded, slid in a full magazine, put a spare in the windcheater pocket. The gun slipped down easily inside her spacious boot. A small sheathed knife slid down inside the other boot. And she had her Browning inside the special pocket in her shoulder bag.

'I could phone Tweed at Santini's, get his opinion,' Monica persisted.

'Don't you dare!'

The icy cold hit her face when she left and climbed inside her car. The heater soon warmed up the interior as she drove towards Baker Street. She didn't expect everyone to be at home in the village but some of them never seemed to leave it. Then a barrier stopped her with a diversion sign.

She could see most of a juggernaut protruding from a building in the course of construction. A policeman she happened to know leaned down as she lowered the window.

'That doesn't look nice,' she said. 'Any casualties?'

'The driver inside the cab. I don't think we're going to find much of him left.' He coughed, feeling he'd said too much. 'Don't quote me, Miss Grey.'

'I've forgotten already what you said, John.'

She gave him a smile as she swung down the diversion. Soon she was racing down the A3, just inside the speed limit. No other traffic. A ghostly moon shone on the frosted fields. She was pleased to be on her own for once. Now she could handle things *her* way.

She had crossed the first Down, swept along the steep hill beyond, when she paused by the inn on the main road, the inn where Buller's car had been found abandoned. What the devil was going on? she wondered as she turned off up the steep, twisting road up into the remote Downs. She felt justified in what she was doing. Tweed had emphasized he thought little time was left before London was subjected to a catastrophic attack.

High up, headlights on full beam, she turned off at the triangle leading to Black Wood. She began to doubt whether she had been wise when trails of mist drifted through the trees as she drove carefully down the 'rabbit warren'. Now she was hemmed in on both sides by high banks. She caught sight of movement.

Something inside the mist close to the road. She stopped, kept the engine running, took hold of her Browning, lowered her window. Now she could *hear* something approaching her car. A crunching of feet on the dead bracken. God! Had she been impetuous? The stealthy approach came closer, the something disturbing the bracken. She checked – yes, she had locked all her doors before starting out.

Her nerves were vibrating. Who on earth could be stalking through Black Wood? Her sense of menace grew stronger. Maybe she had made a fatal mistake in stopping? She thought of driving on. But a bullet fired accurately from above would finish her off. It was too late now to change her mind.

Then the something slithered down the bank in front of her. For a moment it stood in the glare of the headlights. A large fox. With a swift reaction it climbed the opposite bank and was gone. She took off her gloves, wiped both hands clean of the sweat, put them on again, drove on down the gulch road and soon she was climbing the road up to Carpford.

She eased her way round the sharp corner where Mrs Warner's car had been found abandoned. So many reminders of people who had vanished into thin air. Unnerving disappearances. She had little doubt Beaurain was convinced they had all been murdered. But if he was right how had they disposed of the bodies? Carp Lake had been dragged and nothing found there.

Cresting the rise to the plateau on which Carpford was perched, she was not happy to see that the mist was thicker up here, almost a fog. Paula had decided the first place she wanted to check was Mrs Gobble's shop. Was the telescope still there? She drove slowly past Garda, Victor Warner's weird Italianate residence. Lights in all the windows. He must have come up here himself.

Driving slowly on, she passed the futuristic blocks of concrete cubes which were Drew Franklin's hideaway. More lights in the porthole windows. Maybe she had come up on the right night.

No lights in Mrs Gobble's shop. Their absence gave the place a funereal look. Driving a few feet beyond it, she saw a large shed half-hidden behind it. Hadn't noticed that before. She stopped, left the engine running for a quick getaway, got out.

Like stepping into the Arctic, a mist-bound Arctic. The two doors to the shed had a padlock which was not closed. She eased the doors open, Browning in her hand. Extracting her flashlight from another pocket, she switched it on. The place was empty. No sign it had been used for a long time. Then it struck her this was the ideal place to park her car out of sight. Within minutes she was closing the doors with her car inside. Now she needn't advertise her approach.

The door to the shop was open. She entered cautiously, her flashlight swivelling round. It had been searched, by the police she felt sure. An attempt had been made to put things back where they belonged. Male searchers. They could never put things back in the right place. She noticed the four-panelled screen was still standing. No sign of the telescope. It had gone. Taken by who?

She decided to approach Palfry's huge tub of a home first. Following the path she had walked with Tweed, it was only when she was close to it that, because of the fog, she saw there were lights. But where was the entrance? She crept round the side and found steps leading up to an arched door. She swivelled her flashlight up its side and realized for the first time how massive the place was. Mounting the steps, she pressed the illuminated bell, heard chimes pealing inside. The door was opened after sounds of locks being released. In bright light stood Peregrine Palfry.

'Ah, Miss Grey, what a pleasant surprise. Do come in . . .'

His smooth face was smiling, as always. He had greeted her as though this was nothing unusual. Diplomatic training, she thought. He closed the door on the fog as soon as she was inside. Wearing a smart check sports jacket and beige slacks with a sharp crease, his shirt open at the collar.

170

'Just got a hot pot of coffee ready,' He said. 'You won't refuse. Not after walking through that fog. Do sit down after I've taken your jacket.'

He was the perfect host, acting as though he had expected her. The chair he led her to had an Oriental look, large and with comfortable arms. As she sat he was placing soft cushions behind her.

'Now, I'll get the coffee . . .'

She had kept her shoulder-bag, and while alone looked at her strange surroundings. The diameter of the room was enormous. High up the ceiling was masked by a cloth canopy with a peculiar design. The furniture had an Eastern look. Her eyes followed the endless circle of the walls. If you'd had a few drinks you'd soon feel dizzy. By the side of the wall furthest from her a wide massive oak staircase with a banister climbed, disappearing above the canopy. Palfry returned, served the coffee, sat on a throne-like chair.

'What do you think of it?' he asked, waving his hand.

'It's very Oriental. A unique house I'd say. Large enough to house a small army.'

'Excuse me?' His normal gentle eyes sharpened.

'I just said it was large enough to house a small army.'

'Oh, sorry. I didn't quite catch what you said. I suppose it is.' He chuckled. 'Don't let the MoD know!'

'And very tastefully Oriental.'

'So glad you approve. My girlfriend doesn't. Came here once and said from now on she'd meet me in London.'

'You've been to the Middle East?' she pressed on.

'Pardon?' The eyes sharpened again.

'I asked if you'd been to the Middle East.'

'Oh, yes. For a short time. Posted to the Cairo Embassy. I didn't like Cairo. Got out one weekend on a huge barge going down the Nile. It was motorized but a team of Egyptians rowed us up. Strong chaps. Pulled giant oars. Chap who came back recently said they now use a steamer if you leave from Cairo. More luxurious, I gathered.'

171

'Turning to another subject, Mr Palfry . . .'

'Perry, please.'

'Is there any news about Mrs Warner? Have you any theory as to what happened to her?'

'No, to both questions, I fear.'

'Someone said there was a rumour she'd run off with another man.'

'I'm sure she hasn't. She was a real lady, the perfect consort for the Minister. The kind you don't often see any more.' His smile glowed. 'Present company excluded, of course.'

Paula had drunk her coffee and refused a refill. 'Thank you, all the same. Before I came over here I visited Mrs Gobble's shop. The door was open. The place had been searched.'

'By the police. I rushed over when I realized what was going on. Told them she had asked me to keep an eye on the shop if she was ever out. A fib. They don't know how to put anything back properly. I was annoyed.'

'Did they take anything with them? A high-powered telescope, for example?'

'No they didn't. They made a mess taking fingerprints. Left that all brown dust they use. I spent hours cleaning it up. A telescope? Didn't know she had one. Why would she?'

'A woman on her own needs something to occupy her. She did mention to me she was fed up with motor-cyclists arriving at all hours.'

'Can't say I've ever heard them, but this place is insulated against outside noises.'

'Well, Perry, I really came to see if you had heard any news about Mrs Warner. I must go now. Oh yes, I have a car parked nearby. You have been most hospitable. Thank you.'

'The pleasure has been all mine.'

He disappeared to fetch her windcheater. She was standing

172

up by the chair she'd occupied when she heard the sound of a motor-cycle engine clearly. It had gone when her host returned.

'Do come again,' he urged, helping her on with the windcheater. 'You have livened up what would have been a boring evening for me . . .'

He was smiling as he opened the door. A wave of icy fog drifted in. Palfry closed the door quickly. Frowning, Paula turned to her right, walking slowly towards the next house occupied by Margesson. She was recalling her conversation with Palfry. Something wasn't right.

Her visit to Margesson's Georgian mansion, which was a blaze of lights, was very different. It was also much shorter.

The bearded giant, who, more than ever, reminded her of an Old Testament prophet, made his point without any attempt to soften his words, to be polite. She was holding up her SIS folder, open so he could see it.

'I'm Paula Grey, assistant to Mr Tweed, whom you've met . . .'

'The Lord warns us against temptation,' he thundered. 'I would never have a woman in my house after dark. Take your wiles and yourself elsewhere.'

The door slammed shut in her face with a heavy thud. Paula shrugged, put away her folder. A religious fanatic. A man it would be a waste of time to attempt to talk to. Especially after dark! She smiled to herself.

She walked slowly along the road to Billy Hogarth's bungalow. The team which had dragged the lake had cleaned up with care. Mud still clung to the grass verge at the edge of the lake but they had done everything they could to leave Carp Lake as they had found it.

Lights were on in the bungalow behind closed shutters. She took a deep breath, hoping Billy was sober, pressed the bell. She was taken aback when the door opened.

173

Silhouetted in lights behind him stood a tall handsome man. Clean-shaven, tall, in his forties, he was smartly dressed in country garb.

'I know it's late,' she began, 'but I was hoping to have a word with Mr Billy Hogarth.'

'Better come in. It's beastly out there. I'm Martin, Billy's brother. He's had a few drinks. You are?'

'Sorry. Paula Grey . . .'

'Tweed's legendary assistant. No need to show me your ID. Care for a drink? What's your tipple?'

She was inside a narrow hall and Martin had closed the door quickly. He gave her a charming smile, a shade too charming. She mistrusted men with that kind of smile. He took her arm, led her into a large comfortable living-room. A heavily built man with a white moustache and fringe beard stood up out of an armchair. His hair was thick and white, his movements agile as he came forward, hand extended.

'You're an improvement on my boring brother.' The hand he extended was large, like the rest of Billy. She braced herself for a crushing grip. Instead, he pressed her hand gently as Martin called over his shoulder.

'To drink?'

'Just coffee, if it isn't a nuisance.'

'It's a pleasure,' Martin assured her with a smile before disappearing into another room.'

'I'm Paula Grey of the SIS,' she told the brother.

Close up to him she could smell beer. Could see his face was dripping with moisture about to fall on his shirt. Taking out a handkerchief she said, 'Excuse me,' and wiped his face. Not a gesture she would normally have dreamt of performing but she had taken an instant liking to this powerfully built man. He grinned, thanked her, said something about the heating being too high, ushered her to an armchair. Behind his back as he returned to his own chair she sniffed at the handkerchief. Beer fumes. Billy had

174

rubbed beer on his face, pretending to be drunk. Why?

With his strong frame and his appearance she could imagine that, born in the right time, he'd have made an impressive pirate. He lifted his glass off a table, sipped a small quantity of beer, then held the glass in his hand.

'How can I help you, Miss Grey? I'm Billy, to people I like.'

'I was hoping you could tell me something about Mrs Warner. It's over three weeks since she disappeared. There are rumours that she's gone off with another man. I don't believe them.'

'You never know,' interjected Martin who had returned with a Meissen cup of coffee, a jug of milk, sugar. 'Shall I pour? How do you like it?'

'Black, please.'

'And ignore that foul implication Martin has just made,' Billy growled. 'Linda Warner is a lady, something Martin wouldn't recognize. I helped her out with one or two problems. One evening her key wouldn't work in the front door. She came over and I went back with her. Tried kicking the brute of a door and the key worked fine.'

'Before I came here,' Paula went on as Martin dragged a chair next to hers, 'I called on Margesson. Wouldn't let me in – raved on about not having a woman in after dark, slammed the door in my face.'

'He's potty,' Billy said and laughed. 'You wouldn't think he was once a housemaster at Eton. Heaven help his pupils. He wasn't a religious maniac when he arrived here. All this ranting on about Allah . . .'

'About God,' Martin corrected.

'All right, about the Messiah. He's just repeating what someone has brainwashed him with. Thinks it makes him seem important. A real gasbag.'

'Billy,' Martin interjected again, 'I don't think Miss Grey wants to hear about the parochial goings-on in Carpford.'

'I noticed you used the present tense when referring to

175

Mrs Warner. You said Linda Warner *is* a lady. So you feel she is still alive?'

'Jolly well hope so. Not so many like her about these days. Incidentally, Martin, that darned motor-cyclist must still be about. Heard his machine but haven't heard it shove off.' He looked at Paula. 'They park their machines between our bungalows. Never been able to get hold of one of them to tell him to stop it.'

'They?' Paula queried.

'Yes. Recently instead of one of them we get two during the evening, coming up separately. Don't know where they go to.'

'Probably just delivering pizzas,' Martin suggested.

'What, in a large white slim envelope?' Billy protested. 'I don't think you'd get a pizza as thin as that. I know you wouldn't.'

'Billy isn't much of a detective,' Martin sneered unpleasantly.

'I think,' Paula said emphatically, 'he'd make rather a good one.'

She had her left hand perched on the arm of her chair. Martin had placed his hand over hers. She slipped her hand free, careful not to look at him. He seemed to treat it as a challenge.

'Not much fun here,' he started, smiling invitingly. 'Come and have a drink at my place. It's just next door.'

'I wouldn't if I were you,' Billy warned.

'I'd better go now,' Paula remarked after openly checking her watch.

Martin was on his feet in a flash. He disappeared in the direction where he had taken her windcheater. Paula leaned forward, lowered her voice.

'Did you know Mrs Gobble, who has also disappeared? Her telescope, a big job, has gone. I found out the police didn't take it after they'd searched her place.'

'A nice old lady. Very independent. I worry about her.

176

She was not the type to push off without saying something to me. She was lonely. The telescope was her friend . . .'

He stopped talking as Martin appeared with the wind-cheater. She tried to slip it on quickly but he made a ceremony of it, his hands clutching her arms. She pulled herself away, thanked him formally, then turned to Billy who had stood up.

'I want to thank you for a most enjoyable evening. You are the perfect host.'

'I'm not a bad cook either. What's your favourite dish?'

'Shepherd's pie.'

'Next time you come up here call me first.' He handed her a card. 'Shepherd's pie is my speciality.'

Martin accompanied her out into the long hall. They were standing by the door and he was making a performance of opening it when he spoke to her with a sneering smile.

'My boozy brother.'

'I heard that!' shouted Billy. Glancing over her shoulder she saw him standing in the hall outside the entrance to the living-room. 'What Martin won't tell you is that the only reason he can afford the rent for his bungalow and a load of expensive clothes is he was left a legacy by his uncle. I worked for my nest-egg. You'd better go now, Miss Grey. He has crawly hands.'

'Good-night to both of you.'

Paula stepped out into the fog and the door closed behind her. *Boozy brother?* She'd noticed that as Martin brought in the coffee Billy took another sip of his beer and banged the glass down on the table. It was his defence mechanism against his brother. Why was it necessary?

Several yards away from both bungalows, she paused. The mist swirled round her. As she had passed the gap between them she had glanced up the opening. A large motor-cycle was leaning against a wall. A Harley-Davidson she thought. So the mysterious messenger was still here.

'I learned a lot from Billy,' she said to herself. 'So what do I do now?'

She decided to walk round the end of Carp Lake to call on Drew Franklin. Since lights were on in the house of concrete cubes it might be a unique chance to talk to him. She again had trouble finding the front door. It was set into the concrete under an overhanging cube. She pressed the square bell, heard nothing inside. She was just about to walk away when the door opened swiftly. A slim man of medium height with a good-looking but cynical face stared at her.

'Yes, Miss Grey. What is it? Oh, come on in. You look as though you might be entertaining.'

She stepped into a living-room tastefully furnished with antiques. Franklin wore a white polo-necked sweater which matched his white slacks. His neatly brushed hair was brown and intelligent eyes swept over her. His jaw was firm but not aggressive, his mouth smiling. Closing the door, he waved towards a large sofa near a desk with a word-processor.

'I'll take your windcheater. You'll need it whenever you happen to leave.'

She decided to go over on the attack. She'd heard stories about his many conquests with women, some married. Taking off the windcheater, she folded it over her left arm, leaving her right hand free.

'Thank you, but I shan't be here long. And I'm not here to entertain, whatever that implied.'

'Tough lady. I've heard that too.'

'How did you know who I was?' she asked.

'It's my job to know all the key people in our crumbling society. Do sit down.'

'I prefer to stand. I've been sitting too long.'

'Please yourself,' he replied amiably, putting his hands in his trouser pockets. 'What do you want to know?'

He *was* attractive, she was thinking. She'd been wise to be on her guard. Get to the point, she thought. He was a man who disliked small talk.

178

'Did you know the missing Mrs Warner?'

'Come straight out with it, don't you? Yes, I knew her slightly. She didn't like me, but I liked her. She has been gone for three weeks. I find that ominous. I have decided to provoke her fool of a husband. You might like to read the bit in my article for tomorrow's *Daily Nation*.'

He walked over to his desk, took out a red pen, ringed round one short para. She went over to read it. Above and below the para were snippets which were not complimentary about well-known people on the society circuit.

Have the police considered Linda Warner may have gone off with a friend? Just one of other more draconian possibilities. The Minister seems concerned about St Paul's Cathedral. Does he really think September 11 could be repeated here? A quite different form of attack seems more likely. Al-Qa'eda are a very cunning organization.

'Isn't the first sentence libellous?' she wondered.

'Just checked it with our lawyer. He says it's all right.'

'Warner will go potty when he reads the reference to al-Qa'eda. He's trying to keep any reference to them in the press under wraps.'

'May wake up the PM at the eleventh hour. I am a responsible journalist, Miss Grey.'

'You don't think Warner can handle the crisis then?'

'I don't think Warner *is* handling the situation. That para will hit the Cabinet like a bombshell. Which is my motive.'

'You'll drive back to London with this copy in time to get it into tomorrow's edition.'

'You think I'm clueless, Miss Grey?' he said sarcastically. 'I shall transmit it to the editor over the phone tonight. Never missed a deadline yet. Is Tweed beginning to get a grip on his widespread investigation? The energy of your chief.'

'He's pursuing all leads,' she said cautiously.

'Oh, come on, Miss Grey! That's the kind of nonsense

179

statement the police issue when they don't know what they're doing.'

His tone dripped sarcasm. He folded his arms, walked away and sat on the sofa. At no time since she had arrived had he stood close to her, let alone touched her. He crossed his legs.

'Do give me credit for knowing what's going on, Miss Grey. Instead of wasting time in London, examining the mutilated body of an informant called Eddie in Covent Garden, he'd do better to come up here, grill everyone of the sinister lot who live here. Tweed should be here,' he snapped. 'At least you have come. Seen anyone else?'

'Yes, I have. Peregrine Palfry, then Margesson, who slammed the door in my face. After that Billy Hogarth, who happened to have the brother, Martin, with him.'

'Martin? You're on the right track. You've done well so far. Can't remember when I said that to anyone else.'

'I'd better go now.' She was putting on her windcheater. 'I would like to thank you for giving me so much time. You'll want to transmit your latest commentary.'

'Yes, true.' He stood up, a lean athletic figure. 'How are you going to get back to London? It's late.'

'I have my car parked safely away.'

He had accompanied her to the door which he opened. He was close to her as he whispered in her ear.

'There's no safety up here . . .'

She started walking back to the shed where her car was parked. Drew Franklin had a powerful personality. She was almost sorry to leave him. If anything the fog seemed denser, an opaque cloud which swirled slowly round her. Made her feel nervous. She was still close to Drew Franklin's house when she sensed someone was behind her. She was turning her head when it was struck with a ferocious blow. She fell forward, diving into a dark endless abyss of darkness.

24

She woke slowly, had trouble thinking, felt as though she had been drugged. Her eyes were closed. She kept them closed, hoping her head would clear, her brain would start functioning.

Gradually she realized she was stretched out on her back and lying on a bed of hard boards. Feeling was returning. She listened for a long time, eyes still closed. Her arms were stretched out, lying on her body. Something was pinioning her wrists together. She was listening to check whether a guard was with her. She heard nothing. A tomb-like silence.

It was cold. Gently she twiddled her toes. She was still wearing her boots. Where the hell was she? She risked opening her eyes quickly. What she saw was not reassuring. The room was square, the floor paved with stone slabs, no windows. Over to her right a heavy wooden door, a barred window in its upper half, a cover over the window on the other side. She eased herself up, felt terribly stiff. How long had she been lying here?

Her left arm ached, the sleeves of the windcheater had been pulled up. In her forearm where it hurt a plaster had been attached. She *was* drugged. She raised her aching arms, saw the rope binding her wrists together, with about a foot of slack between the rope round her wrists. They had also roped her ankles round the boots. Her legs had swollen. Maybe they'd had trouble trying to take off the boots, had given up trying.

With a great effort, she sat up, twisted her head to see behind her. A stone wall with a pecular plaque, a large circle set into the wall. The plaque carried a symbol she didn't recognize. She made no attempt to read the brief Arabic wording.

She realized they had left her watch on her wrist. She checked the time. Eight o'clock. In the night or in the morning? She had no idea. She lay back in her original position, exhausted. She was hungry. A wave of her helplessness swept over her. No good. She bit her tongue carefully. The pain brought about sudden recovery. She began to think.

She realized for the first time her prison was illuminated by a light in the ceiling, a light protected by a glass box with thin wire bars. Presumably so it wouldn't be smashed by the prisoner. She heard the cover over the window in the door opening, closed her eyes, sagged back. Someone was coming to see her.

Another sound. The turning of a rusty key in a lock. As the door swung inwards she peered quickly through almost closed eyes. The man who entered was hampered, carrying a large plastic container, a glass protected with clingfilm or something similar.

She saw a tall slim man in his late twenties, his face and arms brown, hair cut short. She closed her eyes as he re-locked the door, leaving the key on the inside of the lock. The ceiling light went out. Most reassuring. She heard him approaching the wide bed, putting what he'd been carrying on the stone floor. He was close to her now. He slapped the side of her face, spoke in English.

'Wake up! It must have worn off now.'

Another slap to the other side of her face. She opened her eyes. He held a large flashlight beamed on her head. She groaned, said something deliberately unintelligible. Her next words were clear but hoarse.

'Put on the friggin' light . . . Dopey . . .'

To her surprise he went back to the door, pressed a switch. The ceiling light came on. Returning, he switched off the flashlight, laid it on the floor. She heard it rolling away under the bed. He rasped out his annoyance in a language she didn't understand. She made a great effort to divert his attention.

'You'll . . . go to prison . . . for this. For a long time.'

'You are the one in prison. Whether you ever leave it is dependent on yourself.'

She was staring at him now. He wore a T-shirt and a pair of blue slacks. The forearms exposed by the half-sleeved T-shirt exposed more brown skin. His young face was smooth-skinned, the eyes dark, soulless. He stared at her without expression. Egyptian was her best guess about his nationality. His arms looked strong, wiry. Difficult to tackle. She deliberately exaggerated the hoarseness of her voice.

'I'm thirsty . . . Water . . . I need . . . water.'

He nodded. Took the glass out of its protective covering, poured liquid which looked like water from the canister. He handed her the glass. She snarled at him.

'I've . . . been drugged . . . you drink first.'

'But of course.' He lifted the large container, drank from it. She still held on to the glass without drinking. 'You see,' he continued, 'just water. Nothing in it.'

Her throat was crying out with thirst. She forced herself to drink slowly. When the glass was empty, she shoved it at him. Her movements were difficult with her hands tied together.

'More . . . more,' she croaked.

He refilled the glass, seated on the edge of the bed. She took it from him. Again she compelled herself to drink slowly. She was feeling half-alive now. Her brain ticked over. How to handle him. Every time he spoke his face had the awful blank expression. No emotion whatsoever.

'Now you answer questions,' he told her. 'Information

183

is what I need. What does Tweed know? How far has he got with his ridiculous investigation?'

She stopped herself protesting at 'ridiculous'. Instead she sagged back. She moved slowly, as though completely worn out. She shook her head, slowly. She pretended to try and speak several times before the words came out.

'Can't think . . . feel drugged . . . Mind not working. Sleep . . . must sleep.'

'Then I come back later. Then you answer questions – if you want to leave your prison alive. Answer questions and you are released . . .'

She was staring straight at him as he spoke, at his eyes, so blank of feeling. She knew he was lying. If she had given him information – which she had no intention of doing – she would then be killed. Would disappear like the others.

'Later,' she said, 'I tell you . . . anything I can. Information.'

Her unexpected agreement to cooperate diverted him, as was her intention. He stood up, a lithe athletic young man in the prime of condition. He took the glass from her, picked up the canister, headed towards the door. He was so smooth, his voice and his physical movements. It was frightening. He unlocked the door, took out the key, went out, closed and locked it behind him.

She sagged further back, eyes closed – in case he took a second look through the window in the door. He didn't. She felt she had won a small victory. The flashlight which had rolled under the bed was still there. It might be so useful to her later. She wasn't sure how.

She sat up again. Leaning forward, ignoring her aching body, she held her hands together, used one to feel down inside her boot. The sheathed knife was still there. She eased it out, pushed sheath and knife under her waist band. The Beretta was still inside the other boot, but firing that could be heard by Lord knew what other vicious thugs were inside this place.

184

Where was she? She had asked herself a dozen times. Now her memory was clearing. The last person she had called on was Drew Franklin. It was shortly after she had left his house that she had been clubbed on the back of the head. Those concrete cubes could hide heaven knew what below the ground. But it could have been someone else.

She began exercising. Drawing her knees up into a pyramid, forcing herself to do that twenty times. The exercise was seeming easier. Now for her hands. She clenched and unclenched her fingers thirty times. She worked her arms, drawing them up, pressing them down another thirty times. She thought of using the knife to weaken the ropes tyiing her hands, rejected the idea. He hadn't tested the rope yet, but he might do when he returned.

She had worked out two options for dealing with him, according to the circumstances. One essential was to make him lose his temper, that cold-blooded control she'd seen in those eyes. What had worked wonders for her were the two glasses of water, removing the dehydration. Earlier, for a short time, she had experienced a sensation of overwhelming despair. Now she was feeling a sense of cold fury, an urge to kill if necessary. That was what they had planned for her.

Then an alarming thought occurred. Supposing he came back with someone else? She could never tackle two of them. Maybe she did need the Beretta. No, she couldn't risk the noise of two shots. She relaxed as she heard the rusty key turning in the door. A matter of life or death.

He came back alone, repeated the same drill, locking the door on the inside, leaving the key in the lock. No more water this time. As he came over to the bed she blinked, hoping to hide her drastic change of mood. He sat down again.

'I am Mohammed. So you know who you are talking

185

to. Best to be polite, friendly. What does Tweed know about us?'

He'd thrown the question at her without warning. This was going to be different. She looked puzzled. His right hand reached forward, stroked her face, then suddenly slapped her with such force her head jerked sideways. Her controlled cold fury was not disturbed.

'Who is us?' she asked quietly.

'Who is he investigating?'

'How would I know?'

'I'll cut your face to ribbons. No man will ever want to look at you again.'

The same smooth voice. No emotion. In his right hand he held a large curved knife. He raised it, the tip close to her face.

She broke down. Her expression betrayed hideous fear. She opened her mouth to speak but no words came. She swallowed. She opened her mouth again and this time she spoke in a shaky voice.

'I will tell you everything I know. Give you all information I have. But please . . . please . . . put that knife away. My brain is locked. Put the knife away.'

He lifted the back of his T-shirt, slipped the weapon back inside the hidden scabbard. She sat up straight. Mohammed leaned closer to her, his eyes staring into hers. Now was the moment. As she'd sat up her right hand had slipped underneath her thigh, had grasped the stiletto-like knife. She leaned closer, rammed the knife into him, between his ribs, with all her force.

For a moment he couldn't believe it. He glanced down at the handle protruding from his body, then he let out an agonized groan as blood spurted, poured down over his T-shirt. It was a large bed and she had been dumped on the side nearest the door, leaving half the bed unoccupied. She heaved her whole body upwards, lifting him, then swung sideways. They ended up with his body on the unoccupied area with her on top of him, her knee pressing the knife in deeper. Both her hands, close together, grasped him round the throat, pulled him towards her then shoved him backwards. One side of his head struck the plaque, the other side crashed into the stone wall. She heard an unpleasant sound – bone breaking against the stone. He lay motionless.

Still kneeling on him, she used her knife, jerked savagely from his body, to sever the rope round her wrists, then the rope pinioning her boots. She was free. She was about to jump off the bed when she stared. Where one side of his head had struck the plaque there was a large hole, maybe three feet wide. The plaque had disappeared. She realized it was hinged, opened inwards.

She wiped her knife clean on the coarse duvet she had lain on, climbed off, slithered under the bed, found the flashlight which had clicked off. She turned it on, stood on her side of the bed and peered down into a tunnel.

She was startled by what she saw in the light's beam. A few feet below her was a stationary flatbed trolley on wheels. It was perched on a narrow rail line. She aimed the light down the tunnel, which was oval, built out of stone, sloping downwards until it reached a point where the angle of the rails became steeper. She switched off the flashlight and closed her eyes to accustom them to the dark. In the distance she saw a blurred glow, circular in shape, the end closed off with a wire screen. Presumably for ventilation.

She had a brief thought that the escape route was via the heavy door Mohammed had entered by. The key was still on the inside of the lock. She rejected the thought. Attempting that route, she would probably run into a gang of armed thugs. She dropped through the three-foot wide opening on to the trolley. It remained stable as she landed, bending her knees, relieved to find them working normally.

Switching on the flashlight, she examined the contents of the flatbed. Again she was startled. Old bound books

187

covered with mould. *Tom Jones*, *Vanity Fair*, etc. Old technical manuals on how to fly a jumbo jet, each one torn in two. It was a rubbish trolley – their method of getting rid of what was no longer needed. So where was the dump? Presumably beyond the end of the tunnel.

She took the precaution of easing the Beretta out of her boot, pushed the weapon firmly down inside her denims, leaving the handle protruding. There was a large lever protruding from the side of the trolley. Taking hold of it, she moved it forward slowly. The trolley began sliding forward. Downhill. She pulled the lever back and the trolley again became stationary. She had only pushed it forward half-way.

She settled herself in a seated position after making a space by pushing aside the rubbish. Then she pushed the lever forward and she was moving slowly downhill. In the space she had cleared she saw a large red stain which she was sure someone had attempted to clean. Blood.

The cold was intense. As she approached the section where the line became a steeper gradient, she pulled the lever back, stopped the trolley moving. She aimed the flashlight at the bottom of the tunnel. The exit was barred by the screen of strong-looking wire. She would never get out past that. She felt she must escape quickly. As if to confirm her fears, she heard the distant sound of voices echoing down the tunnel. She looked back and her vision was hit by a blinding searchlight.

'Damn you all to hell,' she said under her breath.

She aimed the Beretta. One bullet did the trick. Above the eerie echo of her bullet she heard glass shattering. The searchlight went out. She swivelled sideways off the trolley into a narrow space between the rail and the wall of the tunnel. Her hand reached out, grasped the lever, shoved it forward as far as it would go. The trolley took off almost like a cannon-shell, racing down the much steeper gradient. It hit the wire screen, which swung open outwards. It must be hinged like the plaque.

She crawled down the tunnel as fast as she could. Sooner than she'd expected she reached the opening. Icy cold. A dense fog. As she crawled into the open air a shaft of sunlight penetrated the fog. She saw the trolley bumping its way down a shallower slope. Below it was a gleaming lime pit. She was just in time to see the trolley plunge into the large pit, its rear wheels upended, sinking out of sight.

Move! Where was she? Instinct told her to turn left. She stumbled over a branch. Picking it up, she used it to test the ground in front of her, walking parallel to where she thought the lime pit was located. The ground was rough but her boots helped her to keep her balance.

She could see nothing beyond the fog. Then a broad beam of sunlight penetrated the fog below her, illuminating a huge abandoned quarry. She heard a rattle at the top of the quarry. Someone up there? She paused, watched as a large boulder slowly toppled from the summit, falling down to join a heap of large rocks at the quarry's base. No sign of anyone. The quarry was unstable.

She plodded on, always using the branch to test the ground ahead. After a while she decided to move up the slope very cautiously. The fog was thinning, was soon a trailing mist. She saw an ancient one-storey building ahead. It seemed familiar. She climbed more quickly, paused, gasped with relief. It was the rear of Mrs Gobble's shed. She was still in Carpford.

In her haste to reach the front she nearly stumbled, recovered her balance. Taking out the padlock, she threw open both doors, praying. Parked inside was her car. She nearly wept.

25

The car started first time. She drove out and turned left, the quickest way to leave Carpford. The mist had cleared from the plateau. If anyone tried to stop her she would drive straight over them. Between Mrs Gobble's shop and Drew Franklin's concrete cubes she saw two figures walking along the road towards her. Tweed, shoulders sagging, behind him Beaurain, erect. She jammed on the brakes, jumped out.

Tweed was already rushing towards her, relief written all over his face. They met and he threw his arms round her. They stood there, hugging each other, her face buried against his chest. She was crying now as he stroked her hair.

'Tweed,' Beaurain told her, 'has almost been out of his mind with anxiety.'

She eased herself out of Tweed's grip and flung her arms round the Belgian. 'God! Am I glad to see you two.' Tweed produced a handkerchief. She released Beaurain and mopped her eyes, her face. She was shaking with relief.

'How are you?' Tweed asked gently. 'Are you all right?'

'I'm bloody hungry. *Starving!*'

'That calls for a full breakfast at the Peacock,' Beaurain decided. 'I'll drive. You sit in the back with Tweed.'

She had her arm round Tweed as Beaurain drove them in her car out of Carpford. At one point Newman, standing by the road, grinning, waved, one thumb up. She waved back and managed to smile. A few feet away Marler, smiling, gave her a little salute as they passed.

Beyond Marler she saw Harry and Pete, who also waved and grinned. She was startled but waved back. Then they were out of Carpford, descending the hill and past the obtruding rock where Mrs Warner had disappeared.

'How many of you were up here?' she asked.

'Everyone.' Tweed was calmer now. 'When I got back from dinner with Eva Brand and read your note I sent up a rocket. I called Buchanan and he's up there, calling on people. I was going to rip the place apart.'

'I'd better call Buchanan,' Beaurain suggested, 'and give him the good news . . .'

Driving with one hand, he hauled his mobile out of his pocket, called the Scotland Yard man, gave him the news. He finished the call and spoke over his shoulder.

'Buchanan is so relieved. Sends you his love, Paula. He said he'd need to question you, but I told him that could wait for later.'

'He's such a nice man,' she said. 'And I've so much to tell you . . . I've found out things . . . Don't have the faintest idea where I was held after they grabbed me . . . I'd just left Drew Franklin's place . . .'

'Later,' said Tweed. 'After you've had breakfast. Had any sleep?'

'Only when I was drugged.' She pulled up the sleeve of her windcheater to show the patch. Beaurain was watching in his rear-view mirror.

'After breakfast,' he said crisply, 'we'll take you to a top-flight consultant, a friend of mine who only recently retired. That needs checking.'

'I feel OK. Just so hungry.'

'Even so,' Beaurain insisted, 'when you've eaten we're taking you to see Mr Manderson. He lives near the Peacock. He can find out what they pumped into you. Don't argue.'

'I won't. I think a minute ago I nearly got hysterical. Sorry.'

'Concentrate on what you'd like to eat,' Tweed ordered.

'Forget about Mr Manderson,' she said firmly. 'I'm OK. When we get back to Park Crescent, instead of burbling on I'm going to type a report about everything.'

'That,' Tweed agreed, 'is a good idea. Then I can quietly read whoever you interviewed. But type your report only after you've had a good sleep.'

'Don't want sleep. While they are fresh in my mind I need to type the record. Sleep can come later. I had a long conversation with Peregrin Palfry, an encounter with that "priest", Margesson, then a pleasant talk with Billy Hogarth, despite the presence of his nasty brother, Martin. My last conversation was with Drew Franklin. It was soon after leaving his house that someone clubbed me on the head. I'll elaborate later.'

'So,' Beaurain said thoughtfully, 'the last person you had seen before the attack was Drew Franklin. Interesting.'

'No more,' Tweed ordered. 'Breakfast is the first item on the menu.'

'Ali speaking,' the occupant of a quiet public phone-box answered as the phone had rung. He made a point of never using the same call-box twice. He carried a list of the numbers and addresses of the phone-boxes, a list the caller also held.

'Abdullah here. We are running out of time on this business operation. Report!' the distorted voice demanded.

'The consignments are ready to be transferred to the transporters.'

The bombs are ready to be moved to their final destination.

'Are the teams ready to be linked up with the consignments?'

'They are in place. They are ready to be moved to handle the consignments when I give the order.'

193

'You have decided the best time for the consignments to be delivered?' Abdullah rasped.

'Five thirty in the evening is a perfect time. The conditions we require will be at a maximum.'

The British casualties will run into thousands.

'And zero hour is when?'

'Three days from now I expect. Height is a factor.'

Ali listened. Again the connection had been abruptly broken. He swore, left the phone-box. His car was parked just outside the sleepy village. He drove back to the farm.

Behind her desk at Park Crescent Paula was operating her word-processor at top speed, preparing her reports for Tweed. She was surprised at how even small details of conversation came back easily. Not knowing what he would regard as important, she included every small item. Her ample breakfast at the Peacock had powered her up again. She looked up suddenly.

'How long was I away?' she asked Tweed. 'I've no idea.'

'About twelve hours.'

'Seems like twelve days. I have ready folders with reports on my interviews with Peregrine Palfry and Margesson. Plus a brief description of my visit first to Mrs Gobble's.'

'Please let me have them. I can start reading. I get the impression of Palfry that he starts talking with caution, then his tongue runs away with him. Right?'

'My impression too,' she agreed as she placed the folders on his desk.

Monica was enjoying one of her rare five-minute 'breaks' reading the newspaper. She grunted, folded a page to a small item, took it over to Tweed.

'It's amazing the things people walk off with. Someone has stolen five of those huge milk wagons which distribute to various dairies. Vanished into thin air. What would anyone want with milk wagons?'

194

'Let me see that,' Tweed said, his voice sharp. He read the item. 'Taken from three different depots in the Midlands. I hope the original drivers are still alive.'

'What makes you say that?' Monica wondered.

'*Large transports.*' Paula glanced up. Tweed was staring into the distance. He continued. 'What could they be carrying – apart from the milk? Or, maybe, they were carrying something lowered into the milk cargoes. They were driving south in the dark when they vanished and radio communication with the depots ceased . . .'

'Can't be important,' Monica commented. 'I just thought it was curious.'

'So curious I want you to get Buchanan on the line so I can draw his attention to this mysterious development. First three people go missing, then five milk wagons. A pattern is developing . . .'

An hour later Paula had finished her reports. Tweed had read them carefully. He sat back in his chair, arms folded behind his head.

'Paula, I know you went through a shocking ordeal. If it's any consolation, the information in these reports is priceless. I don't know yet what the attack plan is but as in a dream I'm beginning to see the outlines of what may be coming. What worries me is I sense we haven't much time left. What is the target? How are they planning to attack London? Who is the mastermind? Those are the questions I need to have answers to. Before it is too late.'

'Is there someone we should question again?'

'Yes, there is.' Tweed had jumped to his feet as Newman walked in, rushed towards Paula, wrapped his arm round her.

'You do know,' he said, 'you are the most valuable member of the team. Up at Carpford I could only wave when the car passed me.' He looked round as Tweed put on his raincoat. 'And where might you be going to? Not on your own.'

195

'To question the one individual who may be able to tell us more than he has done. A certain Mr Pecksniff.'

'Then I'm coming with you. I can drive.'

'I'm coming too,' said Paula. 'I've finished your reports.'

'No,' said Tweed, pausing before opening the door. 'Sleep is what you need . . .'

'Yes!' Paula shouted at him, slipping on her windcheater. 'I will not be left out and I'm feeling alert.'

'I suppose,' Monica interjected, 'Roy Buchanan didn't think much of the missing milk wagons story.'

'On the contrary,' Tweed assured her, 'he is phoning the Chief Constable up there, telling him to organize a dragnet to find those wagons. We must visit Mr Pecksniff *now*.'

During the long drive through heavy traffic Paula asked how Tweed had brought everyone to Carpford in the middle of the night. He smiled grimly, sitting next to her while Newman drove their car.

'When I got back from dinner with Eva Brand and saw your note I organized a general alarm. Called Bob, Marler, Pete and Harry on their mobiles. Ordered them to head at once for Carpford. Also called Buchanan who said he'd drive to the Downs immediately. When I arrived I woke up everyone, which wasn't popular but I was in a grim mood so they soon changed their tune. In this way I traced your movements, confirmed by your reports. The trouble was I didn't leave the dinner with Eva until midnight, so everything was pushed into the middle of the night.'

'How did you get on with Eva?' she wondered.

'Very pleasurably. She was out to charm me. Wore a low-cut dress, drank heavily and tried to persuade me to do the same. Out to extract information from me. It was a duel of wits, and she's a very smart lady.'

'Learn anything?'

'Her mother was killed in a car crash on a motorway five years ago. No other relatives. Refused to talk about a father. I'm intrigued about that. Glided over the missing two years

196

in her life Monica couldn't crack. Doesn't believe Special Branch has the talent to solve the mystery of the people who've vanished. Said she couldn't understand what had happened to Mrs Warner. Described her as a resourceful woman. They'd met at parties, got on well together. Thinks Peregrine Palfry is the Minister's lapdog, an opinion I'm not sure I share. Believes the cleverest man living in Carpford is Drew Franklin.'

'So she didn't slip up?'

'There's steel in that lady. Takes brains to be a top code-breaker.'

'I'm going to have to talk to her again.'

Tweed chuckled, smiled at her. 'You think you can crack the ice maiden when I failed?'

'It's not that. Sometimes women will confide in another woman when they're leery of men.'

No one said anything more until Newman announced they were nearly there. He suggested he parked the car in a side street and walked the rest of the way.

'Incidentally,' he went on, 'last night Harry watched Pecksniff's office until he was contacted by Tweed at close to 1 a.m. The lights were still on, so presumably Pecksniff was working late. No one called on him . . .'

He parked the car and they walked along a narrow street with half the old buildings unoccupied. No one about. No sign of life behind the frosted glass windows of Pecksniff's shabby office. Newman was about to press the bell when he paused. The door was almost closed but not quite. He looked at Tweed who gestured for him to open the door fully. Newman called out but no one answered. Again he glanced at Tweed.

Tweed peered through the stained-glass window in the upper half of the door. No good – it was too filthy to see anything inside.

'Go in,' he ordered.

Newman, Smith & Wesson in his hand, entered, followed

by Tweed and Paula, who was gripping the Beretta. While she had been imprisoned in Carpford they had taken her shoulder-bag, which contained her Browning.

The outer office was empty. There was a sinister silence. Newman pushed open the inner door, walked a few paces inside, stopped. Paula peered over his shoulder. This room, Pecksniff's inner sanctum, was also empty. But the throne-like chair he'd occupied behind his Regency desk was lying on the floor, its back broken. The two hard chairs lay on the floor intact.

Paula put on latex gloves, trod cautiously round the other side of the desk. Near the broken-backed throne chair was a brownish pool on the carpet, a large pool. Blood. The filing cabinet against the wall had been ransacked. It had been levered open with some kind of tool. There were files left in an open drawer. More files were scattered on the floor.

'Pecksniff has disappeared now,' Tweed observed sombrely.

Paula was rifling through the files remaining inside the open drawer. She came to 'M' and then moved to 'P.' 'N' was missing. The New Age Development file, she guessed. She checked the files scattered on the floor. Not there.

'They've taken the New Age file,' she told Tweed.

'Bob,' Tweed said decisively, 'call Buchanan. Ask him to get over here. 'I fear this is the fourth murder.'

Buchanan arrived with his poker-faced assistant, Sergeant Warden, nicknamed by Paula the Wooden Indian. Warden stared round the inner office, then gazed at the latex gloves Paula was still wearing. He raised his thick eyebrows. She gazed back at him. His manner had become like a regimental sergeant major's.

'You haven't been touching anything?' he barked. 'This may turn out to be the scene of a crime.'

'I'm sure it is,' she told him. 'I have been searching for a file on the New Age Development company. It's gone.

So whoever took away what was left of Mr Pecksniff was after that file.'

'What was left of Mr Pecksniff?' Warden's tone was outraged. 'How can you make such an assumption?'

'Furniture smashed to pieces. Files ransacked.' She paused. 'Then there's the blood on the floor.'

'Blood . . .'

'Sergeant Warden,' broke in Buchanan, a bite in his voice. 'Would you be so good as to go now and examine the outer office. You might close the door on your way out.'

Buchanan waited until Warden had gone. Then he waved a hand round the wreckage. Tweed showed him the stained area discovered by Paula. The chief superintendent bent down, used a finger to touch part of the large discoloured patch. He straightened up.

'What do you think this is all about?' he asked Tweed.

'I'm worried that whoever is directing this operation is closing up loopholes. That suggests to me we are dangerously approaching the climax. As for Pecksniff, this is the fourth disappearance – probably the fourth murder.'

26

'You have to go straight over to Downing Street to see the PM,' Howard, the Director, fired at Tweed the moment he walked into his office past Monica.

'There's been a development?' Tweed asked.

'I'll say there has!'

Howard was a tall well-built man in his fifties. He wore an expensively tailored blue suit from Savile Row, a white shirt from a Jermyn Street shirt-maker, a blue Hermès tie and a pair of hand-made shoes. As usual, he sat in one of the armchairs, one leg draped over an arm. He had a large head with recently trimmed brown hair, turning white at the temples, a strong nose under blue eyes and, below an amiable mouth, a jaw suggesting energy but without aggression.

His main function was to keep in touch with Whitehall mandarins he secretly regarded as fools. His bland manner went down well with them and, behind his back, Paula had nicknamed him Mr Bland.

'Tell me,' Tweed said as Paula slipped past him, smiling at Monica before she sat at her desk.

Newman came in last, nodded to Howard and perched on the edge of Paula's desk. Howard's upper crust voice got on his nerves.

'First . . .' Howard waved a manicured hand '. . . I want to tell you, Tweed, I greatly appreciate the way you have kept me fully informed of what has been going on.

Frightening. Better get over to the holy of holies now. Be very blunt with the PM.'

'There's been another disappearance, probably the fourth murder,' Newman said casually when Tweed had left.

'*What!*' Howard jerked upright, his pink face flushing.

Newman explained in as few words as possible their visit to Pecksniff's office. Howard stood up, flicked a piece of cotton off his sleeve.

'Can't get a decent tailor these days. My God, Newman, what is happening?'

'Tweed thinks a major al-Qa'eda attack on London is pretty imminent.'

'Well, it's all down to Tweed. Maybe in the nick of time.'

'What does that mean?' Paula asked.

'Can't tell you, my dear, until Tweed comes back. All hush-hush. Won't be for long. I'd better get back to my office. In case something else blows up . . .'

'Paula,' Monica said, when Howard had gone, 'while you were in the loo, Tweed said your reports had put him on the right track.'

'My report of my interview with who? I visited Mrs Gobble's shop, had a long talk with Peregrine Palfry, a confrontation with Margesson, a friendly chat with Billy Hogarth, a few words with his peculiar brother, Martin, then the last one with Drew Franklin. Which one?'

'He didn't say.' She looked at Paula. 'You really should go home and get some sleep.'

'Think I will. I'm dropping.' She looked at Newman. 'Bob, could you drive me there, then stay in the living-room until I wake up? I'd feel safer.'

'We're on our way now . . .'

Marler, Butler and Nield were in the office when Tweed came back. He was carrying a large envelope and his expression was abstracted. He gave Monica his raincoat, sat down and extracted a typed sheet headed *Downing Street*, handed it to Marler.

'You might as well be the first to know.'

Marler read it without showing any reaction. He handed the document back to Tweed. Taking out a cigarette he then spoke.

'Thank God!'

'What is it?' several voices wanted to know.

'Tweed,' Marler said, in a grim voice, 'has been appointed as commander of all the security services. Including the Ministry of Security, Special Branch, the police and anyone else he wants to rope in.'

'Lordy!' exclaimed Monica. 'It is all down to Tweed.'

'Strictly within these walls,' Tweed explained calmly, 'the PM is scared stiff. He has appointed me Supremo – his word, not mine. I may need the SAS – its commander has been sent a copy of that document. As have the chiefs of all other services. Bob, you know the number. Can you get a senior officer on the line for me?'

'I can get Sarge, the man who ran the unit which trained me when I wrote my article on them. Through him I should get the man you want. I'll try now.'

'The SAS!' Monica said excitedly. 'The balloon is really going up.'

The team was still up to full strength in Tweed's office when the phone rang. Monica seemed to have trouble with the caller. Persistently she asked for the caller's identity was obviously getting nowhere.

'What is it?' Tweed called out.

'Someone on the phone with a funny voice, Cockney, as far as I can gather. Important information they can only give you. Could be a hoax.'

'I'll talk to them . . . Tweed here. How can I help?'

'Got information. Can't 'ang round 'ere much longer.'

'Then tell me.'

203

'Got the name of the boss of Alqueerda. Know what I'm on abaht?'

'Yes.'

'It's Abdullah. Runs that gang of killers.'

'Where is he based?'

'No idea. You've met with it. Got to scarper . . .'

'Wait a minute.'

The line had gone dead. Tweed told everyone what he had been told. So far as he'd been able to tell the caller was talking through a handkerchief to disguise its identity. Couldn't tell whether it was a man or a woman.

'Hoax call,' Newman said dismissively. 'Abdullah is a common Arab name!'

'I wonder,' Tweed said thoughtfully. 'The caller said I'd met with it. I haven't met any Cockneys recently. I'm inclined to believe the caller knew what it was talking about. Also it's odd I should receive that call soon after the mandates giving me full powers will have reached everyone concerned. The PM was sending copies out by couriers the moment I left to come back here.'

'Can't see the significance,' Marler commented.

He had just made his remark when the door opened and Paula walked in, followed by Newman, who spread his hands in a gesture of frustration.

'Don't blame me. She's had less than five hours' sleep but she insisted on taking a quick shower and came straight back here.'

'I feel fine,' Paula said emphatically. 'Ready for anything. Any progress while I was in the land of nod?'

She had perched herself on the edge of her desk instead of sitting in her chair. Dressed in a black trouser suit, she was swinging her legs under the wide kneehole, the picture of energy.

Tweed stood up, walked over, handed her the document he had brought back from the PM. She read it slowly, twice. She looked serious as she handed it back.

'Maybe in the nick of time,' was her reaction.

'We don't know that, do we?'

There was a bite in Tweed's comment. Paula had noticed in the past there were rare occasions when he spoke in that tone. Always when he was concealing great anxiety.

'We have no vital data,' Tweed continued. 'As I keep reminding all of you, we need three things. Target, identity of the mastermind, timing of the attack. We have none of these. So I want all three within twenty-four hours.'

There was a hush in the room. The enormity of their task had dawned on them. Tweed studied each of them. He had jerked them out of any complacency. They were in a state of shock.

He dialled the private number of the Ministry of Security. Of course it would be Palfry who answered, an irritable Palfry.

'Tweed here. I need to know the present whereabouts of the Minister.'

'That's classified information . . .'

'Haven't you received a copy of the PM's directive?'

'Yes. So has the Minister . . .'

'So where is he? Tell me now if you want to keep your job.'

'As far as I know he's at home in his residence in Belgravia.'

'Dammit! Do you *know* he's there?'

'Yes . . .'

'Thank you.'

Tweed put down the phone, got up to put on his raincoat. He spoke as he put it on.

'I must first see Warner, assure myself of his co-operation . . .'

The phone rang. Monica listened, then waved at Tweed.

'Someone to see you downstairs . . .'

'I'm not in. Get rid of them.'

'It's Eva Brand.'

205

'Oh.' Tweed paused. 'Ask her to wait a minute.' His gaze scanned the room. 'This is no time for anyone to be sitting around. Marler, get cracking and interrogate Martin Hogarth. This is not a situation calling for finesse.'

'Got you,' repled Marler. 'I'll phone him first to make sure he's up at Carpford. Won't say anything when he answers.'

'Harry,' Tweed snapped, 'you get down into Soho to that place where Bob warned that call girl a brute was on the way up to her apartment. Belles, wasn't it? Chat to people there about rumours of an attack on London. See if you can pick up anything. Then tackle the girls in the street. They often know things.'

'I'm on my way,' said Harry and left.

'Pete,' Tweed went on, speaking fast, 'you go up to Carpford separately from Marler. Tackle that Margesson. Not gently. Bob will draw a map showing you where he hangs out.'

'Martin's in residence,' Marler reported. 'Give me a sheet of paper, Paula, then I can show Pete Margesson's pad.'

Tweed threw off his raincoat and Monica caught it in mid-air. He went back to his desk and sat thinking for a minute. By the time he asked for Eva to be shown up everyone had gone except Newman.

'Bob,' Tweed said suddenly, 'I want you to prowl Covent Garden, near that Monk's Alley where poor Eddie was found mutilated.'

'I'll do that later.' Newman held up his hand as Tweed was going to rap back. 'No argument. I'm driving you over to Warner's penthouse. There have been two attempts to kill you already.'

'If you must. How long did it take us to drive back last time from Warner's place?'

'At least half an hour. Traffic.'

'So, if Eva has come from there, she'd be at the penthouse half an hour ago.'

'No, she wouldn't,' Monica objected. 'I heard a motor-cycle pull up before I heard she was downstairs. I peered out of the window and saw her parking it by the kerb outside. She'd get here like the wind.'

'Motor-cycle,' Tweed repeated slowly. 'Those couriers which arrive after dark in Carpford. I've just remembered reading a newspaper report about Afghanistan. The Northern Alliance lot were closing in on Kandahar. Omar, the key Afghan who worked closely with Osama bin Laden, escaped from Kandahar just in time. On a motor-cycle. Al-Qa'eda seems to like those machines.' He gazed into the distance, lost in his thoughts, then sat up. 'Ask Eva to come up now.'

Paula was still at her desk when Eva Brand walked in. She had kept quiet, determined to accompany Tweed on his visit to the Minister's home.

Eva Brand was dressed in a black trouser suit, the bottoms tucked inside her motor-cycle boots. Motoring gloves tucked under her arms. At Tweed's request she sat down in an armchair facing him. He greeted her with an amiable smile, the first time he'd smiled since returning from the PM.

'It's good to see you again. Looking as delectable as ever. You bring good news?'

'Flattery will get you somewhere, as the girl said to the predator. And I bring bad news. Which is why I hared over here.'

'Something has happened?'

'In a big way. Victor has blown his top after receiving the new mandate ordering him to work under you. I've never known him so livid. Striding about his office like a maniac. Lifting up vases to alter their position, then hammering them down on table tops. He actually broke one in his fury. He's going to block you off. He's going to phone the PM and ask him to cancel the mandate. Says the idea of working under you will make him look such a fool in the Cabinet.'

'Really?'

'Yes, really. And he's appointed Tolliver as Acting Chief of Special Branch in Buller's absence. Disappearance.'

'Tolliver? Not brilliant but he does what he's told, which can be a help. I appreciate your coming to tell me.'

'I hope I've got his reaction across to you strongly enough. He's acting like Captain Bligh when he realized he had a mutiny on the *Bounty*.'

'I think I get the picture. Again, I appreciate your taking the trouble to dash over here.'

'That's all right.' Eva stood up, very tall and erect. She glanced at her watch. 'And I'd better dash back again before he realizes I've gone out.' She looked over her shoulder at Paula. 'We must have dinner, lunch, tea or something together.'

'I'll call you soon as I can,' Paula replied with a smile.

Then, like a whirlwind, Eva was gone. Paula looked across at Tweed.

'Don't forget I'm coming with you.'

'I was going to give you a job.'

He glared ferociously at her. She glared back. Newman suppressed a grin. When these two battled these days it was worth sitting back to enjoy the duel. Paula got up, put on her windcheater. There was a sound from the street of a motor-cycle starting up. Monica peered out. Eva, at speed, was swinging her machine over at a dangerous angle, saw the main road was clear, disappeared.

'Bob, we can go now,' Tweed said, putting on his rain-coat.

He walked out, followed by Newman with Paula at his heels. During the drive Tweed sat in the back with Paula by his side. They said not one word to each other. Inwardly Newman was choking with laughter.

★   ★   ★

208

Mrs Carson, the housekeeper, opened the door, her expression disagreeable and unwelcoming. She folded her arms. In the background Paula saw Eva approaching. She had changed her boots for pumps.

'What is it?' Mrs Carson demanded.

'We have come to see the Minister.'

'You have an appointment?'

'I'll show them up,' said Eva, appearing beside Mrs Carson. 'You'd better get back to the kitchen – a pot is about to boil over.'

Mrs Carson stomped off, a door banged. Tweed walked in with Paula. Newman had parked the car out of sight round a corner and stayed with it. Eva led the way to the study, via the elevator, knocked on the door.

'Who the hell is it?' Warner's voice barked.

'Someone to see you,' Eva replied as she opened the door and ushered Tweed and Paula inside. Warner was seated on a high-backed chair on an elevated platform with two chairs in front and below the desk. He swivelled round in the chair, saw who had entered, hastily placed a batch of papers in a red box and slammed the lid closed. One document remained in front of him, the directive from the PM.

'I'm surprised you have the nerve to show your face here,' he sneered, adjusting his pince-nez.

Tweed walked forward, occupied one of the chairs, gestured for Paula to sit in the one beside him. The fact that Warner was so lean and tall and perched above them gave him a dominant position.

'I'm sure you won't mind if my personal assistant is with me,' Tweed suggested quietly.

'Oh, no,' Warner sneered again. 'I appreciate you take your consort with you everywhere.'

Inside her gloves Paula's fingers clenched. She could have killed him. Her expression remained neutral. Eva was still standing by the open door. Warner glanced at her.

'Don't just stand there, Eva. You might as well come

in and join the party. There was a time when women, if allowed into the system, occupied only junior positions. In those days they were clerks and pen-pushers. The system seemed to work more smoothly then.'

Eva had picked up a chair. She placed it next to Paula's, sat down, clasped her hands in her lap.

'A visitor from Whitehall has just informed me there is an air of panic abroad,' Tweed remarked.

Eva shifted slightly and nudged Paula. She was expressing appreciation that Tweed was covering for her. Warner sat up straight, glaring viciously at Tweed as he took hold of the directive from Downing Street, waved it in front of Tweed.

'You know what this is,' he rasped. 'I see copies have been sent to all heads of security services. Even to the MoD.' His voice rose, was savagely harsh. 'You think I'm going to put up with this absurd idea? It means I have to take my orders from you! Well, I'm not going to. It is the most outrageous document I have ever seen since entering government. Christ! I'm a senior member of the Cabinet. Also I'm in charge of security – or I was!' he shouted. 'I am going to phone the PM.'

'That is your privilege, Minister,' Tweed replied equably.

Paula frowned. She was taken aback. She had expected Tweed to thunder back. Especially after his combative mood at Park Crescent.

'I'm glad you appreciate that,' Warner commented, his voice several decibels lower.'

'Minister,' Tweed leaned forward, his manner calm, 'I was hoping – still believe you will agree – that we can cooperate in this desperate situation. I look forward to a state of collaboration between us. We do have a common enemy. With our combined forces we will defeat that enemy.'

Warner was taken aback. He removed his pince-nez, exposing his hawk-like nose. He took out a cloth, polished the pince-nez, perched them back on the bridge of his nose.

'There is a lot in what you have just said,' he agreed, his voice now normal, verging on the polite.

Paula suddenly caught on. Tweed was being very clever. Realizing Warner was worried about his position in the Cabinet, he had just been provided with the perfect way to present the development to his colleagues.

Tweed has explained to me the meaning of the document. He says the meaning of the document is to encourage collaboration between all the security services.

'May I make a suggestion about one way forward?' Tweed asked.

'Certainly, my dear chap. I am all ears.'

'My Whitehall visitor had heard a rumour that Tolliver is now head of Special Branch.'

'That is so. With Buller disappearing I had to appoint someone to run that vital service. Tolliver is very able.'

'For some time,' Tweed continued, 'Special Branch officers have worn a kind of uniform – camel-hair coats. So much so that villains recognize them. I suggest a large number of Special Branch officers flood main areas of Central London. Buckingham Palace, St Paul's, Canary Wharf, along the Thames embankment.'

'What a brilliant idea!' Warner smiled, as always an insincere smirk. 'I'll get that organized the moment you leave.'

'Then there are communications,' Tweed went on. 'Whoever is planning this attack has to communicate. It's possible he does so with radio. You have a section which monitors certain radio transmissions. They could be asked to listen for unusually heavy traffic. You have code-breakers. One is sitting next to Miss Grey.'

'You are full of good ideas, even if we are already listening. But I will direct that section to listen for any unusual heavy traffic. Tweed, I think it's time for us to seal our pact with sherry.'

Tweed stood up. 'Thank you for the suggestion. Another time, perhaps. I have to get back to Park Crescent.'

'Of course. Eva will show you out. I must deal with your suggestions urgently . . .'

They had left the study. The door was closed when Eva moved close to Tweed. She squeezed his arm as she whispered.

'I can see even more now why you hold the job you do. I'd never have dreamt you could turn him round the way you did.'

'The first rule,' Tweed told her, 'is self-control. You can then adapt your tactics to whatever situation confronts you.'

'I'm still stunned . . .'

They had left the building and were walking to where Newman had parked his car when Paula squeezed Tweed's arm.

'I'm wondering how Marler will get on at Carpford.'

27

Martin Hogarth's bungalow was a luxurious establishment. The walls were partly made of stone and above this expensive pine planks faced the wall. The front door, massive, was made of heavy oak and had three Banham locks. Pinewood shutters were closed over slit-like windows. In the dark lights from inside filtered through the shutters. Marler hammered on the iron door knocker, continued hammering.

The sound of locks being turned. A blinding glare light over the door was switched on. The door opened and a man in his late thirties was framed in the light, a man holding a gun. A 7.63mm Mauser with a long barrel, magazine capable of holding ten rounds.

'Marler, SIS.'

He was holding up his identity folder open. It could be clearly seen in the glare light. The slim man wore a polo-necked sweater, green slacks. No shoes, his feet were clad in white socks.

'Could you please stop pointing that thing at me?' drawled Marler. 'Guns are dangerous.'

'Didn't you know?' the man sneered. 'We live in a dangerous world. You come making one helluva row knocking on my door after dark. I have no idea what may be waiting for me when I open the door.'

'You know now,' Marler said, tucking away his folder. 'So put the damned gun away. We need to talk.'

'By that,' the man continued sneering, 'you mean you need to talk. Doesn't mean I need any conversation.'

As he spoke he placed the Mauser on a table next to the door. He nodded, indicating Marler could come in – nodded as he might to a tradesman. His thick brown hair was carefully coiffeured and below a sharp nose he sported a trim moustache. Marler had already weighed him up as a con-man, consumed with his own vanity. He walked into an expensively furnished drawing-room. Shaded wall-lights. The walls were painted a pale green. There were framed pictures of girls wearing nothing except inviting smiles. It all fitted in with the personality of the owner.

There was another performance as all three locks on the door were closed. Marler took the opportunity to pick up the Mauser by the barrel, to retract the magazine, putting it in his pocket.

'Just in case we have a disagreement,' he explained, placing the weapon back on the table. 'You are Martin Hogarth?'

'You knew that before you started trying to kick the door down.'

'It could have been a neighbour.'

'Let's get one thing clear from the start. I've already had a visit from your lot. When I was with my brother, Billy, that tart you employ wormed her way in.'

Marler hit Martin. A hard swift blow on the meagre chin. Martin went over backwards, ended up on the deep pile carpet, one hand nursing the chin. His shifty eyes were full of venom as he slowly clambered to his feet.

'I'm reporting this to the Minister, Victor Warner,' he hissed. 'An unprovoked assault.'

'Do that. Waste of time. Don't come under his juris-diction.' Marler's voice was calm, indifferent. 'But clean out that mouth of yours. Maybe a good job I emptied the Mauser? You look put out. While we're on the subject,

214

Miss Grey is a very professional woman, also a very *decent* one. Now, we'll talk.'

Marler perched himself on a silk-covered upright chair. As he did so Martin opened a cupboard, brought out a bottle of fine Scotch, poured himself a stiff one, swallowed it. He returned it to the cupboard without offering his guest a drink.

'You have motor-cycle couriers calling on you at dead of night,' Marler began. 'They bring large envelopes.'

'Nothing to do with me,' Martin snapped as he sprawled in an arm chair, legs splayed out on the carpet. 'They park their damned machines against my bungalow wall at the side. A ruddy nuisance.'

'So why not go out and tell them to park their machines in Carp Lake?'

'I read the newspapers. Britain is as dangerous a place today as Afghanistan. They carry knives, not fussy about using them.'

'You've been to Afghanistan then?'

The shifty eyes flickered. Wandered about the room. Martin reached for his glass, realized it was empty.

'Good Lord no,' Martin replied after a few moments. 'Africa and Asia are full of savages. Trouble is we're letting the blighters in here. They should beat them up when they crawl in here and send them straight back . . .'

'How did you come to buy this bungalow?'

'What? Oh, saw an ad in *The Times*. Rented it, wasn't for purchase. Got it for five years. Rent's extortionate . . .'

'You were vetted by Pecksniff then?'

'Vetted! Don't like that word at all. I did pay one visit to the Dickensian old clot's office in the sewers . . .'

'Your Dickensian old clot has disappeared, probably murdered. Why?'

'Hold on, Sweetie.' Martin got up, fetched the Scotch, poured himself another stiff one. 'Cheers!' he said, raising the glass.

Marler ignored the insult as Martin emptied the glass. He sat very still while Martin sprawled again in his armchair, clutching his glass. The silence continued and Martin felt compelled to speak.

'Was there anything else?'

'Yes, I'm wondering why you chose this quiet isolated spot to live in. Not that it's quiet any more – not with four murders to its credit.'

The shifty eyes again began scanning the room. Almost as though its occupant was checking up to make sure nothing was missing since his visitor's arrival. Martin was clutching his glass tightly.

'Four murders?' he enquired eventually. 'You've lost me.'

'Let me help you.' Marler began counting on his fingers. 'We have Mrs Warner, gone missing. Mrs Gobble, ditto. Jasper Buller, chief of Special Branch, ditto. Now Pecksniff, ditto. Chief Superintendent Buchanan of the Yard, a most experienced officer, now thinks all four were murdered. Why? They knew too much. Maybe about the New Age Development organization?'

Marler's barrage of interrogation was getting to Martin. He shifted restlessly in his chair. Withdrawing his sprawled legs, he sat up straight.

'I never knew any of these people.'

'You knew Pecksniff. You've just told me you met him. And maybe,' Marler went on, remembering what Paula had told him, 'you were worried about Mrs Gobble's high-powered telescope observing what you did, who came here.'

'Telescope? Sweetie, you've lost me again.'

'I think,' Marler decided, standing up, 'I have obtained the information I came for. I'll leave now if you'll kindly go through unlocking all those Banhams again.'

'Information?'

Marler made no reply as Martin went to the door,

216

unlocked it. Opening it, he glared at Marler. 'Information? What information?'

'People never seem to know when they've talked too much.' Marler turned on the doorstep outside and smiled. 'I don't think we'll be calling on you again. Unless, of course, we come with an arrest warrant.'

His last view of Martin was of all the colour draining from his face. Soon as he's barred and bolted the place he'll run for the whisky bottle, he said to himself. A really well-worthwhile interrogation.

The entire team – except for Marler – was assembled in Tweed's office. There was a tense atmosphere as Beaurain walked in. Outside it was a clear, cold night. Beaurain rubbed his finger across his moustache as he sat down, then spoke, his manner grim.

'I think we have very little time left . . .'

'My sentiments also,' agreed Tweed.

'So,' Beaurain continued, 'I am now convinced the brain base of al-Qa'eda is located in Carpford. You disagree, Tweed?'

'No. I have come to that conclusion. Some very suspect people in that strange village.'

'So we must establish our own base there for surveillance of the inhabitants. I have just returned from there – bringing with me Billy Hogarth. I have persuaded him to loan me his bungalow. I've settled him in a small hotel in Bloomsbury I am going to drive up to his bungalow tonight where I shall settle myself in secretly and watch.'

'I agree,' said Tweed. 'We must go over on to the offensive now. The key is in Carpford . . .'

'I'll come with you,' called out Paula. It needs at least two people to mount the death watch.'

'Death watch?' queried Harry.

'Yes. Four people have now disappeared and I don't think any of them are alive.'

217

The door opened and Marler, just returned from Carpford, walked in. His expression was bleak. He told them of his experience with Martin Hogarth. His tone was more clipped than usual as he concluded.

'Something not right about Martin Hogarth. In fact, something very wrong about him.'

He listened while Tweed explained Beaurain's decision. He had only one question.

'Can we trust Billy Hogarth?'

'Yes, we can,' Paula ssured him. 'I had a long talk with him and he's not involved, I'm certain. As Marler said, the rotten apple in the barrel could be his brother, Martin.'

'I think there is more than one rotten apple,' Beaurain rasped.

'We must still keep an eye on Billy,' Tweed decided. 'Make sure he stays in the hotel. Pete, Paula will describe Billy to you. Your mission is to watch the hotel, make sure he stays there.'

'He could still use the phone to call someone,' Newman warned.

'No, he couldn't,' Beaurain to him. 'When I left the hotel I cut the main phone wire outside.'

Paula was describing Billy's appearance to Pete while Beaurain stood up. He began striding up and down the office.

'Think better when I'm moving.'

Picking up a blank pad off Paula's desk, he wrote down the address of the hotel. He added brief instructions how to find it. As Paula ended her description he handed the sheet to Pete.

'Marler,' Tweed ordered, 'I want you to contact every informant you can tonight to spread a rumour. Within days the Army is moving into London. Whoever the mastermind may be, I want to rattle his cage.'

Pete had already left the office. He was followed by Marler. Newman frowned. The atmosphere in the office

218

was growing more electric by the minute. This was what they all wanted. *Action.*

'During the night will Marler be able to find his informants?' Newman wondered.

'Best time,' Harry assured him, grinning. 'He has a string of callgirls who make a powerful grapevine. They operate at night, if you didn't know.'

Paula was opening her case she had hauled from a cupboard, its contents ready for instant departure. Monica had dashed out of the office earlier. She returned later with a large canvas satchel, handed it to Beaurain.

'You'll find a flask of coffee to keep you both going. Plus a batch of sandwiches. Hope you like ham or cheese. Too bad if you don't. Also plenty of fruit.'

'When I was in Billy's place,' Paula piped up, 'I peeped into his kitchen through the open door. He has a cafetière, cans of coffee, cans of beans, bread, butter – all spread out on a shelf under cupboards. We won't starve.'

Harry had also left the office earlier. He came back holding two large violin cases. He opened one, stood aside so Beaurain could see the contents. Beaurain smiled again. He had just called Monica 'the most wonderful woman in the world', had hugged her, the satchel slung over his shoulder.

'Might come in useful,' Harry remarked. 'The other case has the same. You never know.'

Beaurain stared at the Uzi sub-machine gun resting in the violin case. Stacked alongside it were spare magazines. He lifted the weapon out, made certain adjustments, aimed it at the ceiling, pulled the trigger.

'Feels good.' He slapped Harry on the back. 'Thanks.'

'Time to get moving,' Paula said impatiently. 'We've got what we need – enough for a small war. I'll carry the second violin case. You've got your own case you brought with you, your violin which you play so well, I'm sure, and your satchel. So, what are we waiting for?'

219

'Keep me in touch,' Tweed called out as they rushed from his office.

'That leaves me,' Harry said, disgruntled.

'No, it doesn't,' Tweed rapped back. 'Your informants are different from Marler's. Prowl London, spread the rumour Marler is circulating.'

'See you. Some time . . .'

Harry was gone. Newman stood up, went to the clothes cupboard, took out a long black coat. He put it on and it almost reached his ankles. He asked Monica to fetch him another 'violin' case. He peered out of the window.

'Paula and Jules have left in his car. I'll wait a few minutes before I drive after them up to Carpford. I'm going to be the mysterious figure lurking at the edge of Black Wood. Back-up for Paula and Jules. Even if you object I'm still going.'

'Mutiny!' Tweed threw up his hands. 'First Paula, now you. Get up there as fast as you can. Communicate with me on your mobile. When you can.'

Monica appeared. She handed Newman the Uzi inside the case. She pursed her lips.

'Don't go and shoot yourself.'

'What?'

Then he saw the smile on her face. He kissed her on the cheek. She then handed him a smaller satchel than the one provided for Beaurain and Paula.

'Coffee in a flask. Plus a bottle of mineral water. Still. The way you like it. You get thirsty, I know.'

'Bless you. I'm on my way . . .'

The office seemed strangely quiet with only Monica and Tweed left. It was the contrast with the frenetic activity which had taken place. Tweed asked Monica for her book with the list of phone numbers. He first called the Ministry of Security. The dull voice of a guard told him the Minister was not there.

Tweed called the penthouse number where Victor Warner

lived in London. He was taken aback when a soft voice answered.

'Hello?'

'You sound like Eva. Tweed here.'

'Maybe it's because I am Eva,' the sultry voice replied. 'Hold on, don't go . . .' He heard her call out to Mrs Carson that this was a personal call and could she have some privacy. There was plenty to do in the kitchen. A door slammed. 'Old Nosy,' Eva whispered. 'Now what can I do for you? Always a dangerous question for a woman to ask a man.'

'Sometimes. Is his Lordship there?'

'If you mean Victor Wannabe, no he isn't. He drove up to Garda – his hideaway in Carpford. I can give you the number, but don't tell him how you got it. Ex-directory.'

'Thank you, but I won't bother.'

'I'm feeling lonely, restless. Could we meet somewhere? I'd suggest Marco's Love Nest in Lower Cheyne Street. It's off Walton Street.'

'I know it.'

'You do? I'm surprised at you. In an hour's time?'

'See you then . . .'

In a subtle way Eva had sounded seductive. There were many sides to Eva Brand. He phoned the Ministry of Security again, asked for Peregrine Palfry.

'He's not here. Didn't you phone a few minutes ago?' the same dull guard's voice asked.

'No. Good-night . . .'

His new call was to Martin Hogarth. He handled this carefully. A superior voice snapped.

'Yes. Who is it?'

'Martin?'

'Yes . . .'

Tweed hung up. His last call was to Drew Franklin at the *Daily Nation*. He was transferred from one person to another. Then a girl's voice answered.

'Drew?' she said. 'He's shoved off into his country place. Who is calling?'

'Charlie Wilson. Not urgent. Thank you . . .'

He broke the connection. Monica was gazing at him, intrigued.

He drank some cold coffee which had been in the mug for a long time. She pulled a face.

'Don't know how you can swallow that. You've been phoning all the suspects, haven't you? To find out where they are.'

'That's right. The only one I've left out is Margesson, whom Paula called the Priest. We haven't his number but it's probably ex-directory. Doesn't matter.'

'They do say that it's the one you've missed you should have called.'

Despite Monica's protests about lack of protection, Tweed drove himself to the bar off Walton Street. He was glad to be on his own. He could think better without company.

Marco's Love Nest was discreetly advertised. No flashing neon lights. The name simply engraved on a brass plate with a dim light above it. When he walked in he had to pause to get used to the dimness. A long thin room with the bar on his left. The only illumination was a series of wall sconces glowing with a shadowy light. Behind the bar was a thin man clad in a white apron decorated with the name Marco. He approached the bar.

'I was supposed to meet a lady here.'

'She is waiting for you at a table at the back. Arrived ten minutes ago.'

'How do you know she's waiting for me?'

Marco now had a secretive smile. Not a smirk but knowing. He put down the glass he was cleaning, leaned forward and spoke in a low voice.

'She described you, sir. Medium height. Could be in his mid-forties. Wearing horn-rim glasses.'

'What is she drinking? Ready for another, you think?'

'Not yet. She just sips her drink. What will you have?'

'A glass of Chardonnay.'

'Two of a kind. Even like the same drink.'

'Marco, just give me the drink, then tell me the cost, including the lady's.'

'Didn't mean to be offensive. Sir.'

'Had you been, you'd have known about it . . .'

Having paid, Tweed made his way to the back of the bar. By now his eyes had become accustomed to the dimness and he could see her clearly. Sitting at a table in a secluded alcove, one hand slowly swivelling her glass by the stem as she watched him coming. He sat down, facing her.

'Cheers!' He raised his glass and she clinked hers with his. Her outfit surprised him. She was wearing a close-fitting white sleeveless dress, exposing her shapely arms and shoulders.

'Does he know you're here?' Tweed asked suddenly, abruptly.

'Victor? Certainly not. I keep my private life very private.'

'When was he first appointed Minister of Security?'

'Oh, about two years ago . . .' Eva replied.

'Why was he chosen?' Tweed asked.

'He was an MP and had been director of Medfords private security outfit. Obvious choice. The only one with the experience.'

'How did you come to work for him?' Tweed went on in a blank tone of voice.

'Thought you'd have realized that from what I told you when I slipped over secretly to your office. When he was with Medfords I was on the staff. It's a loose arrangement.'

'What does that mean?'

'It means,' said Eva, 'I'm not officially on his staff. So I'm not trapped in that idiotic Civil Service system. I'm paid out of his private income. Victor is a rich man.'

'How did that come about?'

'It came about, Mr Tweed, because it was the only way I would agree to work for him.'

'You have official office hours?' Tweed asked.

'I damned well don't. I come and go as I please. I thought this was going to be a fun evening.' She was still smiling as she had done since he'd sat down. 'Instead I find myself being interrogated. I did a lot of that myself at Medfords.'

Tweed sipped his wine. She waited, her large eyes glowing into his. He had the odd feeling she was penetrating inside his brain. An exceptionally intelligent lady with bewitching looks.

'Where were you born?' he asked suddenly.

'In a small village in Hampshire. Don't ask me the village's name because I won't tell you. My childhood is strictly my own affair.'

'You told me your mother was killed in a road accident. So what about your father?'

'You've hit a road-block. I don't want to talk about him. I will not talk about him.' Still smiling.

'You disliked him?'

'Didn't you hear what I just said?'

Eva lifted her almost full glass, swallowed the contents in two large gulps. She raised the empty glass to the barman, who came hurrying over.

'Same again,' she said.

'You left Medfords before Warner did?'

'As a matter of fact, I did. He contacted me two years later when he became a Minister, offered me the job.'

'And how did you spend those two years?'

'More interrogation.' She was still smiling. 'I was what they used to call a swinger, maybe still do. Cocktail bars and the best night clubs.'

'Miss Brand . . .'

'Eva, please.'

'Eva, I don't believe you. The swinger fairy-tale. Not your style.'

'Then that's your problem.' She waited until the barman, who had brought her a fresh glass of wine, went away. She drank half the glass at one go, then stretched out a hand and took hold of Tweed's resting on the table. 'We are friends, are we not?'

'I would hope so. I've just been doing my job.'

'Good. I asked you here to warn you. When the mandate from Downing Street arrived, appointing you Supremo in the present crisis, at first Victor was livid. Then he came to like the idea,' Eva explained.

'Why?'

'Because if al-Qa'eda launch a successful and devastating attack on London you get the blame, not Victor. He has always operated in this way – had a scapegoat tucked away in a cupboard, so to speak. After all, you are in charge of defeating al-Qa'eda – a point he has emphasized in the Cabinet.'

'So, secretly he's worried about an attack coming? Even though he pooh-poohs the idea in public?'

'Now you've caught on. Warnings about some terrible catastrophe being imminent are beginning to seep into the press. Our nice gossip writer, Drew Franklin, has seen to that. Sometimes I think Drew is not all he seems. He's suave, polite with women, flatters them so he can get what he wants. Reminds me of a smokescreen.'

'You could be right,' Tweed agreed.

'He came after me. But I got the impression his main motive was not the bedroom. It was to pump me about Victor's security measures. I told him I couldn't talk about security – and I wasn't interested in having dinner with him. When he asked, "Why?" I said because I didn't trust him. You ought to pay attention to Drew Franklin.'

'I will. And I appreciate what you have told me. Scapegoat? Interesting.'

'He developed that technique at Medfords. If something didn't work out he had someone else ready to dump

225

the blame on to. He is, in fact, your typical politician. Manipulation is the name of the game. He's an expert.'

'Then maybe,' Tweed suggested, 'you should watch your back.'

She squeezed the hand of Tweed she was still holding. Leaning forward, she kissed him. Tweed smiled, squeezed her hand, then withdrew his.

'You know,' she said, 'I've come to prefer more mature men who have a lot of experience. I can't stand the young macho type who has only one thing in mind with a woman. Plus they're such a bloody bore.'

'I have enjoyed talking to you,' Tweed said amiably. 'But if someone we know comes in here tongues will start wagging and that might hurt your job with the Minister. Shouldn't we call it a night?'

'After I've had another drink.' She waved her empty glass. Marco hustled over. 'Same again,' she told him. 'What about you?' she asked Tweed.

'If you insist.'

'I do insist.'

'Ever been to the Middle East?' Tweed asked suddenly. 'Since one of your languages is Arabic.'

'Don't really fancy the place.' Her large eyes still gazing into his. 'I prefer Switzerland. Everything there works.'

'True.'

Tweed remained silent until Marco had brought the fresh drinks and left them alone. He sipped his wine as Eva swallowed half her glass. He could see no sign that she was getting tipsy. A hard head.

'Do you think you're going to defeat al-Qa'eda?' she asked.

'As the Duke of Wellington once said, a battle may be won or lost until it's over. Not an exact quotation, but it conveys his meaning. I have enjoyed your company, but do you mind if we go in a moment?'

'The man has a battle to be fought.' She drank the rest

226

of her wine. 'I've got my Audi parked round the corner so you don't have to offer me a lift . . .'

'I have been seduced mentally,' Tweed told Monica as he sat behind his desk.

'Only mentally?' Monica was grinning. 'Shame!'

Tweed then told her about their conversation. With his power of recall he told her everything. Monica checked her bun of hair at the back of her head before she commented.

'So three questions arise,' Monica commented. 'She cleverly evaded your asking her whether she'd ever been to the Middle East. She firmly evaded telling you anything about this mysterious father. Finally, the missing two years in her life worry me.'

'I agree. She has a very dominant – without being domineering – personality. Still on your list of suspects?'

'It's a long one. Victor Warner, Peregrine Palfry, Martin Hogarth, Margesson, Drew Franklin and Eva Brand.'

Tweed frowned. 'Come to think of it, we don't know all that much about Franklin.'

'So I'll work fast, put him under my microscope again using the contacts I've left out.'

'Good. You know I don't think you should have included Eva in your suspects list. The Arabs would never take orders from a woman, even one with her exceptional brainpower.'

'Unless they don't know their controller is a woman.'

28

Newman had decided he wouldn't drive up to the village. He wanted his arrival and presence to be secret. He parked his car in the triangular setback off the main climb. The Uzi machine-gun was taken out of its case, which he locked in the boot. He slung the weapon, now fully loaded with a magazine of forty rounds, over his left shoulder. A spare mag went into the pocket of his warm black overcoat. In his left hand he held his Smith & Wesson as he began yomping down the narrow sunken road Paula had called a rabbit warren.

Soon he was enveloped by the dense trees of Black Wood, growing above the steep banks. At intervals he paused to listen. He heard only the sinister silence of the wood. The moon was up but didn't penetrate down into the gulch. He was glad he had brought a pair of night-glasses, which turned everything he looked at green, but enabled him to see clearly. Sarge, who had trained him in the SAS when he was writing an article on the secretive outfit, had recommended them.

Two-thirds of the way down the gulley he paused again and listened. Only the sound of silence. He scrambled up the left bank and plunged into the wood. There was a mixture of big firs, the occasional pine and the leafless deciduous trees which reminded him of skeletons. Why think of that word at a time like this?

His sense of direction was good. He saw the glimmer of

moonlight ahead, knew he was close to the edge of Black Wood. He proceeded more slowly. Then he was looking out across a field at the houses. Before leaving his car he had again studied the map Paula had provided. He had arrived just where he wanted to be.

A huge tall pine loomed above him. He began to climb, using convenient branches as rungs in a ladder. He was high up, near the top, when he found a natural settling place. Sturdy branches splayed out, concealed by the foliage. He perched the Uzi in a safe place, took out the water bottle from his satchel over his right shoulder, drank three modest swallows, capped the bottle. Now he felt full of energy. Sitting down, he pulled aside some of the pine's foliage.

There it was. About a hundred yards across a flat field. The bungalow to his right – Martin Hogarth's – appeared to have no lights. He extracted his monocular glass from the satchel, pressed it against his eyes. Martin's bungalow jumped at him, its rear side. All the windows had shutters closed, but he saw gleams of light between the blades. Martin was still up.

He swivelled the glass to the next bungalow beyond the wide gap between the two buildings. Shutters again closed over all windows, but gleams of light filtering through them. Beaurain and Paula had taken up residence.

'They'll know we're up here somewhere,' Paula warned as she poured coffee. 'I know we drove slowly before we parked the car in Mrs Gobble's shed – where I parked mine when I ended up trapped in that horrible cellar.'

'That's all right.' The tall Beaurain was smiling as he gripped her shoulder briefly. 'We want to stir them up, worry them. That's when they'll make a mistake.'

She found his smile attractive. His air of confidence was also comforting. He'd taken off his windcheater and wore a dark polo-necked sweater. For comfort and dark in case

230

he had to go outside. Make it more difficult to see him, as long as he kept out of the moonlight.

Paula watched him as she drank her coffee. A very athletic man, he couldn't keep still, kept striding round the large living-room, checking the shutters, checking his Uzi which he'd laid, loaded now, on a table near the front door.

'Don't get me wrong,' he said, turning round, 'but you can handle your Uzi?'

'Reasonably well.' She smiled as she glanced at her own weapon perched on the dining-table near the door into the kitchen. 'Barney, the instructor, who gave me a refresher course at the mansion down in Surrey, kept me at it until I blew the bull's-eye area of the target to smithereens. Why are they so keen on Uzis down there? They have an armoury of other automatic weapons.'

Beaurain swallowed the coffee he was drinking. He smiled again. 'Probably because the Israelis, who invented the weapon, are so reliable.'

'Well, now you know,' she lectured him gently, 'you won't have to worry about looking after me if the balloon goes up.'

'I regard you . . .' He bowed '. . . as a totally reliable back-up. That is why, when we arrived, I gave you the key Marler had obtained from Billy, then let you go inside first while I kept an eye on the outside.'

'Just so long as you have confidence in me. I don't like men to feel I'm a liability which needs protection.'

'If the balloon goes up, as you said, you'll damned well have to look after yourself,' he told her with an engaging grin. 'There are two bedrooms. Choose whichever suits you and I'll take over the first watch.'

Ali was becoming bored with waiting inside yet another quiet public phone-box. He snatched up the phone the moment it began ringing.

'Yes?'

'Who is that?' the distorted voice demanded.

'Ali, of course . . .'

'Never again say "of course". You are a mere subordinate. So, who is that?'

'Ali.'

'Abdullah speaking. There are rumours the British Army is moving into London in five days from now. How is your programme for the merger operation?'

'It is still two days from now . . .'

'Keep it that way. There is another problem, an emergency. Two members of the opposition have moved into the bungalow of Billy Hogarth. He was seen leaving, carrying cases to his car. He is staying at a small hotel in London. Since then two members of the opposition have arrived in the village and occupied Mr Billy Hogarth's bungalow. You have any extra men in the area?'

'Four. They are hidden in a deep hole in Black Wood. They are not needed for the merger . . .'

'You can communicate with them?'

'Of . . .' Ali hastily changed his wording. 'Yes, I can.'

'You know which bungalow I refer to? There are two bungalows.'

'I know which which one you mean . . .'

'Then alert the four men. Tell them to kill whoever is inside. *Tonight* . . .'

The phone was slammed down. *Bastard!* It was an English word Ali liked. He would never dare to use it when talking to Abdullah. He took out his mobile phone, pressed numbers and gave the four hidden men their orders.

29

It was 1 a.m. when Beaurain, seated in an upright chair to keep himself awake, heard the approaching motor-cycle. It slowed, the engine was turned off as it reached Billy Hogarth's bungalow, was followed by a hard thump as the machine was propped against the side wall.

Unlocking the front door, his Smith & Wesson concealed behind his back, Beaurain peered out. Strong moonlight. He walked to the end of the bungalow, looked round the corner. The rider was taking a large cardboard-backed envelope from his pannier. He wore the full outfit – black leather jacket and trousers tucked inside his boots. His head was masked by a large helmet.

'Don't park that damned thing there,' Beaurain ordered.

The man swung round, his right hand jumping to the inside of his jacket. Beaurain waited. The man changed his mind, withdrawing his hand empty. Motoring gloves were perched on the saddle.

'You say what?' the muffled voice behind the helmet asked.

Beaurain waved his left hand, first at the machine, then over to the distant side of Martin Hogarth's bungalow. The man hesitated, then spoke again.

'No hurt wall . . .'

'I said move the damned thing over there.'

Again Beaurain used his left hand to gesture at the machine, then at the side of Martin's bungalow. The man shrugged, put on his gloves, tucked the envelope under his arm and moved the machine, propping it against Martin's end wall. He kept well away from Beaurain as he turned, walked up to Martin's entrance. Beaurain walked quickly back to his own entrance, found the door open, the living-room lights turned off. Paula stood framed in the gloom.

She had been woken by the sound of the motor-cycle arriving. When she slipped under the sheets she had only divested herself of her windcheater, her boots and had pulled up her thick woollen jumper out of her trousers. If called, she wanted to be able to dress in half a minute. Now she stood in the dark, her right hand clutching her new Browning. Gently, Beaurain pushed her back inside, followed her, closed the door.

'He's delivering a large envelope to someone,' he whispered.

'There won't be anything inside it. Accidentally, I'm sure, one of those envelopes was delivered through the letter-box to Mrs Gobble. I found it in a trash can. Nothing inside that one.'

'This gives us a chance to check on who he calls on . . .'

He opened the door quietly again and they stood shoulder to shoulder, concealed inside the deep porch alcove. Looking at Martin's bungalow, they saw the glare light come on, heard the door opening. Martin's sarcastic voice could be heard clearly.

'Go to hell! At this time of night!'

A door slammed shut. They stood very still as the messenger walked past, giving not so much as a glance at the alcove. He had taken off his helmet. In the moonlight Paula thought he was youngish, brown-skinned, hair trimmed very short. An Egyptian? A Saudi?

Looking out, they saw him call at Margesson's Georgian house. The reception was even more explosive. The glare light came on. They heard Margesson's deep rumbling voice.

'Frig off! Lunatic . . .'

Another door slammed. Paula was frowning as the messenger proceeded to the huge tub-shaped house where Palfry lived. Another glare light. They could just catch Palfry's smooth voice.

'Not here. Please go away . . .'

A door closed more quietly. The messenger now proceeded round the far end of Carp Lake. The moon shone on the lake, making it appear like a sheet of black iron. Then it was blotted out by clouds. Paula said 'Damn! We won't see what happens on the other side.'

'Yes, we will.'

Beaurain darted inside, felt round inside his satchel, came back wearing night-glasses. His view through them was a luminous green. Enough to see the motor-cyclist walk past Mrs Gobble's residence, then on to Drew Franklin's cube house, where he stopped. Another glare light. Beaurain told Paula his impressions.

'Stayed longer there, then skulked off. Why longer there?'

'Because Drew is noted for his biting tongue. Or did he hand him the envelope?'

'No, still got it under his arm. That just leaves Garda, the Minister's palace. A tall man has opened the door. No glare light. Think light from the moon which has just come out again was reflected off glasses.'

'Pince-nez.' Paula shivered. It was a bitterly freezing night and the air was penetrating their bungalow. It had been warm before, thanks to Billy's good central heating system.

'What's happening now?' she asked impatiently.

'Warner has closed the door. The motor-cyclist is hoofing it back over here. To collect his machine. Still has the envelope under his arm.' He closed the door and Paula turned on the lights. 'Most mysterious.'

'What does it mean?' she asked from the kitchen as she used the cafetière to make them more coffee. She kept on

235

her windcheater until the central heating neutralized the icy air which had drifted in.

'I discussed this with Tweed and he replied with one word. Communications.'

'Still not with you, Jules.'

'It hit me when he said that. You've probably read about the attack in New York on the World Trade Center. No one could understand why such an intricate plan hadn't leaked. Now I'm confident I can guess why, what method was used over there, and is being used here. Nothing is ever written down, in case it gets into the wrong hands. All communication and instructions are by *word of mouth*. That's why the Americans had no warning about September 11 – and why we're getting no warning about their plan for London.'

'So the envelope is for cover?'

'Exactly. The trouble is we've observed where the motor-cyclist called, but we don't know which individual he delivered a verbal message to.'

'Maybe to all of them.' She handed Beaurain a mug of coffee and sat down with him on a sofa, sipping from her own mug. 'All of them,' she repeated. 'Martin, Margesson, Palfry, Drew Franklin and the Minister.'

'Doesn't sound likely. Not Drew Franklin, for example, I'm sure. It's one individual, but which?'

'So we're back to square one . . .'

Beaurain lifted a finger to his lips and she stopped talking. Paula had good hearing but Beaurain's was exceptional. After a minute they heard the motor-cycle's engine start up, then the machine roared off away from the village. Paula drank the rest of her coffee, stood up.

'If you don't mind I'm going to snatch a bit more kip.'

She went to a window at the front, lifted a blind. The view had vanished. She was staring into a dense fog, curling round the bungalow like an enormous snake. She told Jules, reminded him to wake her when the time came for her watch, went back to bed. Nothing more was likely to happen for the rest of the night.

Nestled in his observation point at the top of the pine tree, Newman woke suddenly. His thick black coat had kept out the bitter cold, had made him too comfortable. He was appalled. He had fallen asleep on duty. Something had woken him up. Stripping off his gloves, he reached out, took hold of the Uzi. He moved very little, careful to make no sound. He listened. Then he heard it. The stealthy crunch of feet below, treading down dead bracken.

The trouble was a heavy mist had fogged his vision. He put on the night-glasses, the mist turned green. Cautiously, he pulled aside a screen of foliage, gave himself a window on the blurred world. Four of them, well spread out across the field. Good tactics. No bunching to provide one target.

They were crawling forward, almost as swift as ants on the move. Four men with turbans wrapped round their heads. He thought the turbans were black. Al-Qa'eda. What was their target? He aimed his Uzi through his 'window', waited.

The circle began closing. Heading for Billy Hogarth's bungalow. Paula and Beaurain were their targets. Newman waited no longer. Aiming at one figure in the middle, he fired a shot. It electrified the stalkers. One swung round, raised his weapon, a Kalashnikov, began spraying the tree tops with a hail of bullets. How he'd realized the single shot had come from high up in the trees Newman had no idea. He no longer waited.

He let loose a stream of bullets. The man who had fired rolled over sideways, lay deathly still. Newman swung the muzzle to the next man, who had started shooting wildly at Black Wood, crouched now on his knees. Newman fired again. The shooter was riddled with bullets, dropped his weapon, fell forward. He didn't move again.

237

Newman turned his attention to the other two and was alarmed when he found they had disappeared. They must have taken cover round the sides of the bungalow. Newman hoped to God the fusillades had warned the occupants.

Inside the bungalow Paula had hauled on her boots, grabbed the Uzi she had placed on a table close to the bed. She flung open the door to the living-room. Beaurain was standing close to the front door, his weapon in his hands. He smiled grimly.

'You watch the kitchen door. I'm taking the front one . . .'

He unlocked the door, stood to one side, flung it wide open. Mist drifted in. Not helpful. He listened. The firing at the rear of the bungalow had ceased. The silence was ominous.

No one in the alcove porch. He stepped into it, listened once more. Nothing. He suspected the attackers could move like mice. No warning they were coming. He peered out of the alcove, checking both directions. No one. Then he heard faintly but clearly a voice he just recognized. Newman's, shouting a warning through hands cupped round his mouth. The words, muffled by the mist, just reached him.

'Two of them near you. I brought down other two in the field behind . . .'

Two? Dangerous. If they both attacked at once. To make himself a smaller target, Beaurain sat down outside the porch, a tactic he'd used successfully fighting terrorists over the water. He heard the faint jostle of a pebble to his right. A man appeared, a silhouette in the mist. Holding a Kalashnikov. The barrel came up to kill Beaurain. The Belgian had his Uzi aimed in that direction, fired a long burst. The figure jumped – under the shock of the bullets hitting him – dropped his weapon, leaned against the wall of the bungalow, slithered down it, lay very still. Beaurain's weapon was already aimed to his left. Nothing, no sound.

Inside Paula had darted into the kitchen, paused, facing the heavy back door which she knew was bolted. No one was going to get in through that. She also was listening, now the shooting from the front had ceased. She prayed Beaurain was still alive.

They couldn't get in through the living-room windows – the shutters, closed, were heavy. Newman's shout had just reached her. Difficult to hear but she'd caught the gist of his warning. Was there one more out there?

She wasn't frightened. She had been startled to be woken from a deep sleep by the sound of gunfire. Now her training came to her aid. Her nerves were cold, controlled. She was ready to kill. She held her Uzi across her waist, ready to aim it in any direction.

The back door was bolted top and bottom, but when they arrived the key had been missing, although the door was locked. Billy must had slipped it into his pocket without thinking. So she had no way of knowing a ferocious eye was peering at her through the keyhole.

Some instinct made her back further away from the door. Still she held the Uzi across her stomach, parallel to the floor. Frequently she glanced back over her shoulder. When she had rushed into the kitchen she had hauled down two large pans off hooks, had dropped them at the entrance to the kitchen. She had used the dimmer to lower the lighting. If anyone came through the door from the living-room they would, with luck, stumble over the pans, announcing their presence.

When the attack came it was still a shock. The heavy back door was smashed inwards, breaking free of its hinges, the bolts giving way. A huge figure stood in the doorway, the biggest man she had ever seen. His weight had destroyed the back door as though it were made of matchwood. On his head he wore a black turban. His black beard was glistening with moisture from the mist.

He was grinning savagely. His Kalashnikov was looped over his shoulder. In his right hand he held a horrible-looking curved knife. He was going to slash her to bits. Quite confident – peering through the keyhole he'd seen that her Uzi was held across her waist. His trunk-like legs carried him forward like a juggernaut.

She swung the barrel of the Uzi through ninety degrees, was pressing the trigger, kept on pressing it, emptied the magazine into him. Forty rounds. He stood perfectly still for a mind-breaking moment, then fell forward. She had to jump backwards to avoid this immense body hitting her. It thudded to the floor, caused a shuddering vibration. She forced herself to bend over it, checking the carotid artery in the bull-like neck. He was dead.

Before checking the artery she had hauled out the empty mag, had inserted a fresh one. Behind her she heard a clatter of pans.

She jumped up, her weapon aimed at the entrance into the kitchen. Beaurain's voice shouted.

'Don't shoot. It's Jules . . .'

She smiled wearily, lowered her gun. He came forward and stared, first at the smashed door, then down at the body. He whistled.

'What a giant.'

'It was like something out of *Psycho*. He came in like an express train, waving that knife. My training saved me. He's dead as a dodo, thank God. What a brute.'

Beaurain looped his Uzi over his shoulder, put both hands on her shoulders, pulled her close. She was trembling. He held her like that until the trembling stopped and she released herself.

'I'm OK now. What's the situation?' she asked briskly.

'There were four of them. Newman must have been guarding us, hidden in Black Wood. He got two of them.

I got one. You brought down this bull, who was probably the leader. They're al-Qa'eda. Look at the turban . . .'

He whipped his weapon off his shoulder as he heard someone outside the back door. A voice called in, cautiously. Newman's.

'Are you both all right? Heard you talking.'

'I think we'll let you in,' Paula called out impishly.

Newman appeared. He paused to look down at the intact door lying on the floor. Its heaviness had saved it from any real damage. It had simply given way in one piece under the massive onslaught.

'Tell you about that later,' Paula said with a smile. 'So good to see you. Thanks for the back-up. Now, can we fix the door before we freeze to death . . .'

Between them, Beaurain and Newman lifted the door, slotted it back into place. Newman opened drawers, found a collection of spatulas and large knives. They used these to ram them into the edges of the door, which held it firmly in place. It was a makeshift job but served the purpose.

Paula, who didn't fancy staying in the kitchen with the body on the floor, said she'd clear up her bedroom while they worked. She'd jumped out of bed so quickly the sheets and duvets were strewn over the floor. When she came back Newman was having a long conversation with Tweed on his mobile, reporting what had happened. He paused for a short time, then resumed the conversation briefly.

'That's organized,' he told Beaurain.

'What is?' asked Paula, prodding him. 'I'm still here, you know.'

'Tweed phoned Buchanan while I waited. Roy is rushing ambulances up here to collect the bodies. He also wants to know who up here has reacted – which is something Roy and I have decided to check.'

'We'd better get outside now then . . .'

The mist was thinning when they all left the bungalow.

241

The lights were on in every house. Martin was already outside, using a flashlight to examine the killer Newman had shot down. He looked up.

'What the devil happened? Who is this guy? He looks dead.'

'He is,' Newman told him. 'We had a gang of burglars who came armed.'

'How long have you been out here?' Beaurain asked. 'And I see you're fully dressed at 3 a.m.'

'How observant of you,' Martin sneered as he stood up. 'I don't think we've met before.' He looked back at Paula. 'And what are you doing inside Billy's bungalow? Where is Billy?'

'He decided to take a holiday,' Paula said, smiling acidly. 'Loaned us his place – I don't think he wanted to leave it empty.'

'Didn't say a word to me.'

'Maybe he doesn't always tell you about his plans,' Paula suggested sweetly.

'The police will have to be informed,' Martin snapped. 'I'll call them . . .'

'Don't bother,' the Belgian told him. 'We have already done that. And I'm Commissioner Beaurain.'

'I see. And I dress quickly. Heard the gunshots.'

'Very quickly,' Beaurain commented. 'Down to inserting a clip in your tie.'

'I'm going back to bed,' Martin snapped and walked back to his bungalow. He slammed the door shut once he was inside.

A tall figure came striding round the end of the lake. His eyes glared from behind his pince-nez. The Minister wore a heavy overcoat with an astrakhan collar and a silk scarf round his long bony neck. He stopped close to them, as tall as Beaurain. His hands were inside his coat pockets and his manner was regal.

'Will someone be so kind as to inform me what has

242

happened? I heard gunfire. I also saw you come out of Billy Hogath's bungalow. So what is going on?'

'The police are on the way,' Newman told him. 'Al-Qa'eda sent four killers to attack us. They are all dead.'

'So,' Paula said pointedly, 'al-Qa'eda have arrived in Britain . . .'

'What proof have you that the men belong to that organization? You'd better be careful before you spread that sort of speculation.'

'They have brown skins and were wearing black turbans,' Newman snapped. 'Didn't you know that is their favoured uniform?'

'Must have slipped through our net at Dover,' Warner asserted. 'I repeat, this must be kept very quiet. We don't want to start a panic in London. Incidentally, I have arranged a full security meeting for the morning. Ten o'clock at my place.'

'Penthouse or Whitehall guardhouse?' enquired Newman.

'I find your sense of humour rather crude.' He turned to Paula. 'As Tweed is coming I suppose you'll be there too,' he went on in a tone lacking enthusiasm. 'Then you can tell me what you were doing in Billy Hogarth's bungalow. I shall require a complete explanation of your presence here.'

He turned his back on them and strode off to Garda before anyone could reply. Newman looked furious, while Beaurain was smiling as though amused.

'I presume that is your Minister of Security. Not in the best of tempers.'

'Well, I really am not all that surprised,' a smarmy voice said behind Beaurain.

'Jules,' Paula said quickly, 'this is Peregrine Palfry, the Minister's personal assistant.'

'I was going on to say,' Palfry continued, annoyed at her intervention, 'that the Minister works all hours and gets very little sleep. On my way here I passed a nasty body. I was also woken by gunfire. What on earth has been going on?'

243

'Armed robbers, dear boy,' said Beaurain, who had taken an instant dislike to Palfry. 'It doesn't just happen in London. And before you ask the police are on their way.'

'But what exactly happened?' Palfry insisted. 'You have told me nothing.'

'That burglar tried to shoot me. I shot him first,' Beaurain said in a bored tone.

'How absolutely frightful. How extremely mind-boggling. We thought we were safe here. The people who live in this village, I mean.'

Palfry was dressed as though he'd just got up. Below his overcoat, buttoned to the neck, protruded a pair of pink striped pyjamas. But Paula noticed that below them were were the cuffs of a dark suit. Did he really sleep in his suit under pyjamas? Palfry was lying.

'The gunfire woke you then?' she enquired.

'I'll say it did. Pretty awful way to start the day if you ask me.' He turned to Paula. 'I heard the Minister inviting you to come with Tweed to the meeting tomorrow morning at his Belgravia apartment. You'll be hungry when it's all over. Maybe you would join me for a little lunch afterwards?'

'Kind of you. Let's see how it goes.'

Palfry walked back towards his 'tub' house. Paula noticed he took a route which kept him well clear of the body lying outside the bungalow.

'I wonder whether he will come over to see us?' Beaurain said.

He pointed across the lake to the cube house. A red MG was emerging from a garage under one of the cubes. In the moonlight she could see the distinctive figure of Drew Franklin behind the wheel. The car sped round the end of the lake and drove at speed towards them. Drew braked feet before he reached them. As he alighted from the car he took off his hat and bowed to Paula.

'So, gentlemen, the war has started.'

'We shot a burglar . . .' Newman began.

'Burglar my foot.' His headlights were beamed on the body. 'Native clothes and a black turban? That's al-Qa'eda come to town. The lot of you could have been murdered.'

'Yes, we were lucky,' Beaurain said with a smile.

'That will light a fire under Victor Warner. I've called my editor, told him to delay my column twenty-four hours. The headline? *Al-Qa'eda Strike in North Downs*. How many of 'em?'

'You only see one body,' Beaurain pointed out.

'How many?' Drew demanded again. 'All that gunfire.'

'Four bodies – like that one,' Newman admitted.

'Bigger headline. *Massacre of al-Qa'eda near London*. The Minister will love that. None of you were hit?'

'We hit them,' Paula said.

'Good for you.' He put his arm round her. 'And I'll bet this lady scored a bull.'

'It was a bull – in every sense of the word,' Beaurain replied.

'I'm off. To rewrite my article. Might just bully the editor into reworking the paper so it will hit today's edition.'

He leapt back behind the wheel of his MG. The car roared off towards London and was gone. Beaurain looked thoughtful.

'That Drew Franklin could be the brightest brain up here. I think someone should interrogate him for a long time.'

'I could do that,' Newman said. 'We're both reporters . . .

Paula packed quickly, remade the bed in her room, checked the interior of the bungalow to make sure it looked neat. Swift as she was, two ambulances arrived before dawn. Buchanan jumped out, listened while Beaurain and Newman gave him a quick description of what had happened, where the bodies were. Within twenty minutes, under Buchanan's urging, both ambulances were occupied with their cargo.

'I want to get these bodies out of this village, heading back to London before the inhabitants appear. I know

245

they've been up once but from what you've told me they don't know all that much.'

'Except Drew Franklin,' Beaurain reminded him.

'That's great,' Buchanan said, smiling. 'He'll splash what has happened up here. Finally wake up people to the grim threat al-Qa'eda poses to London.'

'Tweed will be rubbing his hands,' Paula commented.

'And that idiot, Victor Warner, will be wringing his. You will all be leaving, I hope,' Buchanan went on, turning to get aboard one of the ambulances. 'You've done the trick. Rattled al-Qa'eda's cage – and that of the master planner . . .'

They were leaving. Beaurain locked the front door of Billy's bungalow. He paused, his satchel and 'violin' case looped over his shoulder, his case in his other hand.

'You going back to the Peacock?' Newman asked.

'No, I want to get to London. Paula's car is inside Mrs Goggle's shed. What about you?'

'I left my car at the triangle at the other end of what Paula calls the rabbit warren.'

'Then we'll all drive there in my car so you can pick up your car,' Paula decided. 'I wonder how Billy is getting on in some hotel in town?'

30

Pete Nield shifted his position behind the wheel of his parked car. He was stiff. In the Bloomsbury district of London it was still dark. No streaks of another cold dawn appeared in the heavy sky.

For hours he had waited opposite the front entrance to the Pink Hat, a small hotel in a side street. Its frontage was narrow, four storeys high with steps leading up to the entrance, which had a light glowing over it. In front of grubby net curtains a notice hung hopefully. *Vacancies*.

The Pink Hat? Silly name for a building which had stood there since Victorian days. It was the obscure hotel Nield had, in the evening, escorted Billy Hogarth to. On arrival Pete had accompanied Billy to check his bedroom. On the second floor it had only one window which overlooked the street where Pete had parked. No fire escape. Pete had checked that. So the only way anyone could get into the place was up the front steps. Pete was a stickler for details.

He checked his Walther for the sixth time, slid the magazine back into the butt. Something to do, to keep him awake. He didn't expect any trouble but on their way there he thought he'd been followed down from Carpford. Nerves. He slumped down further so any passer-by would assume the vehicle was empty.

The two men appeared out of nowhere. Incredibly silent in their movements. A tall thin man in a grey overcoat, his

247

companion short and tubby, wearing a shabby raincoat. They were too quiet. Reaching the foot of the steps to the Pink Hat, they turned suddenly, went up the steps, vanished inside like ghosts. Pete slipped out of the car, closed the door quietly, crept up the steps in time to hear what they said to the night clerk, a plump dopey-looking woman.

'Our brother, Billy Hogarth, is staying here. We bring bad news. His mother has just died.'

'How awful,' the woman said, not really interested.

'We want to go and wake him gently.' It was Tall Thin talking.

'It will be a shock, so we won't tell him until he's really woken up. Which room is he in?'

'Number 16 . . .'

'Then if you loan us your master key we can be sure not to startle him too much. See what I mean.' Now it was Short Tubby speaking. 'He was very fond of his mother.'

'Not nice,' the dopey receptionist mumbled, reaching for the key, handing it to him. 'Up those stairs, to the second landing, then turn right.'

'We appreciate this,' Short Tubby said in his hoarse voice. He picked up the key.

'Gentlemen, I suggest we discuss this in the parlour – that door over there,' Pete said quietly. His Walther was pressed into the back of Tall Thin. 'This gun holds eight rounds – it will blow you pal's spine into two pieces.'

Tall Thin had frozen. Short Tubby slipped his hand inside his jacket. Pete shook his head at him, his eyes cold as ice.

'You have one second to show me that hand – without anything in it. I'm going to pull the trigger.'

Short Tubby's hand whipped out, empty, even faster than he had inserted it. The night clerk was staring, her mouth open, standing still as a waxwork in Madame Tussaud's.

'Now,' Pete continued in his deadly quiet tone, 'we'll all

248

go into that parlour, sit down and discuss the situation. You go first, Fatty. Walk very slowly.'

'Call the Yard,' Pete said over his shoulder to the woman. 'Ask for Chief Superintendent Buchanan. Tell him where this place is, tell him to send armed men. Now, gentlemen,' he went on, talking to the two men. 'Do walk slowly, I beg you, if you want to see the dawn . . .'

Short Tubby kept both of his hands by his sides, palms outwards as he took slow steps into the parlour. Pete prodded the Walther harder into Tall Thin, who followed his partner.

Inside the small parlour, decorated with a palm plant in a pot, badly in need of water, and a few wicker chairs, Pete kicked the door shut behind him.

'*No!* Don't sit down,' he ordered in the same Siberian voice, as Short Tubby was about to occupy a chair. 'Walk slowly to that wall. Now press your face against it, then lift the hands high above your head, press them against the wall. If you look round I'll be the last person you ever see. You stand very still,' he ordered Tall Thin, his Walther still pressed into the thug's spine.

From behind he used his left hand to pat and feel over his body. Under his left armpit he found the gun, withdrew it from the shoulder holster. A Webley-Fosbery, fully loaded. He continued to search, felt something round and hard in his overcoat pocket. A silencer, ready to be screwed on to the weapon before it was used to kill the sleeping Billy.

Pete's expression became even grimmer. He slipped Tall Thin's gun and silencer into his pocket. Reversing his Walther, holding it by the barrel, he brought the weapon down with savage force on the back of his captive's head. Tall Thin fell forward, unconscious, landed in one of the wicker chairs.

'*Don't look round!*' he hissed at Short Tubby.

Approaching him quietly, he rammed the Walther into Short Tubby's spine. He proceeded swiftly to search him.

Another shoulder holster from which he extracted a Colt .455, also fully loaded. Slipped that into his other pocket and continued searching. Nothing else, no silencer, but he hadn't expected one considering the weapon. He also now had two wallets shoved inside his pocket. They could be examined later. He also had the master key, which Short Tubby had put in his trouser pocket.

'Stay where you are. Quite still. I'm going to sit down and then we can . . .'

He was still speaking when he smashed his gun down on the fat man's head. He jumped back as Short Tubby slid down the wall, collapsing in a heap on the floor. He checked both men's carotid arteries, found them ticking over. He reckoned it would be an hour before they regained consciousness.

Leaving the parlour, he closed the door. The night clerk woman was sitting behind her counter, absorbed in looking at one of the cheaper women's magazines. She looked up, went back to her magazine.

'Did you call Superintendent Buchanan at the Yard?' Pete asked.

'Don't know the number.'

Pete raised his eyes towards the ceiling. She was no longer looking at him. He took a deep breath. There was 999.

'Give me a piece of paper.'

She scrabbled below the counter. Eventually she found a notebook with creased pages. He wrote down the number, Buchanan's name and rank, then his own name.

'This is serious,' he snapped. 'Here is the number, the name of the man you need to speak to, and my name, which he will want. Tell him to send two patrol, cars with armed men. Tell him I said it was *urgent*.' He added that word to the notepad, underlined it. 'Give him the name of this hotel, the address. The two men who came in are waiting in the parlour, don't wish to be disturbed. Do it now.' He took out a five-pound note. gave it to her. She woke up, grabbed the note. 'They will give you more money when they arrive,' he fibbed.

He ran upstairs, followed the instructions she had given the two killers. Billy Hogarth woke quickly, did not seem worried when Pete said he was moving him to another hotel. He dressed quickly, picked up the case he hadn't unpacked, fetched his shaving-kit bag from the bathroom, tucked it under his arm and they went downstairs.

Dopey woman was talking on the phone. Pete listened. She'd garbled his instructions but given enough for Buchanan to react. Pete paid the bill with cash, hustled Billy down the steps and into his car. It was very cold and the first streaks of dawn, promising another unpleasant day, were now visible.

'What's up?' Billy asked, suppressing a yawn.

'I think we were followed here by some undesirable characters. I'm taking you to another hotel in a different area. You'll be saf . . . more comfortable there.'

'Lots more goin' on up at Carpford than round 'ere.'

'What do you mean?'

No reply. He glanced at Billy. His passenger had fallen asleep, his head drooped on his chest. Pete checked the rear-view mirror. No traffic at all. No one was following them this time. But what had Billy seen up at Carpford?

31

Beaurain, with Paula by his side, was driving down the narrow, steep curving lane, descending from the Downs to the main road. Paula had gratefully accepted his offer to drive – she was feeling shaky, a reaction to the violent events at Carpford. They had dropped Newman where he had left his car. Beaurain had let Newman, anxious to get back to Park Crescent, go ahead of him.

It was daylight, of a sort. Murky grey clouds drifted above them and the wind was cold. Beaurain was driving well within the speed limit, cautious as to what might lie round the next corner – in this section there was only room for one car.

A violent honking started behind them, continued non-stop. Paula looked back. She recognized the aggressive driver in his Alfa-Romeo. Martin Hogarth, wearing a base-ball cap. The honking of the horn went on, sending the message: *Get out of my way.*

'This is ridiculous,' Paula protested. 'It's Martin, Billy's brother. How can he possibly hope to pass here?'

'He wants me to speed up,' Beaurain said with a smile. 'How old is he?'

'At least forty and he's wearing one of those stupid baseball caps.'

They turned yet another corner and the road widened. As the honking was maintained, Beaurain steered into the middle of the road, making it impossible for their harasser to pass. Beaurain waved a hand out of his window, indicating he was slowing down, which he did, then stopped.

'Won't take a minute,' he said, still smiling.

Martin slammed on his brakes, left his engine running as he dived out to confront the Belgian. Beaurain stood with his arms folded, smiling. Martin came up close to him, his tone sneering.

'Think you own the bloody road? Time you read the Highway Code. Of course, you're a foreigner.'

Paula had left her car. She stood beside it, watching.

'Actually,' Beaurain said mildly, 'I have read the Highway Code from cover to cover.'

'Didn't do you much good, did it? You're a slob. You need a lesson.'

Martin bunched his right fist, aimed it at the other man's jaw. Beaurain moved his head, the punch went past him, then he did something, the movement so swift Paula couldn't follow what happened. Beaurain now had Martin's right arm gripped in a peculiar angle, pushed him back over the bonnet over his Alfa.

'Watch it!' Martin yelled. 'You'll break my arm.'

'Just keep quiet and listen,' Beaurain said calmly. 'What is your job? That is, if you've got one.'

'I'm . . . a stockbroker . . . if you must know.'

'I pity the people you advise. Doubtless they all lose money. Now I'm going to release you. Don't move until I tell you.'

Martin remained bent backwards over the car. He glanced to his right, saw Paula, averted his gaze quickly. Beaurain had walked round to the open driver's door. Leaning inside, he switched off the engine, took out the ignition key, then threw it into the grass verge, which had not been cut for ages.

'You can get up now,' he called out as he walked back and got behind the wheel as Paula sat again in the passenger seat. He began driving downhill.

'It will take him ages to find that key,' Paula said with a touch of malice.

'Not too long. I could have thrown it into the field, but I don't like overdoing things. London, here we come.'

'Tweed will have been up all night,' she predicted. 'Maybe he has found something important.'

When they walked into the office at Park Crescent it was crowded with members of the team. Newman occupied one armchair facing Buchanan, who sat in the other one. Marler was leaning against a wall, smoking a cigarette. Pete Nield was perched against the edge of Paula's desk, and was speaking. He stopped when Paula walked in with Beaurain. The only one not present was Harry Butler. Nield moved away from the desk as Paula went to sit behind it. Monica, Beaurain observed, was seated behind her word-processor. Paula stared at Newman and her tone was sharp when she spoke.

'Bob, has that Airsight friend of yours flown over Carpford to take pictures? If I could study them I'm sure I can work out which house has the cellar I was imprisoned in.'

'Soon now,' Newman assured her. 'He's taking longer over his holiday than expected. He's the best.'

'He shouldn't take holidays if he's the best,' she grumbled.

There was a knock on the door and Monica jumped up to open it. A middle-aged grey-haired lady, wearing a spotless white apron, pushed a trolley in. Monica gestured.

'Breakfast for anyone who's interested. Fried eggs, bacon, toast, marmalade, coffee. Hands up.'

Every hand went up instantly. Nellie, as Monica called the woman, was going to serve Tweed first but he waved her away. Pointed at Beaurain, Paula, then Newman and Nield.

'Their need is greater than mine. Serve me last. You have plenty of trays. Not much of a breakfast-room in here.'

255

Paula fetched folded chairs propped against the wall, opened them. The door opened again and Eva Brand strode in. She sniffed.

'Any leftovers? I haven't eaten for ages.'

The door opened again and Howard, the Director, strolled in. He wore a smart grey-striped suit, perfectly creased trousers, a pink shirt and a Hermès tie. His plump pink face broke into a smile.

'Smells good. You'll be relieved to hear I've just had breakfast at my club.'

'Well, there's nothing left for you anyway,' Paula said.

He rested a hand on her shoulder, squeezed it gently. 'I've heard about the Battle of Carpford from Bob. I've been told how well you did. Felling a giant.'

'A colossus,' she said.

'Won't interrupt your meal. Any more developments, Tweed? If so, tell me later . . .'

'He's tactful,' Paula said, scooping up egg yolk.

'More than you were,' Newman chided her with a grin.

'He doesn't like people who bow down to him,' she retorted.

'Can I report now?' Nield asked. 'About the Pink Hat and the two gentlemen who called on Billy?'

'Those so-called gentlemen are in custody,' Buchanan remarked. 'You don't know how good a job you did. They're both professional hit men we'd been after for months. Sergeant Warden, who called here a while ago for the evidence bags containing the weapons and bullets, is interrogating them. Separately, of course. Warden can be very tough. Not actually using physical force, of course.'

'Actually?' queried Paula.

'No need to go into the details. Obviously they'd arrived to kill Billy Hogarth. Pete, as he has done before, saved the day, saved Billy.'

'Who,' Pete explained, 'is safely cloistered in a different hotel with Harry parked outside, watching the place.'

'That incident was significant,' said Tweed, wiping his lips with a napkin.

'You mean your breakfast?' Paula asked mischievously.

Tweed was relieved to note her humorous mood. Newman had given him a brutally detailed account of what had happened at Carpford. And it wasn't so long ago since she had been a prisoner in a bleak underground room, uncertain whether she was going to live or die. None of this showed in her appearance or manner.

'The incident I called significant was the attempt on Billy Hogarth's life, his remark that lots had been going on in the village. The mastermind is taking no chances, trying to wipe out anyone with information. The attack on Billy Hogarth's bungalow is even more significant, for the same reason. It suggests the timing of the attack is very close.'

'Communications in al-Qa'eda,' Beaurain said.

'Obviously by word of mouth. The farce of motor-cyclist couriers carrying empty envelopes. Calling on everyone up there. The messages are passed by word of mouth. Who is the real recipient is concealed by the courier calling at every dwelling. I'm convinced the same word-of-mouth technique was used in America. Hence neither the FBI nor the CIA were alerted. More and more I'm convinced that the same mastermind who planned September 11 is planning the imminent attack on London.' He checked his watch. 'Time for us to attend the meeting called by the Minister at his apartment for 10.30 a.m.'

'Why,' protested Paula, 'do we have to go traipsing over there? I'm surprised you didn't insist the meeting should be held here.'

'Tactics,' Tweed told her, 'no point in creating resentment. Warner will be more open with us on his own patch. Heaven knows what he's planning now.'

Newman drove them. Tweed had also selected Beaurain, Eva and Paula to go with him. Mrs Carson opened the apartment door and made a typically tactless welcome.

'You're just on time. He's waiting for you with the others.'

The others? Paula glanced at Tweed as the elevator ascended. He was standing very erect in his most authoritative manner. When the elevator door opened on the penthouse floor Palfry was there to meet them. His expression was important and official.

'This way, gentlemen. Our people are waiting.'

He opened a door into a room they had not seen before. It was probably the dining-room, Paula thought. Very spacious, with a long table that might have been in the boardroom of a large company.

At the far end the Minister sat at the head. Clustered round him on both sides were six men, most of whom Tweed had never seen before. Except for a large man he knew was Tolliver, the recently appointed chief of Special Branch in place of Jasper Buller. At their end of the table Eva Brand sat down to one side of the top chair. She turned round, gave them a warm smile. No mention of her recent visit to Park Crescent.

'Tweed, you sit at the head of your end of the table . . .'

Tweed had not moved. He scanned the unknown men grouped round the Minister. He put his hands in the pockets of his overcoat.

'Before I sit down, who are these strangers? I know Tolliver, so it's all right for him to stay.'

'To stay?' Warner spoke in the booming voice used when he was at the despatch box in the House of Commons. 'They are senior civil servants attached to my ministry . . .'

'We can't have them in on this meeting,' Tweed replied bluntly. 'They can have only a distant view of what is involved.'

'I must insist . . .' Warner began.

'If you do insist we'll transfer this meeting to Park

Crescent. I'm not sitting down until they have left. And I am short of time.'

Tweed turned to Palfry, standing close to him.

'I heard you lock the door. Please unlock it so we can leave now. You can attend, of course . . .'

There was a muted buzz of discussion at the far end of the table. Then the civil servants picked up their files – you had to have a file always if you were Civil Service. They marched out of the room through the door Palfry had unlocked.

Their noses in the air, they made a point of not looking at Tweed as they left. Palfry re-locked the door. Tweed sat down, indicated to his companions they should do the same at his end of the table.

Warner was glaring at Tweed. He had removed his pince-nez, polishing them with a square of wash leather. A moment before, Tweed had removed his horn-rims, cleaned them quickly on a clean handkerchief, had them back on his nose before the Minister made a performance of replacing his pince-nez.

'I suppose,' he sneered, 'this action of yours emanates from the PM's mandate.'

'We are here, aren't we? Under your own roof. I could have asked for this meeting to be held at Park Crescent.'

Eva, now seated on Tweed's left, leaned over and whispered in her soft voice.

'Coffee is available whenever you wish. Drinkable. I made it myself,' she fibbed.

'Thank you.' He patted her hand. 'Maybe later.'

'Another point,' Warner boomed. 'You objected to strangers attending.' He aimed a long bony finger like a gun at Beaurain. 'What is he doing here? Not a member of your team.'

'Let me introduce you. This is Jules Beaurain. Recently Commissaire of Police in Brussels. Prior to that he was

259

the controller of their anti-terrorist squad. He probably knows more about terrorists than anyone else in this room.'

'Then I'll start.' Warner paused for effect. 'Manchester.'

'What about it?'

'Very experienced operatives of Special Branch have cast their net wide among top flight informants. The word is London is not the target. Manchester is. I have stopped the Army moving units south from the Midlands.'

'Manchester!' Newman whispered. 'Stuff that for a lark.'

Eva grinned. Paula kept her mouth expressionless, then winked at Eva.

'You really believe that?' Tweed asked innocently.

'I have to act on information received,' Warner said at his most pompous.

'Then why is it that my network of informants, once described as the most reliable by the present PM, hasn't heard a whisper about this Manchester distraction?'

'Ah!' Very hawk-like, Warner stared at the ceiling. 'You are invoking your position as Supremo.'

'I have never used that word. It is a fact, though, that I have been asked to coordinate the activities of all the security services.'

'The Supremo,' Warner repeated nastily.

'He's all over the place,' Tweed whispered to Eva.

'Situation normal,' she whispered back. She raised her voice. 'Maybe this is time for coffee to keep us alert.' Beckoning to Palfry at the far end of the table, she whispered again. 'It might cool him down if we have a break.'

Palfry came trotting up to her with a wide smile. 'Can I help?'

'You could organize coffee *toute de suite*, if you would.'

'My pleasure . . .'

Tweed leaned to his right as Paula plucked at his sleeve. She kept her voice verw low. 'I think Palfry is sweet on Eva.'

260

'Won't get him anywhere,' Eva, who had more exceptional hearing than Paula had realized, spoke her riposte aloud.

'Sorry.' Paula clasped her hands in prayer to apologize.

'Why?' Eva asked with a smile. 'Proves you are an astute observer. And I could do a lot better than that if I wanted to.'

At the far end of the table a charade was taking place. To cover his confusion Warner was opening files, pretending to consult with Tolliver. The door opened and Palfry walked in holding a large tray with chinaware and a cafetière. He distributed the cups and saucers while Mrs Carson carried another tray to the other end of the table. Palfry placed his last item close to Eva.

'The cafetière,' he said.

'I do know what it is,' she replied without looking at him.

They drank coffee and then talked some more. After a while Warner called out in a far more civilized voice.

'So, we are agreed?'

'Agreed that we continue taking the precautions already put in train,' Tweed said firmly. 'Are Special Branch officers in their camel-hair coats patrolling prominently? Outside Buckingham Palace, St Paul's, Canary Wharf – and in force along the Thames embankment?'

'Your general suggestions have been followed,' Warner replied. 'I think we have now covered everything.'

'We have.' Tweed jumped up. 'Thank you for your hospitality and now we will leave.'

Palfry hurried down the room to unlock the door. As Paula walked out with Eva, Beaurain and Newman followed, Warner strode down the room, plucked at Tweed's sleeve.

'A word with you in private, please, Mr Tweed.'

'You go down to the car,' Tweed called out to his team. 'I will follow in a minute.'

261

Warner, his expression grave, closed the door. His manner towards Tweed was now polite, even respectful.

'There is a most worrying problem you should know about. In my organization there is a traitor. A top secret file has been stolen. Contains names of al-Qa'eda suspects now held at Dover.'

'Any idea who it might be?'

'None at all. It's most disturbing. Better go now.'

Tweed opened the door and nearly bumped into Eva, who was just outside. She appeared to be studying a file. She looked up and smiled.

'I'll escort you to the elevator.'

'No need, thank you. I know the way by now.'

He shook hands with Warner then walked slowly to the elevator. Before pressing the button he glanced back down the corridor, sensing someone was there. Twenty yards away Eva stood, watching him. She tucked the file under her arm and waved. Tweed waved back, pressed the button, the doors opened.

Afterwards he could not remember stepping into the elevator or riding down in it. He stood by himself, his face fixed as though in stone. Could it be possible? Later he couldn't even remember stepping out of the elevator.

Could it be possible?

32

Arriving back at Park Crescent in drizzling rain, they were surprised to see Buchanan's unmarked police car parked near their entrance. Tweed hurried up to his office, followed by Paula, Beaurain and Newman. Buchanan stood up, smiling.

'Well, how did the great war conference go?'

'Waste of time,' Beaurain told him. 'If Warner is typical of your ministers, they're almost as bad as those in Brussels.'

'Don't agree with you, Jules,' Tweed said. 'I found it most illuminating. Provide more links in the chain I'm building up. Trouble is vital links are missing. Do sit everyone.'

Paula realized he wasn't going to enlighten them. Not to be cryptic but because he hadn't decided whether he was right yet.

'What brings you here, Roy?' Tweed asked.

'We have a witness. You remember calling me about those five missing milk tankers? I did take notice. A few days ago I told Warden to call all the radio stations in the Midlands to ask them if anyone who had information would get in touch – information about the missing tankers. One alert lady phoned one station and they informed the locals who, in turn called me. A Mrs Sharp had phoned. I got her number, called her and asked her if she'd come to London to the Yard. Expenses would be paid. Hearing from the Yard excited her and she arrived this morning. After listening to her I brought her over here. She's waiting in that room facing your guard.'

'Monica, ask her to come up,' Tweed ordered.

'Here we go,' said Marler, standing near Paula's desk.

The door was opened by George, the guard, who stood aside and ushered in Mrs Sharp. In her sixties, tall, slim and smartly dressed, her white hair was elegantly coiffeured. Tweed went to meet her, extending his hand.

'We do appreciate your making this journey. Have you come a long way?'

'I live in the village of Gifford, near Milton Keynes, but in the country.'

She saw Buchanan, also standing, walk over to a wall map of England. She joined him. Her firm index fingers pointed to Gifford. Buchanan circled it with a red pen.

'Oldhurst Farm,' she went on, 'is here. It's been abandoned for years. The farmer went bankrupt. It has two huge barns, a smaller one, near the farmhouse and is approached down a neglected lane.'

Buchanan made another red circle. Tweed then asked her to sit in one of the armchairs facing his desk.

'I think Mrs Sharp should tell you her story as she told it to me,' Buchanan suggested.

'Then we'll get it right,' she said with a wicked smile at Buchanan.

She struck Tweed as very well educated, her voice decisive and crisp. A woman of considerable intelligence. He gave her his full attention.

'It would be three nights ago,' she began. 'I hope I have got *that* right. I've been so busy. At three in the morning I was driving back home down the road past Oldhurst Farm. I had been to see my sister who was unwell. Now recovered. As I reached the corner just before the entrance to the farm – I was driving slowly – I was startled to see a large milk tanker turn down that lane . . .'

'Any name on it?' asked Tweed.

'If there was I didn't see it. You see I was just in time to see it turning in. I was worried. I immediately thought of the remote farm used years ago by the Great Train robbers. So I waited, kept my engine ticking over. Then a few minutes later a small white van drove out. I did see the wording on its side. Florist.'

'An old van?'

'No, brand new. Luckily it turned in the opposite direction from where I waited . . .'

'Direction south-east, towards London,' Buchanan interjected. 'And the M1 is not so far away. Would take the van into the heart of London. Sorry to interrupt, Mrs Sharp.'

'That's all right. I'm getting the impression this could be important. On the way down in the train I read Drew Franklin's gossip column. Always do. He's malicious about people, I know, but so entertaining. Now, I think I've told you all I can so . . .'

'So,' said Tweed, standing up, 'have you ever had tea at Brown's Hotel? It is an experience you won't find elsewhere.'

'No, I haven't. Oh, one more thing. I mentioned the three, no, the *two* large barns at Oldhurst Farm. There is a third, smaller barn behind them. Think I mentioned it.'

'Marler,' said Tweed, 'would you be good enough to escort Mrs Sharp for tea at Brown's?' He glanced at his watch, was appalled to see it was afternoon. 'They'll have started serving by the time you get there.'

'I'm going to enjoy this,' said Marler with one of his rare warming smiles. 'Afterwards I can drive you to the station to take you back. No, it's no trouble at all.'

'No trouble indeed,' agreed Tweed. 'Mrs Sharp, have you told anyone else about this except Superintendent Buchanan?'

'Absolutely no one. When I was asked to phone the

Yard I knew it could be serious. You can rely on me to keep quiet. I'll even resist the temptation to tell my sister . . .'

Tweed thanked her again, escorted her to the door, followed by Marler. Before descending the stairs she turned, smiled at Tweed.

'What a nice lady,' Paula commented.

'Shrewd too. What was that reference to Drew Franklin's column about?'

Newman handed over the copy of the *Daily Nation* he had been skip-reading after she'd made her remark. He had ringed a paragraph.

Tweed began reading it, frowning as he read it once more.

A large force of al-Qa'eda have come to town. Their purpose? To launch a devastating attack on the capital, an attack which will make September 11 look like a skirmish. As usual our security chums are in a panic. Just possible the SIS will save the day – and London. They are near professionals.

'Typically,' Tweed commented, 'dear Drew compliments us, then takes a swipe at us. Near professionals.' He looked round the room. 'But this is going to drive Victor Warner mad. He can't retaliate – the Ministry of Security is not specifically mentioned.'

He passed the paper to Paula, who had left her desk and was itching to read the paragraph. Tweed handed the paper to her, then looked at Buchanan.

'Mrs Sharp. Perfect name for the lady. Are you acting on what she told us?'

'Excuse me!' Buchanan was indignant. 'Before I left the Yard I instructed Warden to check out Oldhurst Farm immediately. He's got a marked map like the one I used here. He's taking three patrol cars full of armed men. Strict

266

instructions from me not to use sirens or lights when they're near the place.'

'They'll find the place empty,' Tweed predicted, 'but they may find clues.'

'Manchester,' Newman said suddenly. 'Had a quiet word with Marler while you were talking to Mrs Sharp. 'As you know, he had been out trawling every inform- ant he could find. When he asked the top-flight ones they told him the word on the grapevine was that al- Qa'eda is gearing itself up for some tremendous operation on London. Only two second-raters said the target was Manchester – both suspects I'm sure are fed by Special Branch. Manchester!'

'Decoy,' said Beaurain.

'Smokescreen,' agreed Tweed. 'It's getting dark already. I think now Jules, Paula and Bob should come with me on a tour of London. As with Mrs Sharp, we got lucky. Now we need one more piece of luck.' He took out an evidence envelope from his pocket. It contained the simple drawing the poor mutilated Eddie had clutched in his dead hand in Monk's Alley. He called out to Paula, who was reading Franklin's column for the third time.

'Come and look at this again.'

Without taking it out of the protective envelope, he smoothed out the drawing. He shrugged in frustration.

'What *does* this remind you of?'

'A canoe.'

'I see. And their weapons will be paddles.'

'You did ask me,' she snapped.

The phone rang. Monica answered, nodded to the phone on Tweed's desk. 'It's Harry calling on his mobile.'

'Another emergency? Tweed here, Harry.'

'Just to report all's well so far with my patient. He stays in all the time, eats at the place. I got him a batch of paperback thrillers. He never stops reading them.'

'Thanks for calling . . .' Tweed turned to the others.

'That was Harry reporting that everything is quiet where Billy is cloistered in his new hotel.'

'I have an idea,' Buchanan said. 'From what you've told me about Billy Hogarth he's trustworthy. I'll send Jean to question him, see if he has seen anything unusual up at the village.'

'Jean?' Newman queried.

'A clever and attractive policewoman. He might feel more comfortable with her.' He took the card Tweed gave him with the hotel's address.

'Just so long as he doesn't get too comfortable with her,' Newman remarked with a straight face.

'Time we prowled London after dark, looking for canoes,' Tweed decided.

He ignored the dirty look Paula gave him.

Beaurain, who had earlier been studying a detailed map of central London, drove them. Alongside him sat Paula, while Tweed and Newman occupied the rear seats. He had his headlights on full beam. Paula soon realized he was heading south-west.

They eventually emerged on to a main road and he turned east. The traffic was heavy. Beaurain was leaning forward over the wheel, his gaze turned to his right. Signalling, he suddenly swung right off the main thoroughfare on to a wide, badly made track.

They quickly left the main capital behind, bumping over potholes as they were driven slowly through a wilderness. An area which had never been developed, with scrubby fields on either side. No buildings, and the fields were littered with rubbish a short distance back from the track – abandoned and rusty wrecks of cars, old metal buckets, a mix of rubbish which showed up in their headlights as Beaurain turned the car round corners.

'Why on earth are we going down here?' grumbled Newman.

'Leave him alone,' chided Paula.

She had sensed that Beaurain had an instinct for exploring the most unlikely locations. He was driving very slowly now, his eyes scanning left and right. He crawled round another corner, the track straigthened. He stopped. Ahead a woman was walking her poodle on the scrubby grass.

'We're still well upriver from the Albert Bridge,' Tweed complained.

'Do keep quiet,' Paula snapped. 'Please,' she added.

Beaurain switched off the engine, climbed out, walked towards the woman. She was well-dressed, in an expensive raincoat and leather boots. Still holding the white poodle on its leash, she turned as Beaurain approached her. Tweed had also got out, following Paula who was near the Belgian. With a snort Newman left the car.

'Excuse me,' Beaurain said as he bent down and stroked the small dog, 'we are searching for some rather dangerous men. Have you seen anything odd going on round here?'

Tweed backed up Beaurain by shining his flashlight on his identity folder which he held open for her to see.

'SIS,' she exclaimed. 'I read about you in Drew Franklin's column this morning. He's witty, but sometimes he goes too far. No need for that last remark.' She turned back to Beaurain. 'Excuse me, I must answer your question. I come here because it's quiet to walk the dog. Earlier, when it was dusk. Down there . . .' she pointed further down the track '. . . peculiar-looking workmen were carrying something heavy and cumbersome out of a white van. The men have gone but it's still there. You can see now the moon's come out.'

They all stared down the track. Perched broadside on was a small white van. Across its side one word was inscribed. *Florist.*

'My God!' Newman whispered under his breath.

'Can you describe this heavy and cumbersome object?' Beaurain asked.

269

'Do my best. It was shaped like a fat shell, much wider in diameter than an ordinary shell. My departed husband was an officer in the Artillery, so I've seen real shells. In other ways it looked like a vertical torpedo, hunched down in the metal platform which supported it. It took six men to carry it to a large motorized trolley, then they secured it with. Afterwards it was driven off further down the track. I was scared stiff they'd see me. I knew something was wrong. I froze still, worried that any movement would catch their attention. I had Pooh on a tight leash, so he kept quiet then.'

'Then?' queried Beaurain.

'All the workmen had disappeared with the trolley except one large man. He turned round and saw me, began to walk towards me. Pooh started growling and snarling. He can make a lot of noise for a little fellow. The large man stopped, obviously changed his mind, went behind that van and must have got on his motor-cycle. He reappeared and it roared off with him over that field to our left. Funny that they left the van.'

'This would be about an hour ago – when you first walked down here?'

'Yes, it would be. You don't know who I am. Mrs Wharton. My address is . . . About an hour's walk from here.'

'Jules Beaurain. One more question. What is there further down this track?'

'Eventually you come to the Thames. That new building you can see in the distance is a powerhouse they finished several months ago. Coal-fired to save money. It's on the other side of the river. It serves a plant which makes some kind of advanced equipment. Something we could do without, I'm sure.'

'Mrs Wharton, I cannot thank you enough for the information you have given us,' said Beaurain. 'Could I ask you on no account to mention this to anyone else in the world?'

'Top secret. I know. I promise you I won't tell a soul. My husband's work was classified and I've learnt to keep my mouth shut. Now, if that's all, I think I should go home.'

'We could squeeze you into our car and drive you there.'

'Thank you, but I like walking. So does Pooh. He can walk miles and miles. I wish you luck with your project.'

'We may just have had the luck we needed from you,' Tweed assured her, holding out his hand and smiling.

Tweed borrowed Newman's mobile and called Buchanan, who had left Park Crescent when they did. He phrased what he said carefully. Buchanan said he was coming out with a special team immediately. Beaurain waved to say something.

'Tell him I'll park your blue Audi at the entrance to this track, otherwise he'll miss it . . .'

They drove back the way they had come in silence for a shirt while. Then Paula couldn't resist turning round to speak to Newman.

'Well, Bob, in future maybe you'll have more faith in Jules's instincts.'

'Yes. Jules, how the devil did you decide to come down this way?'

'Observation. Before we reached the entrance I'd noticed on the main road a series of oil leaks. They were particularly noticeable at the entrance to this track. Beyond it on the main road they ceased.'

'I'll eat my hat,' Newman responded.

'Since you don't wear one,' Paula told him, 'I'll be sure to buy you one tomorrow.'

They had parked at the entrance to the track for only a few minutes when a patrol car came racing down the main road, siren screaming, lights flashing. It stopped. Behind it came a car with Buchanan at the wheel and behind him a large truck carrying specialized equipment.

271

Beaurain backed, swung his car on to the scrubby field, the convoy drove in and passed down the track. They got a brief wave from Buchanan.

'Now proceed to the right,' Tweed ordered. 'I want to check whether Warner has Special Branch patrols along the embankment as I suggested . . .'

Again it was a crawl in dense traffic. They passed the Albert Bridge and Beaurain gazed fixedly at it while waiting for a chance to drive on. Paula noticed the intensity of his gaze.

'What is it?' she asked.

'Always like this?' he asked.

'Always,' Tweed called out. 'Rush hour. Not a thing moving on the bridge. Bumper to bumper. It's 5.30 p.m . . .'

They drove on, past Chelsea Bridge, Vauxhall Bridge, Lambeth Bridge and reached Westminster Bridge. All of them were packed solid with motionless traffic. And each time Beaurain gazed at the crush with his fixed stare.

'Now,' said Tweed, sitting up right, 'keep your eyes open for men strolling along in camel-hair overcoats.'

'The Special Branch patrol,' Paula commented.

They reached Blackfriars Bridge and hadn't seen one man in a camel-hair coat. Once again they were stationary, locked in the floodtide of traffic. Paula twisted round to look at Tweed. His expression was grim.

'You're not pleased,' she said.

'Not a single Special Branch man patrolling the embankment. Warner has deliberately ignored one of my key requests. I know why. He'll have a number outside Buckingham Palace. Now we'll check St Paul's. My guess is there'll be a flock of them there.'

'It's Warner asserting a little authority, trying to show he still counts,' she remarked.

Tweed didn't reply. The traffic was about to get moving again. Newman leaned forward, called out to Beaurain.

'I'll navigate from here, get you to St Paul's.'

'When I can I go up Ludgate Hill. I did study the map,' the Belgian said quietly.

Paula twisted round again, gave Newman a certain look. He raised both hands in a gesture of resignation.

'I do realize I have become surplus to requirements.'

When they approached St Paul's, Tweed counted six men in the camel-hair overcoats. Three at the top of the steps, watching visitors as they entered. Three more apparently drifting round in the street below. He grunted.

'He's probably got half-a-dozen inside the place. So he had plenty to patrol the embankment. You were right, Paula. He's demonstrating he is still Minister. Might as well get back to Park Crescent, Jules. Wonder what's waiting for us there?'

Martin Hogarth was waiting for them. George told Tweed he had put him in the waiting-room, that he had protested fiercely about being locked in.

'I would like to arrive back once and find no one waiting for me,' Tweed remarked. 'Give us a few minutes to settle in, then send him up. But escort him like an unwanted guest, which he is . . .'

Tweed had just settled himself behind his desk. Marler was leaning against a wall. Pete Nield was seated in one of the armchairs. Beaurain sat in a hard chair in front of Paula's desk. The door opened and George ushered in their visitor.

Martin Hogarth stormed in, his face very red. He glared round at everyone, then plonked himself in the other armchair in front of Tweed's desk, without being asked.

'Where have you got my brother Billy imprisoned?' he yelled.

'Calm down,' Tweed said, clasping his hands together.

His suggestion only added petrol to the flames. Martin had trouble getting the words out. Then he shouted.

273

'You have kidnapped him. I'll inform the police, get myself a lawyer.'

'How did you find this address?' Tweed asked quietly.

'I've a friend who knows the kidnap business. He said you ran a business negotiating the release of rich people who had been grabbed. Gave me this address. And I thought you were SIS. But you have a bloody plate outside – General & Cumbria Assurance. The Minister, whom by the way, I happen to know, will be interested to hear you impersonated the SIS.'

'You could always complain to him. His Ministry is in Whitehall. Martin, why are you so worked up? I'm sure you have not yet told us your real motive.'

'What . . . do you mean?' Martin's mood had changed. He was now on the defensive. 'Real motive,' he sneered.

'What is it?' Tweed leaned forward. 'Better tell me now.'

'Tell you what?'

The change in Martin's mood under pressure from Tweed was startling. The raging accuser had become a frightened man. Unsure of how to handle the situation. Tweed gave him no time to recover.

'Your real motive. Money, isn't it?'

'Money . . .'

'Collecting the huge sums from Carpford sent abroad – then returned here.'

'Huge sums . . .'

'Thousands of pounds. So bulky they may have to con-vert them into Swiss francs. The Swiss have one-thousand-franc banknotes. Pecksniff was the link – he checked them when you brought the huge sums to him.'

'How did you . . .'

'How did I know?' Tweed finished for him. 'I have a lot of professionals digging up information, interrogating people. Including Pecksniff.'

'I want to leave,' Martin protested feebly.

Newman stood behind him, looming over Martin. His tone was savage.

'You can answer Tweed – or you can leave here. In handcuffs when Superintendent Buchanan and his men come to pick you up. They are not so gentle at the Yard as we are. So answer Tweed's question or I'll bloody well call the Yard now.'

'Pecksniff was working on behalf of al-Qu'eda when he arranged for you to fly abroad to pick up the money,' Tweed snapped.

'I had no idea Pecksniff was working for them . . .'

He had slipped up badly. First, he had not asked who Pecksniff was when Tweed used the name. Second, he had now admitted he had had dealings with the Dickensian solicitor. Paula was fascinated by the way Tweed had, with flashes of inspiration, led Martin into the trap. Monica mouthed the word 'coffee' and pointed at Martin's back. Tweed shook his head. Nothing must disturb the mood.

'Well, now you know he was working for them,' Tweed continued. 'So you might as well tell us the huge amounts you brought over from the Bahamas trips you made.'

'Bahamas . . .'

'Get on with it, for heaven's sake. I'm losing patience.'

The phone rang. Monica answered, beckoned to Newman, who went to her desk. He kept his voice low.

'Newman here. Who might this be?'

'Recognize your voice. Rick Pendleton here, your friendly bank director in the Bahamas. Just got back from a great holiday. Mexico. What's your query?'

'I desperately need to know who has collected the money sent to you from Aruba. The New Age Development Corp. I know you don't like revealing details of accounts. Keep this under your hat. London is facing an imminent catastrophic attack from al-Qa'eda. That New Age money financed it. Who was the courier who collected the money – maybe made several trips?'

'Jesus! Hang on while I check. I remember the guy. The sums were so large it came over to me. Hold the line . . .'

The door opened and Marler strolled in. Tweed reacted instantly.

'The Yard reacted very swiftly. This is the gentleman you may be taking away for intensive interrogation.'

Marler caught on immediately. He laid a strong hand on Martin's right shoulder.

'I'll cuff you when we're ready to leave.'

Martin looked up, stared into Marler's face, wearing its bleakest expression.

'You still there, Bob?' Pendleton's voice, speaking quietly, came back on Newman's line. 'Good. Three visits by a Martin Hogarth. October 15th 2001, November 20th 2001, January 10th 2002. Amounts drawn in sequence. £250,000. £750,000. One mil. Total, two million. All converted into Swiss francs. I wish you all luck in bringing down the bastards . . .'

Newman rewrote the figures he had scribbled down on a pad he'd been given by Monica. Tweed would now have no trouble in reading the data. The phone rang again, Monica answered, handed the phone to Newman.

'Newman here. Who is it?'

'Your friendly bank director again. Sorry, but I double-checked, found two sheets had stuck together. Third and last amount given to Martin Hogarth should be four mil. So total is now five million. He had the authorized documents from Gerald Hanover.'

'Any idea where that guy is?'

'No. We should worry. With commission like that. *Adios!*'

Newman quickly changed the two figures, underlining *total is five million pounds, converted into Swiss francs*. Then he beckoned to Tweed.

'Don't move an eyelash,' Tweed warned.

Marler again rested a hand on Martin's shoulder. Tweed took the sheet, raised his eyebrows. He memorized the

276

data in a few seconds, folded the sheet and went back to his desk.

'That was Superintendent Buchanan,' Newman called out loudly. 'He's getting impatient to see the prisoner.'

Seated back behind his desk, Tweed studied the man opposite for a short time. Martin Hogarth was a broken man. His face had lost what little colour it had had when he stormed into the office. His hands were twisting, couldn't keep them still.

'Pecksniff checked each tranche of money in front of you,' he began. 'Right?'

'Yes . . .' Martin was croaking hoarsely. 'He unlocked the small case I gave him after I'd given him the key. Then he took out the Swiss banknotes stack by stack, counted them aloud. Now, I'd originally answered Pecksniff's first call to Carpford inviting me to visit his office . . .'

'You made three trips to New York. Each time you had a first-class return ticket to the Bahamas. I imagine that way you avoided the long slog through Customs and Passport Control. You simply moved to transfer, caught the flight to the Bahamas.'

'Yes.' Martin looked taken aback. 'How do you know that?'

'I'm asking the questions. How much money? On each trip?'

'£250,000 first trip. £750,00 second trip. Four million pounds on the last one. Altogether five million pounds, all converted into Swiss francs.'

'You must have had a bad time arriving back at Heathrow.'

'I was careful to be about two-thirds the way along the queue. Each time. All three aircraft were crowded. When I reached the counter I plonked down the smaller case with the key on top. Then I quickly hauled up a huge case full of rubbish presents. They ignored the small case, then went through the big job as though looking for drugs. It worked on each trip.'

'And Mr Pecksniff paid you how much for your trouble?'

'Do I have to tell you?'

'You do.'

'Fifty thousand pounds in Swiss francs. I'm not a rich man . . .'

'Of course you're not. But I'm sure you've got a lot more. You have a Rolex on your wrist, a diamond pin in your tie. Get to hell out of here.'

'What?'

'He's telling you that you can go now,' Paula called out.

As soon as the door closed on Martin's frantic departure Tweed nodded to Marler.

'Follow him. Where he goes. Anyone he contacts.'

'I'm on my way. Keep in touch with reports on my mobile.'

      ★   ★   ★

'Is that Ali?'

'Yes, it is.'

Ali had one hand on the loose phone-box door, which the wind kept blowing open.

'Abdullah here. You have a photo of Martin Hogarth, along with the others photographed at Carpford?'

'I have. In my pocket.'

'Send your best man immediately to SIS HQ at Park Crescent. Martin Hogarth has just left the building.'

'I have a good man watching that place.'

'Then tell him to kill Martin Hogarth. Urgently . . .'

33

Tweed sat behind his desk, tapping his pen. Paula knew he was bothered by something. When he continued tapping the pen, gazing at the closed blind which masked the distant view of Regent's Park, she felt sure.

'What's disturbing you?' she asked.

'I'm thinking of phoning the Minister and demanding to know why there are no Special Branch men on the embankment.'

'Don't! You were right before. You decided not to arouse any resentment. Let sleeping dogs lie.'

'I suppose you are right. I won't call him.'

Beaurain was pacing the office, restless, while Newman sat at ease, reading the *Daily Nation*. Beaurain put on his coat and Tweed looked up.

'Going somewhere?'

'I feel it would be wiser if we checked that embankment again. I can tell you're in two minds whether to contact Warner or not. You'd look silly if there are camel-hair coats patrolling now.'

'I'll come with you,' said Paula.

'Restless people,' Tweed commented.

'Yes,' snapped Paula, 'we're all restless, expecting something terrible to happen and no idea what it is, where it will take place. Jules, let's get out of this claustrophobic atmosphere.'

It had stopped drizzling and was icily cold as they reached

her car. Beaurain asked if he could drive again and she agreed. He headed straight down Whitehall for Westminster Bridge. Traffic was still very heavy but he drove with great skill, slipping through gaps.

As he turned left along the embankment he noticed cars were still slow-moving on the bridge. He turned to Paula with a smile, nodding towards the bridge.

'Does it go on like this much longer?'

'It can start in the late afternoon with people trying to beat the rush. Then it can go on until nearly eight. It gets worse day by day.'

'Who would be a commuter?'

'Not me.'

Glancing at him, she saw his penetrating gaze was focused on the embankment walk by the river. She started studying the same area. They had driven a short distance when she let out a gasp.

'Look. That's Martin Hogarth walking along the embankment, away from us. I recognize his walk, his clothes. So where the devil is Marler? He's suppose to be following him.'

'If you can see Marler he's doing a bad job. He'll be nearby. Marler impresses me.'

'Don't see him anywhere . . .'

A dozen yards behind Hogarth a businessman was walking in the same direction. He wore the conventional City outfit. A black jacket and black trousers. His head was protected with a black hat and he was carrying a bulky briefcase.

'That's the "uniform" the City gent wears these days,' Paula explained to Beaurain. 'Black suit, which I think looks so dreary, and the fat briefcase to emphasize how important and busy he is. Hundreds of them dress just like that. At one time they wore a variety of smart suits, now this ghastly outfit.'

A large barge was proceeding upriver. It was laden almost

to the gunwales with powdered black coal. A distance behind it was another big barge, also carrying coal. Beaurain stared at them as Paula enlightened him.

'My guess is they're headed for that new power station the lady with Pooh told us about. The tide is coming in but it will rise much higher during the next two days.'

'First I've seen since leaving Belgium. They ply the river near Liège. Much smaller jobs than those.'

'Still no sign of camel-hair coat types,' she said. 'That fool of a Minister is just asserting his authority.'

'Hogarth is still plodding along the promenade,' said the Belgian, glancing in his rear-view mirror. 'Wonder where he's going? It's a cold night to be out.'

'Marler will find out,' she said confidently.

'Do you know how to get us to the East End? I'm looking for a pub where the locals gather.'

'I'll guide you.'

She would like to have asked what Beaurain had in mind but she desisted from speaking. He always seemed to know what he was doing.

Marler, the businessman, was still following Hogarth. Earlier his quarry had gone into a pub for a drink. Marler had slipped into the pub's cloakroom, locking himself in a cubicle. Opening the briefcase, he had taken out the crease free black suit. Marler could change in less than a minute. Stuffing the clothes he'd been wearing into the briefcase, he walked back into the crowded pub, ordered a beer. Hogarth was still drinking further down the bar. When Hogarth left, heading for the embankment, Marler, the businessman, walking in a different way from his usual stride, took up a position twenty yards behind him, his eyes everywhere.

Halfway along the embankment Hogarth crossed the road when the lights were in his favour. On the far side he plunged uphill into a maze of quiet streets. Marler crossed before the green light changed at the pedestrian crossing.

After the muted roar of the traffic it was very silent and dark. Very few street lights, and those there were at long intervals. A walk in the shadows up the narrow climbing street. Heading for the Strand, Marler decided. He transferred his briefcase to his left hand. Something about this area away from the world he didn't like. He walked faster, his rubber-soled shoes making no sound as he got closer to Hogarth.

His quarry turned another corner, slowing down as he went on up the steep hill. Marler heard a vehicle crawling up the street behind him. He dodged up some steps into an entrance alcove. He waited.

A cab crept round the corner. No light up, showing he could not take a fare. No passenger in the back. The window on the far side from the driver open. Marler couldn't see the number-plate but felt sure it was the same cab he'd passed earlier, parked just beyond the end of Park Crescent.

The driver had his cabbie's cap pulled well down, increased speed a little. Marler ran after it. Round the corner Hogarth was still plodding uphill. Marler arrived as the cab stopped alongside Hogarth. Hogarth had paused, tired by his exertions.

Marler raised the Walther he held in his right hand. The cab driver was aiming a gun point-blank at Hogarth. Marler fired one shot. The driver sagged, his hand losing his grip on his gun. Hogarth, who had looked at the driver when he stopped, was terrified.

'You!' he said, recognizing Marler.

'Keep quiet. Sit on those steps.'

'He was going to . . .'

'Shut up, for God's sake. Sit!'

Marler slipped gloves on to his hands after sliding the Walther back inside his hip holster. While Hogarth sank on the steps, Marler opened the cab's front door. His single bullet had struck the hitman in the chest and blood covered his jacket.

Avoiding any contact with the blood of the dead man, Marler searched his pockets. Nothing to identify him. Figured – with a professional. He left the killer's automatic on the floor, used a folded coat by the side of the seat to cover the blood-soaked corpse's front, climbed out, shut the door. Then he grabbed Martin by the arm.

'Now we're walking back down the way you came. We get out of here fast. On your feet!'

He hustled Martin back towards the embankment. With his hand gripping Hogarth's arm, he was half-carrying him. As they walked he gave his captive instructions.

'Did you drive in from Carpford? You did. So where is your car parked?'

'In a multi-storey near Baker Street . . .'

'I'm taking you there. You will then drive straight back to Carpford and sit tight inside your bungalow. Have you any weapons in the place?'

'A shotgun. Use it to shoot rabbits . . .'

'Keep it by your bed when you go to sleep. Make sure everything is locked up. If there's an alarm, call Tweed at the number for General & Cumbria Assurance. *Do not return to London.*'

'Where is Billy?'

'In a safe place, I have been told. Two hitmen attempted to kill him but they were thwarted. Billy is all right . . .'

They had reached the embankment. Marler flagged down a cab. As they climbed inside he whispered his last instruction.

'Give the cabbie the address of that multi-storey car park.'

At Park Crescent Tweed was making notes, writing down a list of suspects. He was trying to link them up. Newman looked up from reading the *Daily Nation*.

283

'This is the weirdest obituary I've ever read. A Captain Charles Hobart. The weird thing is he died – was killed – almost two years ago. The MoD must have put a D notice on it. First time in history.'

He handed the paper to Tweed. Sighing, Tweed pushed his note book aside, spread the page out, read it carefully.

Captain Charles Hobart served with a well-known regiment. He soon developed the reputation of being a maverick, a quality overlooked by his superiors since he always proved to be right in his unorthodox views and behaviour. It is rumoured he worked closely with an Intelligence officer. Popular with his men – unusual for a maverick – he trapped large numbers of enemy troops. Serving in Yemen, nearly two years ago, he left his headquarters to locate another body of the enemy. He walked into an ambush and was killed instantly. There were rumours that he had been betrayed – vehemently denied by the MoD. There are still soldiers who insist he *must* have been betrayed by someone holding authority.

Tweed studied the photograph of Hobart in uniform. A handsome-looking man with shrewd eyes, he wore an Arab head-dress.

'Sounds like a minor Lawrence of Arabia,' he commented. 'It also sounds as though the MoD really clamped down on this one. I've always regarded them as a bunch of crooks, their first priority being to cover themselves . . .'

He looked up as Marler entered the office. Wiping his hands, as though rid of something unpleasant, he leant against a wall.

'That's got rid of Martin Hogarth . . .'

He gave them a terse account of the incident, as he

284

called it, near the embankment. Tweed listened until he had completed his account, then jumped in.

'That Walther used to kill the hitman. Are you still carrying it?'

'Of course not. The police have a very good Ballistics Department. So I went into the basement before I came up here. Gave them the Walther, watched while they crushed it with their machine into nothing. The remnants are now on their way to our training mansion in Surrey for total disposal. I also collected this from their weapons store.' He produced a Walther.

'Not brand new?' Tweed checked.

'Does it look it? They worked on it while I watched. Looks just like the one I carried for months.'

'The police will find the body,' Tweed explained. 'So just in case someone saw you on the embankment – a patrol car with an officer who knows you – what were you doing down there?'

'What you asked me to. Checking for Special Branch men. Not a single one.'

'You said the hitman cab driver was originally parked near the end of the Crescent here. Wake up, Newman. Those two new men who may join us – Wilson and Walker, the twins. They are still along the road at our Communications Branch learning discreet ways of communicating?'

'They are,' Newman agreed.

'Get along there now. Instruct them to patrol the area outside, looking for anyone watching this building. I wonder what on earth has happened to Paula and Jules?'

'Charming district,' Beaurain commented. 'Streets hardly wider than alleys, not a coat of paint for years on these shabby buildings. And women clearing stuff off stalls, then folding the stalls up. At this hour, in this cold. Who on earth would be out buying in this cold?'

'This is Wapping,' Paula told him, amused. 'Deep in the

285

East End, which is what you wanted. As to the stalls, men who work the river get back late and buy on their way home. I thought this is what you wanted.'

'It is. And there's a pub. The Pig's Snout. So tasteful, but it's the sort of place I want to go into. I can't leave you in the car but, taking you in there . . .'

She punched him on the shoulder. 'Stop being so protective. I've been in worse places than that.'

'Where do I park? Safely?'

He was looking at a gang of boys, ages from ten to sixteen, Paula estimated. They were quite well-dressed but they were watching him as he parked, his front tyres squelching over discarded fish. He turned away from them, took out his wallet, extracted three five pound notes, shoved the wallet back, carefully buttoned up the pocket.

'You know what you're doing,' Paula said, surprised.

'Certain areas of Brussels, all Liège and Antwerp. I can sense where I am. Why that ten-pound note tucked in your glove? I'll be paying.'

'Jules, leave this to me.'

She got out, followed by Jules, who had run round the car to join her. The tallest, tough-looking lad, stood in her way, his bare hands on his hips. She showed him the ten-pound note which he reached out to grab. She snatched it out of reach.

'Whats your name?'

'Jem. What's yours?'

'I'm giving you this ten-pound note to make sure no one gets near this car. I've got one more tenner, then I'm out of cash. You get that if the car is untouched when we come out.'

'You're on, lady. Toffs come down 'ere to see 'ow the other 'alf lives. They leave without their wallets. Watch it in there. A redhair called Sammy.'

'It should be OK,' Beaurain said as they approached the pub.

'Any of them approach the car and Jem will smash them to pulp.'

It was crowded inside, a babble of voices, the air filled with smoke. Beaurain noted a number of the men wore oilcloth coats. Seamen. This was the right place. His arm round Paula, he shoved his way to the bar. He was so tall, his face so weathered, people let him through. He hoisted Paula on to a stool, sat on the one beside her. On his right sat a man wearing an oilcloth. He studied the bottles behind the bar.

'What's yours, mate?' a burly man asked.

'Have you any wine?' Paula asked.

'You look like Chardonnay. French. The good stuff.'

'My favourite drink.'

'Had it before?' the barman asked Paula, looking Beaurain up and down.

'I like to experiment.'

'Then you'll end up on the floor . . .'

The barman brought the drinks, took the notes Beaurain produced from his trouser pocket, slapped down the change, headed for another customer.

A red-haired lad pushed his way between Beaurain and the seaman. He had a cunning smile as he slapped down an envelope, grubby all over.

'Interesting photos. Girls doing different things. You'd never believe it.'

'Shove off.'

Beaurain swept the envelope off the bar on to the floor. It burst open, spilling lewd photos. Redhair swore, using filthy language.

'Shouldna 'ave done that.'

His hand reached inside his soiled windcheater, came out with a knife. Beaurain grabbed his wrist, twisted. Redhair let out a scream. Beaurain released his grip and the hand was limp, the wrist at an unnatural angle. Broken. The barman appeared, holding a large leather-covered sap. He leaned over the counter.

'Get out of 'ere, scumbag, before I break the other wrist.'

Redhair used his shoulder to push his way through the crowd, out of the pub. The seaman got off his stool, picked up the photos, crammed them inside the envelope, pushed it over the counter to the barman.

'Trash can.' He turned to Beaurain. 'You 'andled that well. He's dangerous.' He grinned. 'Was.'

'You're off the river?' Beaurain asked with a smile.

'That's right. I've worked freighters, ferries, barges, the lot.'

'I'm thinking of buying a barge for my business,' Beaurain continued. 'Saw what I need going upriver laden with coaldust.'

'They'd be goin' to the new powerhouse, other side of the river. Built by Dixon, Harrington and Mosley. We calls it the Dick powerhouse. Got a plant next to it for makin' machine tools. New design. And new design of barges. Made to order.'

'Could you do me a rough drawing of the design? Then I can get one for myself?'

Paula, who had sipped cautiously at her wine, surprised to find how good it was, pushed a fresh notebook along the counter to Beaurain. The seaman reached for it, took out a small stub of pencil, began drawing, talking as he worked.

'There's a sort of lid made of metal you can unroll to cover your cargo. From bow to stern. In the middle, 'ere, is a very big hatch you can open so a crane can lower bales into the 'old. A smaller hatch near both bow and stern. Like this. Control bridge is perched up at stern, of course. The skipper then 'as a good view of where 'e's goin', which is rather important.' He chuckled.

'Does the Dick director use the roll-over metal cover?'

'No. They needs as much coal as they can pile in.'

'Have I got this right?' Beaurain queried. 'Dick had both the powerhouse and the barges built?'

'Yes, 'e did. To keep down cost 'e gets a firm in Austria to build the barges. You could find out the name easy – name of the firm.'

'Austria makes sense. They have a lot of barge traffic on the Danube.'

'You're right there. I've taken barges all the way to the Black Sea.' He pushed the notebook with the barge plan over to Beaurain. 'Makes sense?' Beaurain nodded. 'I think the lady is interested,' the seaman said, pushing it further along the counter.

'Thank you,' said Paula. 'I'm Paula.'

'Never gave you my monniker. Sharkey.' He grinned, showing neat white teeth. 'Nothing personal. They call me Shark. On the river we've all got funny names. Got what you want? I'm not a dab hand at drawing.'

'The details you've given me are crystal clear. I see you like Black Jack.'

He ordered another one for Sharkey, his way of saying thanks. They touched tankards and Beaurain swallowed the little left in his glass.

'I was fortunate to sit next to you,' he remarked. 'Seeing as you've had all that experience with barges.'

'Not really. See that fat chap at that table by the wall with his mates? He's a bargee too. Good luck . . .'

As they walked outside Paula had a ten-pound note folded inside her fist. The gang of lads were still outside. One of them sat on the pavement, nursing a bloody nose. Jem appeared, his hand held out. She gave him the tenner.

'Thanks for looking after the car.'

'Good thing you hired me, 'e was goin' to use a coin to scratch your door.' He pointed towards the lad using a blood-stained handkerchief. 'Door's OK.'

'Oh dear,' said Paula.

'That's what you paid me for. Safe trip back to the smoke.'

Beaurain had to manoeuvre a three-point turn to go back the way they had come. He drove more quickly now the market stalls had been removed.

'What I'd like to have done now,' he said, 'was to visit Mrs Wharton, the lady who told us about those men carrying some kind of machine away on a motorized trolley. Down that track to nowhere. But we've no idea of her address.'

'Yes, we have.' Paula smiled, opened her shoulder-bag and extracted a small gilt-edged card from a side pocket. 'She gave me that on the quiet just before we left. 50 Upper Cheyne Lane. I could guide you there.'

'Do it. I want to persuade her to provide a drawing of that machine they put on the trolley. I'm a man for detail.'

'Where are we going with this?' she asked.

Looking at Beaurain, she saw his eyes were gleaming. He was excited about something.

'We're going to 50 Upper Cheyne Lane,' he replied, grinning at her. 'Calling at Park Crescent en route.'

She punched him gently on the arm. He was as bad as Tweed – wouldn't reveal what he was thinking until he knew he was right.

34

'Ali here . . .'

'Abdullah. Zero hour is close.'

'I know. We're on the site of the merger. We should be ready for the demonstration to our client.'

'The equipment is in position then?'

'We're at phase two. By tomorrow morning we'll be at phase three. Gives us a margin on timing of the demonstration.'

'The guard worries me. He knows his job?'

'He's ours. We know his wife too. A man followed the guard home yesterday. So Vince Proctor . . .'

'No names! So he is happy, knowing his wife has someone with her until he gets off his long spell of duty.'

'He is happy. His wife is happy. We are all happy.'

Abdullah once more slammed down the phone. Ali shrugged. He was getting used to it. He left the public phone-box and stepped into the heavy mist. He walked slowly back to the 'site'.

Inside a small terrace house in a side street in Balham, Mrs Proctor sat on a heavy chair in the kitchen. The chair had been brought from the parlour by the man who had earlier rung the bell, then forced his way in, holding a gun in one hand, the index finger of his other hand pressed to his lips.

She now sat with her wrists roped together, another rope

imprisoning her ankles. A third rope was tied round her waist and to the back of the chair. A pleasant red-faced woman in her fifties, she was terrified.

When her captor had arrived he'd worn a waterproof slouch hat, concealing his face, and a long raincoat. Since then, after tying up Mrs Proctor, he had removed the hat and the raincoat. He was now clad in a camouflage suit and she could see his complexion was brown, his hair trimmed short. He was an Egyptian and his name was Haydar. Information he had not provided Mrs Proctor with.

'We have Peter,' he'd said when she was tied to the chair. 'As long as you do nothing silly he will not come to any harm. Do something silly, like trying to warn a neighbour, and he will be shot.'

Saying which, he produced a photo of her husband seated in a chair. His hands were clasped tightly in his lap and his expression was tense. A hand, holding a gun to his head, also appeared in the photo.

'Oh, no,' Mrs Proctor had gasped. She swallowed. 'Where is he? At the power station? Who are you?'

'Questions,' Haydar explained quietly, 'come under the heading of being silly. I shall feed you, give you something to drink. Sit quiet and all will be well when we have moved the drugs hidden on one of the barges. You will then be free, your husband will be freed and will come home unharmed. He is in a safe place. Does anyone come here at night?'

'Sometimes Mrs Wilkinson from next door visits for a chat. Not every night.'

'What will Mrs Wilkinson do if you don't answer the door?'

'She'll think I'm having a nap and go away.'

'Then we have nothing to worry about,' Haydar went on lying.

The truth was Mrs Proctor would never leave the house alive. Once the operation was completed he would shoot her in the back of the head with his silenced gun. The same

292

fate awaited her husband, trapped inside Dick's power station.

Haydar would know when the operation was completed. He had turned on the small TV set screwed to the wall with the sound turned down but still showing a programme.

He had been told that when the operation had taken place all normal programmes would cease. *Breaking News* would start. As it had done in New York on September 11.

35

Buchanan walked briskly into Tweed's office and sat in the armchair facing him. Paula could sense he had a lot to report, but before he could open his mouth Tweed spoke with emphasis.

'I've just closed down City Airport. I sent the Controller a copy of the PM's directive by hand yesterday. Now I need you to despatch a squad of armed men to guard it. Urgently.'

He waited while Buchanan used his mobile to pass the order to the Yard. Closing his mobile, he looked at Tweed.

'In thirty minutes the squad will have arrived. In patrol cars, sirens screaming, lights flashing.'

'Thank you. Now for a confrontation. I'm calling the Minister to inform him of what I've done. He'll be pleased, don't you think?'

'No, I don't . . .'

Tweed first had to go through the usual channels when he called the Ministry in Whitehall. Palfry took the call, started to dither, to say the Minister was in Cabinet.

'Then get him out, for God's sake. Now! Go on, do it.'

Tweed hadn't long to wait. The haughty voice of Victor Warner shouted down the phone.

'Tweed, I was in a Cabinet meeting . . .'

'Gabble, gabble, gabble – then no decision taken. I know what goes on there. Now, *listen*, please. I'm calling to tell you I've just closed down City Airport . . .'

'You've done *what*? Why? I can see absolutely no reason . . .'

'I can. We have to guard against al-Qa'eda landing a large body of men there. In aircraft seized from private flying schools. Heaven knows there are enough of them scattered outside London.'

'I'm outraged. You should have consulted me . . .'

'I'm informing you now. Within minutes of the airport being shut down. Didn't you read the PM's mandate?'

'Tweed! I'm going straight back into Cabinet to report what you've just said. Including your gabble, gabble remark.'

'Please do. The PM has a sense of humour. Something I suspect you forget. Goodbye . . .'

'Sorry about that, Roy,' Tweed said to Buchanan. 'I sense you have news. My turn to listen.'

'I've been tearing round like a cat chasing its tail. But to some purpose. First, I flew with some of my specialists to an airfield near Oldhurst Farm. Mrs Sharp, the lady who travelled all the way down here to see me – then I sent her on to you – has all her wits about her. We found the lane leading to the abandoned farm. It does have two monster barns. Guess what we found inside. Two missing milk tankers parked side by side in one barn, two more tankers inside the second barn. Attached to the place where you get inside each of them was a cable with a handle – to haul up what was concealed inside!'

'Any trace of al-Qa'eda?'

'Do let me tell this in my own way,' Buchanan insisted. 'Inside the smaller barn Mrs Sharp mentioned – not so small – we found a pile of used sleeping-bags.' He paused. 'Thirty of them.'

'Thirty?'

'You look taken aback. Thirty sleeping bags – thirty men at least. They had cleaned up but we found this.'

Newman had been sitting in a hard-backed chair by Paula's desk. He had not spoken a word but he sat leaning

296

forward, watching Buchanan intently. His mouth compressed when he'd heard this but he made no comment.

Tweed examined the torn piece of cloth inside the evidence envelope handed to him. Then he beckoned to Newman who walked over, took the envelope. He pursed his lips, handed the envelope back to Tweed.

'I'd say that could have come off one of those black turbans worn by al-Qa'eda. Thirty is a powerful strike force.'

'That's my conclusion,' Buchanan agreed as Newman returned to his chair. 'We also found bits of food which I've sent for analysis. Bless Mrs Sharp. But there's more, down that track where we saw the white van and Mrs Wharton with Pooh.'

'How did you get there also in the time?'

'Flew back to City Airport.' Buchanan grinned. 'We must have landed just before you closed it down. Then waiting unmarked police cars took us to Mrs Wharton's bleak track. The white van is no longer there. Unfortunately a heavy mist was coming in off the river. We walked all the way down the track until we reached the Thames. There's a wide ramp leading to a long landing stage. Across the river, a bit further up it, we could just make out the new power station. Alongside it is a big wharf, Dick's wharf they call it.'

'See any trace of the enemy?'

'No, it was difficult. The mist was getting denser. I used night glasses but the result was a blur. I did see on either side of the wharf three huge barges moored.'

'You mean six barges altogether?'

'That's what I vaguely made out.'

'Any sign of activity at all?'

'None. Lights were on inside the power station, but you'd expect that.'

'I suggest we act at once,' Tweed said, standing up. 'You assemble a large force of heavily armed police, commandeer boats for us to cross . . .'

'Hold on. There were two big launches also moored to

297

the wharf. And you don't know London as well as I do,' he said grimly.

'What's the matter? You don't look happy about my suggestion.'

'But,' said Buchanan, looking at Newman, 'you might like to see this.' He produced from his pocket a map which he unfolded and spread out across Tweed's desk. It showed the district they had visited when they encountered Mrs Wharton and her poodle. Beaurain stood looking over Buchanan's shoulder as the superintendent used a pencil to trace the track's route to the river.

'With me?' he asked.

'So far, yes,' Tweed replied.

'This building on the other side is the Dick power station. Now look at the large building very close to the station. It is St Jude's Hospital. Over four hundred patients, overflow from the collapsing NHS. When Dixon, the owner of the power station development, called Dick by the river men, obtained permission to build he had to sign an agreement that any smoke from the station would pass into the most sophisticated filter system. Nothing escapes. You see the problem?'

'I do,' said Beaurain. 'If al-Qa'eda *have* taken control of the power station we can be sure they have a vast amount of high-explosives. If they see us coming they'll detonate those explosives. Can you imagine what they would do to that hospital? Over four hundred patients.'

'We can't risk it,' said Tweed grimly. 'We're checkmated.'

When Victor Warner returned to the Cabinet room he reported exactly what Tweed had said. To his great annoyance the PM *was* amused. He closed the folder on the table in front of him.

'Gentlemen, I think we ought to end this meeting now. No more gabble . . .'

Warner returned to his Ministry, fuming, a folder under his arm. He encountered Palfry just before entering his office.

'I'll complete this work at home. You do have my car ready for me, I presume . . .'

Arriving inside his penthouse, he walked straight into his large study. Eva was working at her own desk, decoding a signal as Warner plonked his file down on his own desk. Warner dragged a chair over and sat beside her. Clad in a black trouser suit, she sensed he was in a bad mood. She didn't feel at all prepared to put up with it. So his approach took her by surprise.

'When this crisis is all over I think we need a holiday.'

'Good idea. I'll be going off to France.'

'No you won't.' His strange mouth was twisted in a smile as though contemplating something pleasurable. 'Instead you'll be coming with me to Bermuda. How do you fancy that?'

He placed a hand on her forearm, squeezed it. She removed the predatory hand without looking at him.

'The Elbow Beach Hotel,' he coaxed. 'It's the height of luxury. Has an enormous swimming-pool. Two weeks.'

She gathered up her papers and the code-book. Standing up, she looked down at him, no expression on her face. She really is a beauty, he was thinking.

'I've booked for France,' she told him. 'They can take me whenever I phone them.'

'We can hire bicycles from the hotel,' he continued. 'Get away from cars for a change. Explore the scenic wonders.'

'I don't like cycling,' she replied.

'It's pretty flat. Not hard work. You glide along.'

'Sounds idyllic,' she said in an indifferent tone.

'You'll need new clothes. Just give me the bills and I'll cover the expense.'

'I'll have to think about it.'

'It's an expression of appreciation for how well you look

after me. You are a decoding genius. In Arabic too. Has the missing code message turned up?'

'I think they've sent a second copy as requested. It's on your desk. Since it's marked highly confidential I've left it for you to decode.'

'Damn embassy in Cairo is not very efficient. I'm going to complain to the Ambassador. Now, what we were talking about?'

'I'll have to think about it,' she repeated and left the room, closing the door quietly behind her.

Warner moved his chair back to his desk to deal with the message. He was smiling to himself. Women were all alike. They played hard to get. She would come round to his viewpoint.

36

No. 50 Upper Cheyne Lane was secreted inside a short cul-de-sac of small houses. As they drove in Paula quickly realized they were all conversions.

'They used to be garages,' she told Beaurain. 'Now they're nice little houses which probably cost a fortune. I think she must be at the end – even numbers on our right, odd ones on our left.'

Beaurain drove very slowly, bumping over the cobbled lane. He pulled up at the end where No. 50 was on the right. Two storeys high, the frontage was slim and painted white. The front door was blue. It was a neat, well-cared-for house.

Paula jumped out, followed by Beaurain, and pressed the brass doorbell, which gleamed. Inside they heard a dog start barking its head off. Paula smiled. Pooh was on guard. She pulled the collar of her windcheater up. It was almost dusk and the temperature was falling rapidly.

Mrs Wharton opened the door and Beaurain bent down to stroke Pooh who, recognizing them, stood up on his rear portion, with his front legs dangling. He was panting, hopefully with pleasure.

'Sorry to bother you,' Paula began. 'But Jules has something vital he needs to know urgently.'

'How nice to see you again. Do come in . . .'

Closing the door, she led them down a short narrow hall into a very small room, tastefully furnished. Space was clearly at a premium. She invited them to sit down on tapestry-covered chairs, offered them tea, which they both refused.

'Time is now against us,' Beaurain explained. 'I wonder if you could describe again that machine carried from the white van to the motorized trolley?' He took out a sketchpad Paula had handed to him in the car.

Mrs Wharton carried over another chair to sit alongside her guest. Paula produced from her satchel a fold-up ruler which she unfolded. Intuitively she had guessed what Jules was after. He smiled wrily at her.

'Reading my mind? As I suspect you do with Tweed.'

'Sometimes.'

'Measurements are important,' Beaurain explained, turning his attention back to Mrs Wharton.

'I'm not much good at them, I'm afraid.'

'I think we'll get there,' he assured her. 'It took six men to carry this machine. How wide would you say the support base was – the base the machine was perched on?'

'Show me by stretching your hands apart,' Paula suggested.

'Yes. I think I could do that.'

She stretched her hands wide apart. Paula leant forward, used the ruler to measure the distance. She whistled. 'At least two feet wide.' Beaurain began drawing, starting with the base support.

'Now,' Beaurain continued, 'how tall would you say the machine was – from the base to the tip of the shell or vertical torpedo, as you described what it was supporting?' Mrs Wharton held one hand close to the floor, stretched the other hand as high as she could into the air. Again Paula measured. 'About two and a half feet at least.' Beaurain drew the outline of a monster shell, tapering to detonation tip, writing in the measurement once more. He showed her his drawing. 'Anything like that?'

302

'The body of the shell was fatter.' She held out her hands apart. 'About so much.'

Paula measured the distance. 'Lordy, the main diameter of the shell was over a foot wide.'

Beaurain re-drew the main body of the shell, increasing its size, then showed it to their hostess. She stared for a short time.

'You know,' she said, 'I think you've got it perfect. Evil-looking thing.'

'We are dealing with evil men,' Beaurain told her as he wrote in the measurement in his neat hand. He then swivelled the sketchpad so she could see it clearly.

'Yes, that's the *thing*,' she said with a hint of vehemence.

'Mrs Wharton,' Paula said, 'we can't thank you enough for all the help you've given us. This is top classified data . . .'

'Don't worry.' Mrs Wharton smiled. 'I can keep my mouth shut. And I will. I do think you've got what you need. I do have a good visual memory. Won't you stay for tea?'

'Love to,' said Beaurain, standing up with Paula. 'But we have to get back quickly. Thank you again.'

As she led them back to the door Beaurain remembered to bend down and stroke Pooh, trotting happily along beside him. As she opened the door grey mist seeped in. It was going to be a foggy night.

'What do you think?' Paula asked, as Beaurain three-point turned their car ready to drive out of the cul-de-sac.

'I don't like it, don't like it at all. I just wonder how many of those *things*, as Mrs Wharton called them, al-Qa'eda have.'

Inside the power station Ali stood close to Proctor, the guard. He held an automatic close to his forehead, touched him with the tip of the weapon.

'You told me your chief, Mr Dick, calls you once in the evening to make sure everything is all right here. Now when he does call I want you to remember your wife. Her life is in your hands. If you sound nervous, or in any way make Dixon suspicious, you'll only see your wife when they ask you to go to the morgue to identify her.'

'I can do it,' Proctor said hoarsely. 'But not if you're holding that bloody gun at my forehead.'

'That was not quite your natural voice, Mr Proctor. Try again,' he ordered, holding the gun behind his back.

'I can do it.' The hoarseness was now absent.

'Much better. Imagine you are talking to your wife when the time comes.'

Within minutes the phone rang. Proctor didn't move. Angrily Ali gestured for him to pick it up. Proctor shook his head, stared at Ali.

'He wouldn't expect me to be sitting next to the phone. Why don't you shut your filthy mouth and let me handle this?'

After a minute had passed, during which Ali had trouble not waving the gun at him, Proctor picked up the phone.

'Mr Dixon?'

'Yes, it's me, Vince. Is everything all right down there?'

Ali was leaning close to Proctor, so he could monitor what was said.

'Everything is tickety-boo, sir. The three engineers are down with the plant, just keeping an eye on things, although it is automatic.'

'Good. Get plenty of sleep when you come off duty tomorrow. Good night.'

'Good night, sir . . .'

'What was that friggin' business about the engineers?' Ali demanded in a fury. 'A secret warning?'

'Don't be stupid!' Proctor shouted. 'I always mention them. They're just a stand-by. Not really needed since the system is automatic. But I always mention them. He'd

304

have thought it odd if I hadn't friggin' mentioned them. Satisfied?'

'Don't yell at me. Your meal is being prepared by Mehmet so you can eat soon.' Ali smiled. 'You're being fed in case Dick makes an unprecedented extra call later.'

Ali didn't feel it necessary to inform Proctor the three engineers had earlier had their throats cut, the bodies then weighted with chains and thrown into the river.

At Park Crescent Tweed had drawn up a list of suspects living in Carpford. He read out the list to Newman.

'Victor Warner
Drew Franklin
Peregrine Palfry
Billy Hogarth
Martin Hogarth.'

'You've left out Margesson,' Newman commented.
'If you say so.' He added Margesson's name.
'And Eva Brand,' Newman told him.
'She doesn't live up at Carpford,' Tweed objected.
'No, but I'll bet she visits Warner at his house up there with work.'
'All right, if you insist.'

He then called Jim Corcoran, Chief Security Officer at Heathrow. While he was doing so Buchanan was calling someone on his mobile, seated at Paula's desk.

'Jim? Good. Tweed here. I've got a tricky one for you. I'm not going to be your pin-up of the month. In fact, I'm not sure you can do this . . .'

'Do get to it, Tweed.'

'I have a list of people here and it's important for me to know if they've flown to the States during the past five months.' He read out his list, spelling some names. 'If I had dates that would be helpful. Shall I call you back?'

'No. Hold on. For security reasons, after September 11, and even before then, we have all the passenger manifests on the computer . . .'

He came back quicker than Tweed had expected. He chuckled.

'Bet you thought I couldn't do it. Sharpen your pencil. Here we go. Warner – flew to New York August 20, then back to New York October 12, back to NY November 16. On that trip he flew back from Boston. Palfry – flew to NY September 3 and September 9. Drew Franklin – to NY September 8, back to NY September 18. Nothing on Billy or Martin Hogarth. Nothing on Margesson. Eva Brand – to NY September 9, back to NY January 24 2002. All the previous ones were 2001. OK?'

'A miracle. Now could you carry out the same exercise for the same names flying to the Middle East up to now?'

'Hang on . . .'

Again he was back more swiftly than Tweed could ever have expected.

'Computer was warmed up, which helps. Thse people do travel. Victor Warner – flew to Cairo January 4 2002. All these flights are 2002. Warner flew again to Cairo January 29. Palfry, oddly enough, flew to Cairo each day after Warner had done. Drew Franklin made one flight – they're all to Cairo – on January 30, then on to Tel Aviv, back to Cairo, returned here February 2. Again, oddly enough, Eva Brand flew to both the cities on the same dates. That locks it up. I'll send you my fee. Better still, give me dinner at the Ritz.'

'Will do. You really are a miracle man . . .'

'The computer is. Got to go . . .'

Tweed handed the careful notes he'd made to Newman. Looking up, Newman pulled a face.

'This is going to take some sorting out.'

'Bob,' Tweed played with his pen, 'I suggest you look for anything that strikes you as odd.'

'Which means you've found something and you need me as a back-up check.'

'Something like that.'

He looked across at Buchanan, who was obviously waiting for a chance to speak after his long phone-call.

'Tweed, they have found two of those white vans. Dumped into the river. A fisherman saw vague figures shoving in one van. It was dark, so he huddled down the bank until the men had gone. Probably saved his life, Then, further upriver, he heard a second one being shoved in. When it was quiet he went to the first one. The rear was still protruding from the water, so he took the number plate. I've sent Warden with teams equipped with lifting equipment to haul them out. We should have news soon.'

'Another piece of luck. Now I'm holding nothing back. My next call is to Hereford, the SAS base. I want them alerted.'

Half an hour later Newman reported to Tweed after Buchanan had left for the Yard. Tweed could tell from his expression that he had been struck by something.

'What's the verdict, Bob?'

'The oddest thing is Eva Brand appears to have flown to Cairo, on to Tel Aviv – that's a guess – and back again with Drew Franklin. I don't get that.'

As he spoke Marler walked in, stared at both of them.

'What's up? I can tell something is.'

'I know you've just come in,' Tweed told him, 'but now I have another job for you. I want you to trace the present whereabouts of Eva Brand, then follow her.'

'She could be either at the Ministry in Whitehall or at the Minister's penthouse in Belgravia,' Newman objected.

'So,' Marler told him, 'I phone both places, ask for her and don't say who is calling. Then I'll track her. If I think it's a good idea can I take her out to dinner at the Ivy?'

307

'Typical,' Newman said sarcastically. 'Probably she won't like you.'

'I'll make her like me, Uncle,' Marler quipped, patting Newman's shoulder.

He then skipped quickly out of the door as Newman, furious, got up to hit him. Newman was only five years older than Marler but if the latter wanted to rattle Newman he called him 'Uncle'.

The door reopened and Buchanan appeared again. He remained standing as he spoke to Tweed.

'I've changed my mind about going back to the Yard. I think we should drive down to the river, take a look at those two white vans dumped into the Thames . . .'

He stopped speaking as the door opened again, admitting both Paula and Beaurain.

'I'm glad you're here,' Paula said to Buchanan. 'We have data you ought to see . . .'

Beaurain pulled out the notepad with the diagrams he drawn in Mrs Wharton's house. He placed them on Tweed's desk while Buchanan and Newman joined them. In as few words as possible he explained the drawings. When he had finished Tweed looked at Buchanan.

'What do you think of this?'

'Don't like it one little bit. Still think we should all go down to the river, check those vans. Is the location easy to find? It was tricky before.'

'No,' said Beaurain, 'so I'll drive us down there.'

37

'Lord, it's a heavy mist,' Paula exclaimed.

With Beaurain behind the wheel, they were driving down the bumpy track after turning off the main road. Paula sat beside the Belgian while Buchanan and Tweed occupied the rear seats. The Superintendent was peering out of the window.

'Worse than mist,' he commented. 'It's fog.'

During their drive there Tweed had produced his map of the district. He pointed out how close the power station was to St Jude's Hospital. Buchanan's mouth compressed. He shook his head.

'*If* al-Qa'eda are inside that power station we can't launch an attack to check out the place. They'll have a ton of high explosives. If they set them off that hospital – and all of its patients – would end up obliterated. Beaurain, can I suggest you dim your fog-lights? In case they have someone watching on this side of the river.'

'Yes, I can. Then I won't see where we're going . . .'

'Hold it,' Buchanan went on. 'Turn over the ground to your right. I've just seen a figure waving a torch. Could be Warden.'

Earlier, while in the car, he had used his mobile to contact Warden. He had warned him they would be coming. Beaurain had manoeuvred the car off the track on to the sterile ground to their right. At Buchanan's request he stopped.

309

Paula was on edge about the situation. The fog was like a dense murky blanket. She could just make out the torch being waved. Buchanan spoke as he opened the door on his side.

'Wait here. I'll check. Don't follow me if you hear shots fired,' he warned, a Walther in his hand as he left the car.

'Take care,' Paula called out.

'My motto . . .'

The torch was still shining but had stopped waving as Buchanan stealthily approached the vague silhouette. He crouched low.

'Who is it?' a familiar voice called out.

'Me, Warden,' Buchanan replied as he recognized the voice. As he came close to Warden he saw he was now holding the small torch in his mouth. This had enabled him to use both hands to grip the sub-machine gun aimed at Buchanan. 'And I appreciate it if you'd lower that weapon.'

'Sorry, sir. You always say it's better to be safe than sorry.'

'How far away is the first van you've hauled out?'

'A few hundred yards. The winch boys have really worked. The second van has also been hauled up on to the bank. Further on.'

'We want to see both. Come back with me to the car and guide the driver to the first vehicle . . .'

With Warden ahead of him, showing the way with his torch pointed at the ground, Beaurain drove slowly forward. The ground was even rougher. Paula thought it was her idea of a nightmare. Drifts of fog, like ghostly hands, swirled over the windscreen. She felt better when Warden held up a hand, illuminated it with his torch. Beaurain stopped, switched off the dimmed headlights and the engine. They all got out, following Warden in a crocodile.

Policemen with automatic weapons stood near the van. There were also two frogmen, still in their kit. Through

310

their goggles they stared at Paula. They hadn't expected a woman. She gave them a cheery wave and walked with Tweed to the rear of the van. Both rear doors were open.

She put on latex gloves and leapt up inside the van. Tweed hauled himself after her, his hands also protected with latex gloves. Warden followed, switched on his powerful torch.

'Douse that!' Buchanan snapped. 'It could be seen across the river.'

Paula switched on her smaller torch. She was slowly checking the floor of the van, which seemed strangely clean. Then she stopped, aiming her torch.

'Look at this.'

She was kneeling, with Tweed crouched beside her. In the light from her torch they could make out four screw-holes, well apart from each other. She hauled out from her satchel the fold-up ruler, measured the distance between the screw-holes.

'Just under two feet from one hole to the next one.' She looked up at Beaurain, who had joined them with Buchanan behind him. 'Jules, at Mrs Wharton's we decided the base plate was about two feet wide.'

'So,' Beaurain replied, 'while the van was transporting the devilish device here it was held firm, kept still by the base plate held firmly to the floor.'

One of the frogmen had arrived. He had taken off his helmet, exposing red hair plastered to his skull where water had dripped off the helmet when he removed it. He addressed his remark to Paula.

'Only one of those in this job. Two of them in the other van we hauled out upriver.'

'Like to look at that one in a minute,' suggested Beaurain.

'I know they used four vans,' Tweed said, standing up. 'Tell you how I found that out later.'

'Four vans,' Beaurain repeated. 'That suggests to me about six devices brought down here.'

311

'And six barges,' Tweed said almost under his breath.

They drove to where the second van had been hauled out. A short distance away was a large winch machine with a drum holding a cable. At the tip of the cable was a strong hook.

Both rear doors were open and again Paula was the first to leap inside it. She swivelled her torch slowly round the floor. By its light she saw another four screw-holes to the right side of the vehicle and near the back. Further in, nearer the front, she found four more, this time to the left side.

Again she used her ruler to cheek measurements. She looked up at Beaurain.

'Same as in Van One. Don't see why the two holding points are on different sides of this van.'

'Balance,' he said. 'Assume they drove a distance to bring the devices here. In this van having one device at the right side, the other at the left – and spaced apart – it would give balance. The devices must weigh a lot. We know they do. Mrs Wharton said it took six men to carry one from the van to the motorized trolley.'

'You've had lab experts go over the floors?' Tweed asked Warden.

'Yes, sir. Nothing. No fingerprints. The only element they noticed was a smell of a strong cleaning material.'

'That's it then.' Tweed looked at Buchanan. 'Now both vans must be shoved back into the river, the way they were.'

'What?'

The exclamation came from the red-haired frogman who had spoken to Paula earlier. He looked appalled.

'Sorry,' Tweed said firmly. 'But the dangerous villains involved may send a man back to make sure the vans are no longer visible. The tide has risen. We can't take a chance on this one.'

'Do it, Warden,' Buchanan ordered. 'Quickly. And move that winching apparatus out of the area. Now. Understood?'

312

'Yes, sir . . .'

They went back to the car and Beaurain drove them back to Park Crescent. The mist was clearing as they reached the track and turned up it to head back for the main road. As it did so Paula glanced down the track, wondering what hell might be going on at the power station.

Ali was supervising operations on the three barges moored on the east side of the wharf, the side the team led by Tweed and Buchanan could not see while checking the vans. The hard cover had been rolled over the interior of the barge. Before this action had taken place Ali had insisted the small wheels attached to the underside of the cover were oiled. This had been planned earlier – so when the cover's wheels were rolled along the rail-like tracks on either side they would make no noise.

As six of his men carried the device to place it in position, he climbed the ladder to the main hatchway, which was open. He peered down, gesturing for them to place the device in the perfect position – below the hatch opening. The hatch was more than wide enough to allow safe passage when the huge bomb lifted off its base, streaked through the hatch, aimed with all its explosive power at the target.

He descended the ladder – which would later be thrown overboard – and ordered them to screw the base plate firmly to the bottom of the barge. When they had completed the task he picked up a screwdriver, tried to tighten the four screws at each corner of the plate. He couldn't move any of the screws. This barge was ready, as were the two alongside it. Ali had been chosen by Abdullah for his meticulous attention to detail.

'Now we deal with the other three barges,' he ordered. 'It will be foggy so no danger of anyone seeing us.'

He had listened to the weather forecast for the next day. Very cold, no overcast, clear skies. They would have no trouble seeing the targets. Allah was on their side.

38

Marler had been waiting half an hour, parked in Belgravia where he could see the exit from Warner's penthouse. He had earlier phoned the Ministry, asked for Eva Brand when Palfry answered.

'She's not here,' Palfry had replied in his superior Civil Service voice. 'Who is this speaking?'

'Not urgent,' Marler had said abruptly and put down the phone.

His next call had been to Warner's penthouse. It was Eva who had answered. Saying nothing, Marler had hung up, now he knew where she was. So he had waited patiently. Little over half an hour later she had appeared at the front door, wearing a blue overcoat over her black trouser suit. She had closed the door, then stood there, scanning the area. Marler knew she would never see him and guessed his brief phone-call had alerted her. Smart lady.

She suddenly ran down the steps, ran to a blue Saab, dived inside, switched on headlights and moved off. Marler followed her cautiously. He soon realized she was heading for Whitehall. Going back to the Ministry? No. She turned down a side street, stopped outside a small restaurant which had a chalked board advertising *Tea. Coffee. Full meal if required.*

Leaving her Saab parked half on the pavement, she had gone inside the place. Marler adjusted his rear-view mirror, put on a pair of spectacles with blank lenses, a peaked hat

315

on his head. His appearance was transformed. He followed her inside.

He had a surprise. A man was just pulling out a chair for her. Palfry, smirking. He sat opposite her. Marler chose a table giving him a good view of them. Only Tweed at the SIS knew that Marler had trained himself as an expert lip-reader. The place was half empty. He removed his hat and ordered coffee when the waitress arrived. He could make out most of their conversation.

'I'm worried about Victor,' she said,

'Why? He's as fit as a fiddle. You know.' He pretended to play a fiddle with a solemn expression. She laughed dutifully.

'But how long can he keep it up?' she persisted. She kept quiet while their waitress served them both coffee. She continued as soon as they were alone. 'He pushes himself to the limit. He gets very little sleep. In the evenings he's always dashing off up to his place in Carpford. No guards.'

'What do you mean?' Palfry asked, managing to look worried.

'One of his guards told me they got into a car in the evening and followed him when he'd told them he didn't need them. He pulled into a lay-by on the A3, flagged them down. Then he gave them hell, said when he needed them he'd tell them and they could just drive straight back to London. Did you know this?'

'Not my job to tag along when he doesn't want me. Occasionally I do travel with him to Garda, his place in the village. And I always carry a revolver.'

'Could you use the damned thing if it came to it?' she snapped.

'Well . . .' He smirked. 'Probably end up shooting myself.'

'A lot of use that is,' she snapped. 'Go up there on your own sometimes? You've got that great big tub-like house. Must be room for twenty guests upstairs.'

316

'Well, sometimes I have a party. Maybe twenty guests. They can end up blotto so not fit to drive. Then I can give them sleeping accommodation for the night. Ask you up some time.'

'Drunken orgies aren't my style.'

'They're hardly that,' he protested. 'You could come up on your own one evening.' He smiled knowingly.

'That's not my style either. Now, getting back to why I asked you to meet me here. Victor *is* under great pressure and it's showing. He gets bad-tempered with me. Not that I can't handle that. I can. I thought you ought to know.' She leaned forward. 'And if you ever tell Victor about this meeting I'll see your job goes down the drain. Now, pay the tab and leave. We don't want anyone seeing us together outside. Go on.'

Meekly, Palfry paid the bill and walked out, looking baffled. He passed close to Marler's table without noticing him. Eva then stood up, put on her overcoat, walked towards the exit. She stopped by Marler's table.

'Why are you following me, Marler?'

'For protection. How did you know?'

'You're pretty good.' She gave him her warmest smile. 'I spotted you only once. Don't forget my time with Medfords. I was trained to follow people myself – and to know when someone was following me.' She smiled again. 'At least you weren't able to eavesdrop on our conversation.'

'Hardly close enough.'

'It would have bored you.' She picked up his hat, put it on his head back to front, giggled. 'You do look funny. Take care.' She bent down, kissed him on the cheek and was gone.

Marler didn't think it had been the moment to ask her out to dinner. In any case, he wanted to get back to report their conversation to Tweed.

At Park Crescent Tweed had decided to call Dixon, the

317

owner of the power station and a millionaire. He had spoken to him earlier.

'I've just spoken to Harry,' Nield spoke up. 'He's happy to keep on guarding Billy Hogarth but maybe I ought to relieve him.'

'Stay here while I make this call . . .'

'Mr Dixon, this is Tweed again. The drug dealers we thought might be near your power station are elsewhere. Everything all right at the wharf?'

'Proctor, the guard I mentioned to you, told me over the phone everything is normal. So nothing to worry about. After all-night duty he'll be glad to get back to his wife in Balham.'

'His wife lives in Balham? Give me a moment . . .'

Tweed sat thinking. He doodled on his pad, decided, picked up the phone again.

'Mr Dixon. This is highly confidential. The big operation to trap key drug dealers is taking place in Balham. Our men are armed. I don't want to risk upsetting Mrs Proctor. Would you mind giving me her address? Then we won't call at her house.'

'Very considerate. I will, of course, keep this under my hat, the one I never wear. I won't contact her but here is where she lives . . .'

'Thank you,' said Tweed, after writing down the address. 'I won't bother you again . . .'

He looked at Newman and Nield after showing them the address.

'I have spent a lot of time visualizing how I would conduct this spectacular operation, imagining I was the mastermind behind the planning. As regards Dick's wharf, they will have intimidated the guard, Proctor, so he said the right thing to the owner when he phoned Proctor this evening. These are the most ruthless and merciless enemies we have ever faced. I have little doubt they now hold Proctor's wife as hostage in his house. What will they do just before the operation

318

is launched? Kill Proctor. They will also kill his wife. You know the area now you have the address?'

'I do,' Nield replied who had been studying a map of Balham. It's a side street, probably terraced houses.'

'We must try to save Mrs Proctor. I don't expect a hitman is holding her at this stage. It will be some al-Qa'eda terrorist. It will be tricky.'

'Even dangerous,' Newman said doubtfully. 'Supposing the man holding her has time to phone the leader at the wharf?'

'Go with Nield. Your job is to see he doesn't get the time to do that. Kill him . . .'

Newman drove across Albert Bridge with Nield, navigating, by his side. There was heavy mist and still a lot of traffic. Prior to leaving Park Crescent Nield had collected certain tools, had wrapped them in a leather sheet, now rolled up and in his lap.

'Going to take us all night to get there,' Newman grumbled.

'No, it won't,' Nield said cheerfully. 'You concentrate on driving while I deal with navigating. After my original training session down at the Surrey mansion when they half-murdered me they brought me up here to Balham. Learning to track a suspect, watch a house opposite for two days without falling asleep. All that stuff.'

'Understood, Pete,' agreed Newman.

They had left the bridge behind and the traffic began to thin out. Nield spoke suddenly.

'Slow down, turn right down the next side street. We can get there quicker . . .'

Nield directed him through a maze of turns past old terraced houses with dim street lighting outside. Without consulting the map, he guided Newman, ordered him once again to turn right.

'Crawl,' he ordered after the turn. 'This is the street. So

319

where is No. 12? There it is. Park further along and we'll walk back and do a recce.'

When they walked back in their rubber-soled shoes they found No. 12 was at the end of the terrace. A narrow alley led down its windowless end, since it was the last in this block. No mist here. Just a deadly silence.

Steps led up to the front door direct from the street, and the old front door had stained glass in its upper half. There were lights behind the front bay window, which had curtains drawn closed across it. The frontage was only one window wide and they could hear nothing inside. No lights in the upper window.

'I want to call at another house like this one,' Nield said.

'What on earth for?' whispered Newman.

'To get an idea of the interior plan. They'll all be alike. You keep out of sight. And tuck this tool-kit under your arm . . .'

He walked up the block five houses, paused while Newman took up a position across the road in the shadows. No street light for a distance. Nield pressed the bell hard. Nothing, until he saw through the stained-glass window a large figure approaching. The Yale lock was turned, the door opened. A man in his shirt sleeves with his collar open at the neck glared.

'If you're selling something you can shove off. I'm watching football on TV.'

'Sorry to bother your, sir,' Nield began with his engaging smile. 'I'm lost. Car parked down the road. Trying to find Albert Bridge.'

'You are bloody lost . . .' The man gave swift instructions to reach Albert Bridge, then slammed the door shut.

While the door was open Nield had seen a lot. A narrow hall with a kitchen beyond an open door at the other end. A back door leading into the kitchen. A partial view into a living-room at the front.

He walked back and Newman joined him. Nield explained what he had grasped of the general layout. Under a street lamp he paused, took back the rolled-up leather case, spread it out on the bonnet of their parked car. He extracted pick-lock instruments, a small can of oil, handed them to Newman.

'You'll check, of course, but I think the front door has a Yale lock like the house I visited.'

'Of course,' Newman said sarcastically.

'First, let me dive down that alley and look at the back door. When I get to the other end I'll do a rehearsal – flash my torch twice quickly. That tells you I've checked the back door. Next time I flash the torch twice I'm ready to go in through the back door. Your cue to ring the bell. When Chummy opens it I'll be inside at the back. We'll get him in a crossfire. But if I've shot first you hold your fire. I don't want your bullet passing through him to hit me. Would spoil my breakfast . . .'

While Nield made his way down the alley, Newman went to the front door, used his small torch to check the lock. A Yale. His pick-lock could open that in no time. If there was also a chain he'd use his weight to smash the door down.

As on earlier expeditions with Nield, he was impressed with how cool Pete was. As though he was on a training exercise. He darted back to the end of the alley. At the far end a torch flashed twice. He waited there. Less than half a minute later the torch-flash signals were repeated. Newman rushed to the front door, pressed his thumb against the bell, held it there. He'd decided on a better strategy.

A very large man appeared behind the stained glass, jerked the door open swiftly. Over six feet tall, wide-shouldered, his face was brown-skinned, his hair trimmed short. He was wearing a windcheater and corduroy slacks. His eyes were dead as he stared at the visitor.

'Been . . . drinkin' . . . I'm lost . . . wanna get to . . .'

The giant had his right hand behind his back. His

321

expression became a sneer. A drunk. He sensed something happening in the kitchen, swung round, his right hand holding a Mauser with a long barrel. He aimed it at Nield. Newman's hand had appeared from behind his back. He fired his Smith & Wesson three times. The brute tried to turn round, the three bullets embedded in his body. Newman pulled the trigger twice more. The brute fell face down along the hall.

Newman jumped inside, closed the door behind him, bent down, checked the carotid artery. Nothing. Blood was welling out down the windcheater. Newman chopped his left hand down, indicating to his back-up that the al-Qa'eda thug was dead.

Nield ran into the living-room. Mrs Proctor was tied to a chair, scared witless. Nield smiled as he asked the question quickly.

'Was he the only one?'

She nodded, unable to speak. Nield smiled again, 'We were sent to rescue you. I'm going to cut the ropes round you with a knife. Just sit tight. Can't do much else, can you?'

They left when they were sure she had recovered quickly. No, she didn't want a neighbour to keep her company. Mrs Worthington would never stop talking all night long. Should she phone Vince, her husband? They persuaded her that wasn't necessary, would only worry him, so she agreed. They told her the intruder was a drug dealer they'd been after for months. They'd take him away.

'All I want,' Mrs Proctor said, 'is a cuppa tea, maybe two, then I'm off to bed. Probably sleep in, take a couple of pills. They'll knock me out. Would you like tea?'

'Thank you,' Nield said, 'but we're short of time.'

'Excuse me, must dash to the toilet . . .'

Newman had asked Nield to take over the wheel. There was something he had to do. Between them, after Newman had

322

driven his car up to the house, they had carried the great weight of the dead Saudi – at least Newman thought he was – and arranged it in the boot.

They were approaching Albert Bridge when Newman told Nield to turn left. He did so, raising his eyebrows.

Above the name of the road they had turned down was another sign. *St Jude's Hospital*. Nield said nothing until Newman took a medicine pack from the car pocket, removed his jacket, started wrapping a bandage round his forearm.

'You wouldn't like to tell me what this is in aid of?' he suggested.

'I'm walking wounded when I go into the hospital.'

'Tweed will skin you alive. We're supposed to keep well clear of that place.'

'You wait outside for me.'

Newman took a small non-flash camera from his pocket, an advanced version invented by the boffins in the basement at Park Crescent. Took very detailed pictures and no flash to give the photograph away. His mouth tight with foreboding, Nield parked near the hospital, which was a blaze of lights.

'See you soon,' Newman said, leaving the car.

Approaching the entrance, he had his jacket folded over one arm, the other exposing a lot of bandage. An ambulance had just pulled up and the rear doors were being opened. A lot of nursing staff, two men holding a stretcher waited, so no one was bothered when Newman walked into the entrance.

White-coated doctors hurrying, stethoscopes dangling from their necks. Newman moved to the right, the side nearest the power station. He walked down a long corridor, turned left when he realized he'd reached the end of the hospital building. He was now walking down a very long corridor with few lights and no one about except a grim-looking nurse coming towards him. She stopped as he reached her.

323

'Can I help you?'

'Not really, thank you. Just seen the doctor who fixed me up. Told me to take a good walk inside, then come back to him so he could make sure I was OK. He wasn't worried.'

He resumed his walk and she went her way. Near the end of the corridor he could see the power station and its wharf through large windows. He looked up and down the corridor. No one about except himself. He gazed down on the wharf. A huge canvas screen had been erected. As he watched, the screen was moved. A thin man in camouflage clothes stood on top of the roll-over cover drawn over the interior of a barge. He stood near a very large open hatch in the middle of the barge. The tide was still coming in, shifting the barge towards the hospital. Newman took seven quick shots. As he was doing so three more men in camouflage kit appeared after climbing up a ladder from inside the barge. Slipping the camera back inside his jacket pocket, he walked rapidly back the way he had come. The dragon of a nurse with the superior attitude appeared, asked him the name of the doctor attending him. He ignored her, walked out to where Nield had the car parked, the engine running.

'Drive like hell,' he said. 'Get us out of here.'

39

'What!' Tweed demanded fiercely. 'You disobeyed my order not to go near that hospital, St Jude's? What madness got into you? The key to the success of our operation was not to risk letting al-Qa'eda know we knew their location. You've taken leave of your . . .'

Newman, jaw jutting, eyes blazing, stood up from the chair he'd been sitting in. He had just started explaining what Nield and he had accomplished. He was furious. He leaned forward, put both hands on Tweed's desk.

'So tell me how you knew, really *knew* that al-Qa'eda were at Dixon's wharf? Positively and without doubt. You *assumed* they were there. You made a really dangerous assumption . . .'

'The white vans dumped in the river,' Tweed retorted.

'Those vans could have been dumped in the place least likely to be found. But al-Qa'eda could have been based miles away. The damned vans proved nothing . . .'

'You're forgetting,' Tweed fumed, 'Mrs Wharton saw them transferring a device on to their motorized trolley . . .'

'And what the hell did that prove?' Newman roared. 'Simply the movement of the device towards the river. There's a ramp at the end of that track. They could just as easily have been putting them aboard a vessel to transport it either further upriver – or downriver. Up to this moment there has been no absolute proof that al-Qa'eda was based on Dixon's wharf. So every detail of your counter-operation was based on an unproven assumption. Right?'

Paula, seated behind her desk, was fascinated by the explosive confrontation between the two men. She had only once in the past seen Tweed and Newman at each other's throats. And what an audience they had. Buchanan had returned, was seated in front of her. Beaurain, perched calmly on a hard chair, was watching the two men with keen eyes. Nield, keeping quiet, was seated on a hard chair near Monica's desk. And at that moment Marler walked in. Sensing the atmosphere, he strolled over to lean against a wall. Now only Harry Butler was absent.

Newman was leaning forward over Tweed's desk, almost over his chief. Tweed, gazing up at Newman, sat back in his chair. He folded his arms. When he spoke his voice was normal, almost quiet.

'Based on an unproven assumption, you said. Actually, you could be right. I can see that now. Maybe you'd like to sit down and tell me what happened from the moment you left here with Pete Nield. I'll just listen.'

Newman sat down. He drank the glass of water Monica brought him, thanked her. In a controlled voice he explained where he had been with Nield, this time starting in the right sequence with their confrontation with Mrs Proctor's captor in Balham.

Tersely, he painted a vivid picture of their encounter with the al-Qa'eda killer. The aftermath when they had left Mrs Proctor calmed down. The body still in the boot of the car.

'It's downstairs,' he explained. 'Maybe Superintendent Buchanan should send an ambulance to collect it. Take it to the best pathologist, Professor Saafeld, if I may suggest that.'

'Saafeld is a good idea,' agreed Buchanan. 'I'm using my mobile to call Warden to deal with it at once . . .'

Newman then explained their trip to St Jude's Hospital,

326

his idea. His venturing inside the hospital, the taking of the photographs when the screen aboard the barge was moved. He took out of his pocket the self-developed prints, laid them out on Tweed's desk.

Everyone got up to gather round and study them. Tweed picked up one, the picture taken when the barge heeled over and gave a view down the main hatch. Taking out a magnifying glass, he studied it for several minutes. He then handed it to Buchanan and Beaurain with the glass.

'Think you ought to see this. We can get it enlarged downstairs in minutes, get a clearer pic of the object below the hatch.' He looked at Newman. 'I think you showed extraordinary initiative and courage collecting this vital data. Thank God you disobeyed my orders. Now we are sure where the al-Qu'eda cell is.'

He looked across to Marler.

'Marler,' he explained to the others, 'has just returned from following Eva Brand. Anything to report, Marler?'

'Yes and no . . .'

Marler, drawing on his remarkable memory, proceeded to recall every word of the conversation he had heard between Palfry and Eva. Tweed sat very still, his eyes fixed on Marler until he had concluded.

'Intriguing,' he began. 'And valuable. Sounds as though Mr Victor Warner is feeling the pressure. Maybe why he's glad to hide behind me. But two items could be significant. The Minister's trips off without any guards. And the fact that Palfry's tub-house, as Eva called it, can house up to twenty guests. I wonder. No signs of intimacy between the two of them?' he asked.

'The reverse,' Marler told him. 'Eva dominated Palfry from the word go. Wasn't exactly polite.'

'Another piece of the jigsaw slotted in.'

'I read Paula's report on her ordeal at Carpford,' Buchanan interjected. 'Am I right,' he asked, turning to Paula, 'that when you escaped out of that horrible tunnel you saw a

327

huge abandoned quarry? More to the point, you saw one big boulder tumble down from the crest, joining a whole shambles of fallen rocks?'

'Yes, I did. The shambles, as you called it, was at least ten feet deep and covered a large area. A lot looked as though it had collapsed recently.'

'At the moment,' Buchanan went on, 'we have four bodies which have disappeared in that area. Mrs Warner, Mrs Gobble, Jasper Buller of Special Branch and Pecksniff, the crooked solicitor. I say bodies because at this stage I fear none of them are still alive.'

'You think they're buried under the quarry rock-fall?' suggested Paula. 'Then send a team to search there.'

'I'd like to but there are obstacles. My enquiries show that a large area of that land, including the quarry, are the joint property of Victor Warner and Drew Franklin. Since I can't yet show probable cause for the search no legal figure will sign a search warrant.'

'That's a curious arrangement,' said Tweed. 'I thought Drew rented his cube house. Yet you say he owns land.'

'I know.' Buchanan shrugged. 'The transfer document drawn up by the New Age Development Corp must be complex. If we could ask Pecksniff we'd find out its terms. But Pecksniff is no longer available, to put it mildly.'

'You know, Bob,' Paula said, staring hard at Newman, 'really we do need those aerial photos Airsight are supposed to be taking one day.'

'Tomorrow,' Newman said with a grin. 'The outfit's owner, whom I've told you is the best man, flies over there shortly after dawn tomorrow, takes his pics, rushes them them to us here.'

'I hope,' Tweed intervened, 'he doesn't make a great song and dance when he flies over. I don't want suspicions aroused up there.'

'I've already talked to him about that,' Newman assured him. 'He's clever. He'll take his shots when he first flies over, then he'll do a loop-the-loop manoeuvre before he pushes off. Anyone seeing him will assume he's a macho young pilot showing off.'

'That should cover it,' Tweed agreed.

'When I study those pics,' Paula remarked, 'I should be able to spot which house has the cellar where I was imprisoned.'

Tweed stood up, began pacing the limited space left in his office. He talked as he paced.

'We are so close to the moment when al-Qa'eda will launch its attack our on our city. Tomorrow, I'm sure.'

'Today,' Newman corrected. 'It's just after midnight.'

Tweed was pacing when Buchanan stood up to leave. He kissed Paula on the cheek, said he must get back to the Yard.

'I'll come down with you,' Tweed said. 'Don't argue . . .'

At the bottom, of the stairs he asked George to unlock the door to the visitor's room. Taking Buchanan by the arm, he ushered him inside, closed the door.

'Secrecy is vital,' he said.

'You have a plan to destroy al-Qu'eda, haven't you?' Buchanan suggested.

'Yes. It will involve a lot of cooperation and perfect timing.'

'Then I might as well tell you I have alerted the police anti-terrorist squad for an imminent operation. No details.'

'I'd like you to station them on the right bank of the Thames. Between Albert Bridge and Waterloo Bridge. As many marksmen as you can muster. They can go there now in plain clothes and pick spots where they'll be concealed, but with a clear view of the river. Give you more later. Also, at 4 p.m. when it's nearly dark I want all the street lights on both sides of the river switched off . . .'

'There'll be a riot. People will want to get home.'

'You haven't heard the worst yet. Well before 4 p.m. I

329

want all traffic diverted away from the river, the embankment. I want traffic banned from crossing those bridges. You'll have to get cracking. They can drive down the Strand.'

'I'll need a reason.'

'Announce by policemen on foot that a major police exercise is being conducted. That it will last for several hours, duration unknown. That's only part of it. You and I must keep in the closest touch by secure communication.'

'Is that all?' Buchanan asked cynically.

'For the moment only, yes. I know the target. Strictly between us, I'm in touch with the SAS. That goes no further.'

'Understood. I *had* better get cracking.'

'Just before you leave, I've been in touch with the Home Secretary and got his blessing. Couldn't say anything else – he's had a copy of the PM's directive. And I'll be paying the PM a brief visit. I know he'll signal his agreement.'

'Take good care of yourself, Tweed. I smell great danger.'

Tweed ran up the stairs, entered his office, stood behind his desk. He waited while everyone watched him.

'I'll explain the plan to wipe out the al-Qa'eda cell at 3 a.m. So everyone must be back here by then. Paula, have you ever seen all six barges coming upriver to the power station? You get about a lot.'

'Yes, I have, it's like a huge convoy.'

'Explain in more detail. The distance between the barges.'

'Not more than a hundred yards, at a guess. It really is an impressive sight. I've also seen them going downriver.'

'Same formation?'

'I'd say the distance between one vessel and the next is greater. Two hundred yards. Another guess.'

'Close enough, thank you. Now, Nield, drive to where Harry is looking after Billy Hogarth. Between you get him

330

out of bed, bring him back here. Monica, he can sleep in the camp bed I use in that cupboard. When you've settled him lock this office door, keep the key. Any trouble with him – unlikely – call on George for help. Give him coffee or tea to drink. No alcohol. I don't think he'll want any – he pretends to be drunk according to Paula, to get rid of his brother, Martin. Send out to the deli for breakfast and lunch. The official line for Billy is he's being moved to a safer place . . .'

'Anything when we get back?' asked Nield, putting on his windcheater.

'Yes. Both of you go to the basement, assemble an armoury. Sub-machine guns, tons of ammo, explosive grenades, plenty of night-glasses, personal water canisters, hand-guns to your choice, dark clothing with large SIS patches on the backs and tear-gas bombs. If I think of anything else I'll let you know.'

'I'm off,' said Nield and disappeared.

'Forget sleep,' Tweed continued. 'There won't be any. Newman, drive up to Carpford, knock on all the doors, wake them up if necessary. I want to know who is up there. And while you're there, check every rooftop. You're looking for elevated radio masts. Then report back to me here. Urgent.'

'On my way,' Newman replied and left.

The phone rang. Monica took the call, gestured to Tweed.

'Buchanan's back, says he won't keep you a minute.'

'Get him up here . . .'

'I forgot to show you something,' Buchanan said, the moment he was in the room. 'Only take a tick. I have a photo sent to me from New York after the first abortive attempt to bring down the World Trade Center which didn't work.'

'I remember that incident.'

Buchanan placed a photograph on Tweed's desk. Tweed

331

stared. then he beckoned Paula and Beaurain to come and look. Paula gasped.

'My God, it's the same thing.'

Tweed opened a drawer, took out the sketch Beaurain had drawn on Mrs Wharton's description of the 'machine' she'd seen six men carry from van to motorized trolley. The photograph of the device was the exact replica of Beaurain's drawing.

'Giuliani sent a note with this,' Buchanan explained. 'He said this one didn't detonate. They took it to pieces. It was packed with Semtex and another explosive which would have increased its power. So now you know what you're up against. Must dash . . .'

'What's the target?' Paula asked.

'I remember this first attempt,' Tweed replied. 'They planned to destroy the ground struts holding up the buildings. It did not work when the other devices were detonated, but it made a helluva mess. I can use this photograph.'

'What's the target?' Paula repeated.

'Wait until the 3 a.m. meeting here.'

'I guessed you'd say that.'

Tweed suddenly frowned. 'I could have made a mistake. Try and delay Newman from leaving . . .'

He had hardly finished speaking when Paula flew out of the door and down the stairs. George saw her coming, had the front door unlocked and open. She ran down the steps, saw Newman just taking off in his car. She ran like mad, ran in front of him. He braked suddenly, swore, switched off, dived out.

'You idiot! I could have run you down . . .'

'Shut up! You're needed upstairs . . .'

'Sorry, Bob,' Tweed said as a flushed Newman dashed in, followed by Paula. 'But I may need you here before you go up to the village.'

'Anything I can do?' Beaurain asked with a smile.

'Yes. It would help me if you both went down to the

waiting-room while I make a highly confidential call. Not my idea.'

'A chopper's landing in Regent's Park,' Paula reported, looking out of a window. 'That's odd. Looks like a Sikorsky.'

'Let me make this vital phone-call,' Tweed said after checking his watch. 'I'll call you all up when I've dealt with this.'

Paula left, followed by Monica, Beaurain and Newman. Now Tweed had the office to himself. He pressed the numbers from memory, the numbers which would put him through to SAS HQ at Hereford. A bored voice answered.

'Yes.'

'Tweed here. Able is expecting me to call now.'

'Never heard of the name. Hang on . . .'

'Who is this?' a crisp well-educated voice asked.

'Tweed, SIS.'

'Codeword?'

'Pagoda.'

'Fire away.'

'I need a contact from you here. I cannot discuss this on the phone.'

The phone made a strange noise. Tweed frowned, decided to check.

'There's a strange noise on the phone.'

'That's a system to ensure we cannot have the line tapped.'

'I can tell you now. Be on red alert.'

'I see,' Able replied calmly. 'As to the contact, we foresaw you'd need one. He'll arrive any moment. You will confer with him alone. Unless Robert Newman is available. He can sit in.'

'What about Beaurain?' Tweed spelt the name.

'Christian name, please.'

'Jules Beaurain . . .'

'His credentials, please.'

333

'Former chief of the Brussels anti-terrorist squad. Later he was Commissaire of Brussels police.'

'We know him. He can sit in with Newman. No one else.'

'Understood.'

'Target known?'

'Yes. Central London. Will be precise with contact. Zero hour is today. Probably after four in the afternoon.'

'Thank you, sir. Good luck, Mr Tweed . . .'

Switching off all the lights, Tweed went to the window and pulled a curtain aside a few inches. A tall man was walking out of the park from the direction where the Sikorsky had landed. Switching on the lights again, Tweed sat at his desk, called George.

'Ask Newman and Beaurain to come up immediately. Not Paula. Give her my apologies. Tell her I had no option.'

The door opened and Newman walked in, followed by Beaurain. Tweed asked them to sit down, then he gave them the news.

'A contact from the SAS is due to arrive any moment. The commander at Hereford gave permission for you both to be present while I outline the plan of attack. Ours, that is.'

'I'm surprised,' Newman replied. 'I know I did the course when I was writing an article on the SAS . . .'

He stopped as Monica called him on the phone. He listened as she spoke.

'George says a very suspicious character is asking for you. He's down here now.'

'Ask him to come up, Monica. Please join Paula in the visitors' room . . .'

The door was opened by George, who ushered in a very tall man. He was dressed in civilian clothes and a scarf concealed most of his face, leaving his mouth exposed. He stared quickly at everyone in the room.

334

'I guess you're Mr Tweed,' he said approaching the desk. 'You are expecting me.' He held out an identity folder.

'Sarge!' Newman had jumped up. 'Recognize your voice. You put me through hell on that training course.'

'Sarge also trained me,' said Beaurain, standing up, holding out his hand. 'Welcome.'

'Maybe we should start right away,' replied Sarge, occupying the armchair Tweed had gestured to.

40

Before beginning, Tweed apologized to Sarge, told him he had brief vital instructions to give, left the office. He ran down and entered the visitor's room. Paula, Marler and Monica were seated at the bare wooden table, drinking coffee. Tweed spoke rapidly.

'You both heard the orders I gave to Newman to drive to Carpford, to check who is there. Since Newman is occupied upstairs I want you, Marler, to take his place. Paula, go with him. Don't forget to check the rooftops for an elevated aerial mast. Then get back to report to me. Urgently . . .'

He returned to his office, sat down behind his desk. He began explaining the situation. Sarge listened without saying a word. Tweed showed him a detailed map of the Thames area, pointed out the power station, St Jude's Hospital.

He showed Sarge Beaurain's drawing of the device, then the photo from Mayor Giuliani Buchanan had left with him, the photos Newman had taken from the hospital of the wharf. Mackie, the most brilliant boffin in the basement, had since provided blow-ups of Newman's photos. Sarge was most interested in the pic Newman had taken looking down inside the main hatch.

'Took that one,' Newman said, speaking for the first time, 'as the barge tilted towards me. A big police launch moving upriver had sent out a large bow wave, causing the tilt. The device you can now see clearly placed

337

below the hatch is like the photo Giuliani sent from New York.'

Sarge nodded his agreement. Tweed explained the measures being taken by Buchanan along the embankment later. He covered all the information they had obtained, his plan for eliminating the al-Qa'eda cell. Sarge nodded again. He had taken no notes.

When the time came for him to leave he asked for all the photos and Beaurain's drawing, together with Tweed's map. He put them inside the briefcase he'd been carrying – more cover as a businessman. He told them the SAS unit would number about thirty, got up to leave. 'We should meet here again. Midday? Good.' Then he left, after shaking hands.

41

Paula swore to herself as Marler drove over the crest into Carpford. A dense fog blotted out the village. She navigated as he drove very slowly, partly because of the fog and partly to make as little noise as possible.

'You see the lake?' she began.

'I do. Driving any faster and we'd have been in it.'

'Follow the road to the left. We'll start with Martin Hogarth's bungalow. I'm sure he'll be so glad to see us . . .'

Marler drove the car off the road on to the open field when he saw the dim outline of the bungalow. Switching everything off, he followed her towards the entrance. He gripped her by the arm, stopped her, whispered.

'He's up. Glow of light from between the shutters closed over the windows.'

Turning on his powerful torch, he aimed it at the roof. A slim aerial mast protruded upwards. Reducing the strength of the beam, he went up to the door, examined the locks. A well-known make. He handed his torch to Paula, gestured to indicate he needed her to shine it on the lock.

Taking out a small folded leather tool-kit, he extracted an oilcan, a pick-lock. He squirted oil first on the lock, then a smear on the pick. He heard the tumblers drop back, put his tools back in the leather holdall. Very gently, he turned the door's handle. His acute hearing had caught the sound of a voice speaking inside. He pushed the door open a few inches. No creak. The door's hinges were well oiled.

Paula stood next to him as light flooded out from the narrow opening. Martin's voice came to them clearly, speaking emphatically.

'I tell you Billy is not here. I have checked his bungalow and it's empty. What? No, I don't have any idea where he is. And no, I've no idea where he might have gone. Must go now . . .'

Marler realized Martin had been alerted to their presence by the drop in temperature as icy air percolated in from the outside. He walked in, Walther in his right hand, followed by Paula. Martin had his back to them as he put down a telephone on a table. His right hand reached inside his jacket.

'Don't do anything stupid, Martin,' Marler ordered.

Turning round slowly, Martin rubbed fingers across his mouth as though considering how to respond. He was fully dressed in a grey business suit. He dropped both hands, exposing them palms outwards, demonstrating he had no weapon.

'What the devil are you doing here?' he hissed. 'Breaking and entering? A crime. I'll put you both behind bars . . .'

'Martin,' Marler interrupted in cold voice, 'who were you calling on that phone?'

'None of your damn business.'

'But it is our damn business,' Marler told him, moving closer. 'You're mixed up with the New Age people – and something far worse.'

'Prove it,' Martin snapped with a feeble show of bravado.

'I'll leave Superintendent Buchanan to do that. You're already linked to New Age for starters.' With his left hand Marler produced a pair of plastic handcuffs, recently issued. Locked on wrists, they clicked tighter and tighter if the prisoner struggled with them. 'Turn round,' Marler went on. 'Hold both wrists close together behind your back.'

The next minute was horrific. Martin twisted his lips in

340

a strange attempt to look defiant, then crunched on something in his mouth. His face twisted again into something almost unrecognizable as his hand darted to his throat. He let out a terrible half-choked scream, fell sideways into a chair. It became a gurgle of unbearable pain. His eyes bulged. Paula rushed forward. She had only seen this once before.

'He swallowed something. He put it in his mouth when his back was turned to us.' She sounded desperate as she reached him, bent down.

'Water,' said Marler. 'With salt. An emetic . . .'

He was heading for the kitchen when Paula shook her head. By now Martin was thrashing his legs and arms, still in the chair. Paula stopped Marler.

'No good. He's gone. I caught a whiff of bitter almonds from his mouth. He swallowed a cyanide pill. We can't save him.'

Martin's thrashing body suddenly became motionless. He sagged in the chair. His eyes were open. Dead eyes. Marler came back, looked down at him. He realized he was still holding the Walther. He slipped it back inside his holster.

'Why on earth did he do that?'

'My guess,' Paula replied quietly, 'is he knew he'd be linked to al-Qa'eda. That he'd face a sentence of thirty years in prison. Couldn't face it.'

'I'll inform Buchanan at once,' Marler decided, taking out his mobile. 'We'll need an ambulance up here urgently. And no screaming sirens up here – or flashing lights . . .'

He was lucky. When he pressed Buchanan's private number at the Yard, the superintendent answered immediately. Marler explained the situation in as few words as possible. The superintendent said he was on his way to Carpford with an ambulance at once.

'Buchanan's coming himself,' Marler told Paula.

She had forced herself, after putting on latex gloves, to go through the dead man's pockets. Inside a thick wallet she found credit cards, driving licence, five hundred pounds in five-pound notes. She also found a one-way ticket to the Bahamas via New York. She showed the ticket to Marler.

'Look as though he was about to flee. The Bahamas. That suggests Gerald Hanover.'

'Isn't he the man who is controlling the whole operation?'

'Yes. Or the woman.'

They continued the search while waiting for Buchanan. Marler closed the door to Martin's bungalow but left the door unlocked.

The door to Billy Hogarth's bungalow was closed but also unlocked. Which Paula found strange and said so to Marler.

'An obvious explanation,' he replied. 'We heard Martin say on the phone to someone that he'd checked Billy's place. Anything strike you in here?'

'Nothing.' Paula went on checking. She worked quickly and had the reputation at Park Crescent of being an expert when it came to searching. After checking living-room, kitchen and the two bedrooms she came out, held out her hands in a dismissive gesture.

'Nothing anywhere. Nothing I wouldn't expect to find. A gap in his wardrobe, but they'll be the things he took with him to London. Palfry's tub-house next. No, we'll call on Margesson first. Tweed keeps dismissing him as unimportant.'

Marler first pressed the bell after pretending to admire the outside of the Georgian house. There was a light on in a first-floor room. They both heard the heavy thump of footsteps coming down a staircase. The door was flung open and Margesson, clad in a strange robe which fell almost to his ankles, glared out. Even his beard seemed to bristle. Marler was holding up his identity folder.

342

'Do you know what time it is?' Margesson fulminated.

'Yes, we do,' said Marler. 'But you obviously were not asleep . . .'

'I was praying. Does that mean nothing to you? This is the state the world has collapsed to. No discipline. No courtesy. You wonder why the revolution is coming?'

'Which revolution is that?' Marler enquired. 'And we can listen to your views more comfortably if you invite us in. It is bitterly cold out here – and the cold is getting into your magnificent home,' he said with a rare smile.

'You like it?' Margesson's mood changed. 'For a few minutes then.' His mood changed again. He pointed at Paula. 'She can't come in. Only one woman is is permitted to enter my home.'

'Thank you.' Marler pushed past the large figure, holding Paula by the hand. 'Thank you,' he said again.

Confused, Margesson closed the door. As he turned round the folds of his silken robe swished. He waved towards a sofa.

'You may sit.'

Marler sat down with Paula beside him. He gazed round the spacious room, furnished with expensive sofas and chairs, all covered with Oriental designs of a weird character. The big man sat down in a high throne chair facing them. Paula also looked round the strange room.

'This is so beautiful,' she commented.

'I have spent time on my surroundings. It is probably a sin. The world is full of sin.' His voice had risen, his arms waving. 'Society in the West has fallen to the depths and there is no structure, no discipline, just orgies of the most frightful behaviour. Even the children are polluted.'

'Excuse me,' Paula said, leaning forward, her eyes fixed on Margesson's, 'but I have the strongest feeling that you are repeating, by rote so to speak, what someone else has preached to you. Rather like listening to a record, if I may say so.'

343

Margesson blinked. He was confused again. He stared round the room as though seeking help. So far he'd made no effort to deny what Paula had suggested. He gazed down at both of them as though not seeing them. As though drugged.

'So,' Paula continued in the same quiet voice, 'who is it that comes to see you? The person who propagates these ideas to you so forcefully you are convinced this is the real truth. One of your neighbours, perhaps?'

'I think I have to ask you both to leave now,' he mumbled. He looked at Paula. 'Who are you?' Then he lifted a large hand. 'No, please do not tell me. I do not wish to know.'

'We do have to leave,' Marler said, standing up. 'Thank you for allowing us in to your holy house.'

Margesson rose slowly, as though really he was reluctant to see them go. As he unlocked and opened the door, Marler asked his question suddenly.

'You see much of Palfry?'

'Palfry?'

'Your neighbour living in the round house.'

'He comes occasionally.' His reply came after a long pause. 'My blessings . . .'

The cold hit them like a hammer. Marler looked thoughtful as they made their way to the tub-house. As they got closer it looked enormous in the fog.

'That was very clever of you,' Marler remarked. 'He has been brainwashed by some unknown person. Maybe Palfry – you noticed how long it took him to answer my last question.'

'Or the unknown woman, the only one permitted to enter his house.'

No lights in Palfry's home. They walked all round it before approaching the front door. Paula was surprised by the dimension of its circumference. It was a *very* large place. Marler decided there was no one inside. Using his tool-kit, he dealt with the lock, opened the heavy door, stepped inside, felt round, found the switches, turned them all on. Paula gazed at the interior, taken aback by what she saw.

One vast room with circular walls. A kitchen area over to her right. Curved counters, curved cupboards against the wall, an immense American-style refrigerator, a stove, cooking utensils hanging from the wall behind the huge counter. No antiques, but plenty of tasteful chairs and sofas scattered around. On the far wall a curving staircase led up to a gallery.

I'd soon get dizzy living here, she thought. Marler had a nerve, breaking into the place. Supposing Palfry was sleeping upstairs, appeared with a shotgun. Then she noticed Marler had his Walther in his hand.

It was very warm and so silent. The only sound the faint gurgle from the curved radiators spanning the walls. She wended her way between the furniture, ran quietly up the carpeted curving staircase to the gallery. One heavy door with another lock. Carefully she turned the handle. Locked. She hissed down to Marler, beckoned.

It took him less than two minutes to deal with the lock. He turned the handle slowly, pushed the door open. Paula crept after him. This was the dangerous moment. Again Marler found the switch panel, turned everything on. A corridor curved off in both directions, a corridor with closed doors at regular intervals.

'You go that way, I'll go this way and we'll eventually meet. Check every room . . .'

None of the doors were locked. She had her Browning ready as she opened doors. Each room had a bed made up and in a corner a shower room. The beds were made up neatly. She felt the sheets but they were cold. She made her discovery in the last room. Neatly piled up in several stacks were piles of sleeping-bags. She counted. Twenty of them.

Emerging from the room, she met Marler coming from the other direction. He took her by the arm.

345

'Time we got out of this *Ideal Home* place.'

'I don't think they'd allow it to be shown at the exhibition,' she whispered back.

She even welcomed the cold when they were outside. Marler used his pick to relock the door, turned to her.

'What do you think?'

'I could never live in a place like that. I'd go mad.'

'Find anything?'

'Only in one bedroom. All the others had the beds made up with new sheets. In this particular bedroom stacks of sleeping-bags. Twenty of them.'

'Twenty sleeping-bags. Twenty members of al-Qa'eda en route. So where to next?'

Paula insisted on checking Mrs Gobble's cottage. It had the feel of any empty house. She even peered behind the folding screen. No telescope. She found it strange that the front door had been closed but not locked. She felt a sadness for Mrs Gobble. Was she gone for ever? Buchanan thought so.

'Now for Drew Franklin,' she said to Marler after closing the door on the cottage. 'Brace yourself . . .'

They kept close together because, if possible, the fog was now denser. It even muffled the sound of their footsteps on the road. Paula felt they were ghosts in a dream.

'Lights on Drew's first-floor window in that cube,' Marler said. 'Think this time I'd better ring the bell.'

'If you can find it.'

After trying several paved pathways they found the entrance. Marler pressed the bell, folded his arms. Very quickly the door was thrown open. Drew stood framed by the hall light behind him, fully dressed in a business suit. He glared.

'Yes?'

'We'd like a word with you . . .' Marler began.

'Then make an appointment to see me at my office in town,' he rasped at them.

346

The door was slammed shut in their faces. Marler shrugged.

There were no lights in the palatial Garda, home of Victor Warner. Marler shrugged again, said they'd better not push it this time. They were walking back to where he had parked the car when a figure loomed up in the fog. Marler had his Walther in his hand instantly. A familiar voice called out. Buchanan's.

'Don't shoot the postman, he's doing his best.'

'You've found Martin Hogarth's corpse?' Paula asked him.

'No. That first bungalow you come to is – was – his? Right?'

'Yes.'

'No body inside that place. No sign there ever was one. We've checked the next bungalow – Billy Hogarth's, isn't it? Nothing in there. Somebody, an amateur, had forced open the front door of Billy's place. Nothing. No body.'

'That's Number Five,' Paula said slowly. 'Disappeared up here. Or am I losing count?'

42

The battle meeting, as Tweed called it, began at Park Crescent at 6 a.m., brought forward from the original timing of 3.30 a.m. This was to give time for Paula and Newman to return from the journey to Carpford.

They had arrived earlier and Tweed had met them in the visitors' room. He listened in silence while they described what had happened, what certain people they'd encountered had said to them. He showed no reaction as Marler described the suicide of Martin Hogarth, the subsequent disappearance of his corpse. As Marler concluded his story Tweed merely nodded as he stood up. He said only one thing.

'It all fits with the suspicions I sensed a long time ago. You did say there was no sign of Palfry?'

'I did,' Marler confirmed.

'Then it is time now for us to attend the meeting. They are all waiting in my office. Everyone who will play a key part in the plan to destroy al-Qa'eda . . .'

Entering his office, Paula was surprised to find the furniture had been changed and a number of people present. Rows of chairs faced Tweed's desk, which he went to sit at. With Newman she had a seat in a fold-up chair in front of his desk.

Next to Newman sat Buchanan. On her left side sat Jules Beaurain, very upright. He smiled, squeezed her hand. On the seat beyond the Belgian Howard sat back with folded arms. In rows behind them she saw Marler, Harry Butler, Pete Nield and Monica. Tweed stood up. He spoke in a quiet voice, his eyes constantly switching from one member of his audience to another.

'This battle meeting is to brief you on how we shall defeat the al-Qa'eda cell based at Dick's wharf on the far side of the Thames.' He paused. 'The target is six key bridges spanning the Thames. In this order of expected attack. First Waterloo Bridge, then Westminster, followed by Lambeth, Vauxhall, Chelsea and Albert Bridges. Anyone may ask questions as I brief you. The attack will be launched by six huge barges, at present stationed at Dick's wharf.'

'Excuse me.' Newman held up a hand. 'How can you be so confident the bridges will be attacked in the sequence you suggested?'

'Because I have spent many hours visualizing, as the mastermind, how I would conduct the operation. The six barges will proceed downriver in a convoy, each barge spaced well behind the one in front. If they attacked, say, Albert Bridge first that would give warning of what was coming. By blowing up Waterloo Bridge first they proceed in logical sequence.'

'And the method of attacks?' Paula enquired for the benefit of the others.

'I was coming to that. Each barge has a roll-over metal cover. All these covers will be shielding the interiors. In the centre of each cover is a large hatch which will be open when the convoy sails. Below this open hatch will be a device of great explosive power. As a barge passes under a bridge this device will be fired. It will travel vertically, pass through the open hatch, detonate when it strikes roughly the centre of the bridge above it. It will be a projectile of enormous explosive power, a mixture of Semtex and another explosive. The entire bridge will lose its stability, will collapse into the river, shattered.'

'And how do we prevent this happening?' Beaurain

350

asked with a smile. Again for the benefit of everyone present.

'I can now tell you the SAS will be present on the embankment. They may already be here, knowing them. They have perfected a new sophisticated mortar, very accurate. Practised on a remote lake in Scotland. First, a large rubber ball is fired, to gauge range and target position. Followed almost immediately by the firing of a powerful bomb, aimed to drop down the hatch. This will detonate the al-Qa'eda device inside the barge, blow it to smithereens.'

'Supposing the mortar bomb misses descending into the hatch?' Beaurain suggested.

'The SAS have a back-up team. Each barge is controlled and steered by the control room at the stern. In case of such an emergency another SAS unit will aim a long-distance rocket at the deckhouse. The barge will then be out of control. Impossible to continue steering it towards its target.'

'This has been well thought out,' Beaurain commented.

Tweed swivelled his gaze across his audience. He sensed rising tension. His next words would intensify that atmosphere.

'I am surprised no one has questioned the timing of the crisis. As yet, I'm sure you have not realized the catastrophe, the horror we seek to prevent. A catastrophe to make the terrible World Trade Center attack in New York seem like a tactical prelude.'

'Barges,' Paula told them.' That's what poor Eddie, murdered in Monk's Alley, was showing us in his crude drawing. *A barge.* Tell us then,' she invited Tweed, 'about the timing.'

'I am sure it will be between 5 p.m. and 6 p.m. Say 5.30 p.m.'

'Oh, my God!' Paula gasped. 'Rush hour . . .'

'Exactly,' Tweed agreed. 'At that time each bridge is crammed with traffic – cars, buses, coaches transporting schoolchildren home from the various exhibitions I hear

351

that they will be visiting, so the casualties would run into many thousands – the key to the al-Qa'eda plan. A spectacular atrocity on the largest scale they have achieved anywhere so far.'

He waited. A deathly silence had gripped his audience. They had grasped how much was at stake. Beaurain decided a little reassurance was called for.

'So we realize how vital it is to destroy those barges one by one before they reach their targets. Which we will do.'

'Monica,' Tweed called out, 'please pass round photocopies of the device drawn by Commissaire Beaurain with Paula's help. Also pass round photocopies of the picture Newman took from the hospital when the barge tilted, giving a clear view down inside the main hatch.'

He sipped a glass of water, still standing, while everyone examined the pictures. Paula stood up, moved from one person to another, explaining anything they were not clear on. The tension in his office was subsiding. Now everyone realized what was involved, their expressions became more determined, grimmer. Tweed found this reaction very satisfactory.

'I've grasped it,' Harry Butler called out in a calm voice. 'But what about the traffic on the bridges?'

'I wondered when someone would ask that question. There will *not* be any traffic on the bridges. There won't be any driving along the embankment on either side of the river. In a moment Superintendent Buchanan will explain what he has planned. The SAS will be the key element in this operation. A large force will be based along the embankment.'

'Then what do we do?' Nield called out.

'You will also be situated at key points on the embankment. So that the SAS do not shoot you the special clothes you wore once before are waiting in the basement. The black clothing with a large "S" in white on the back. To

352

identify you to the SAS. When I use the word "embankment" I refer to the left bank looking downriver. Newman will place you later. That is why Harry has assembled a formidable armoury in the basement.'

'Our targets, please,' asked Nield. 'The barges?'

'No. Not the barges. We know the al-Qa'eda cell numbers at least thirty men, probably more. They will start out on board the barges. But when the dogfight starts – and when it does it will be ferocious – I expect men from the barges to try to reach the embankment. Possibly in motorized dinghies. They will be your targets.'

'Some of them suicide bombers?' suggested Paula.

'*All* of them suicide bombers, I suspect. You have to kill them before they get close to you. I checked with the SAS contact. "Take no prisoners?" I asked. "Of course," he replied.'

'Good,' said Newman.

'I now come to the worst part,' Tweed said. He paused. It was not something he liked to say but it had to be revealed. 'Earlier I named six bridges. The SAS can only save five of them with the resources at their command. One bridge must be allowed to go. That is Albert Bridge.'

There were gasps. Tweed looked very serous. He waited for the question he knew must come.

'But what about all the people who live near Albert Bridge?' Paula protested. 'Cheyne Walk and other areas nearby. Pieces of the blown bridge may hit their buildings.'

'I agree. I would now like to vacate the platform to Superintendent Buchanan. Among other factors he will explain how he is dealing with that problem. Roy, it is all yours.'

He left his desk and sidled his way to the chair Buchanan had vacated to occupy the chair behind the desk. Like Tweed he remained standing as he spoke, tersely in his clipped voice.

All residents near Albert Bridge were being evacuated. They were told a major gas explosion was expected, were being transferred to a number of hotels. He had already stopped the movement of traffic along either embankment, giving the same reason. A major gas explosion. His anti-terrorist squad would occupy the right bank, on the opposite side of the river to the SAS and the SIS. His men would be heavily armed. They would shoot to kill.

Traffic could move along the Strand, past Trafalgar Square and along the Mall. It would mean gridlock on a vast scale and many would not be able to return home that night. Where it was possible traffic would be diverted downriver to Blackfriars, Southwark, London and Tower Bridges and the Rotherhithe Tunnel. So some would get home, albeit rather late.

'What if one of the barges breaks through and reaches Blackfriars?' called out Nield.

'No barge will break through. If necessary it will be sunk by the SAS, using advanced missile launchers. Once this al-Qa'eda cell has been liquidated we can start guiding the traffic back over all bridges.' He paused. 'Except for Albert Bridge.'

He then answered a number of relevant questions before returning to his seat. Tweed stood up to occupy his desk seat when Harry also stood up, his voice powerful.

'Now, you useless lot, down to the basement with me to collect your weapons and ammo. You may get some sleep while you're waiting on the embankment so we have stockpiled cushions. Don't ever think we don't look after you.'

'One more vital question,' Paula called out in a commanding voice which froze everyone where they were. 'Since Albert Bridge will also be closed to traffic, won't this al-Qa'eda scum notice the absence of traffic from the very start?'

'Good question,' Buchanan replied, standing still. 'Which

354

is why we have arranged for a trustworthy firm dealing with old cars destined for the crusher to transport them on to Albert Bridge, placed on the upriver side. After that they'll be too busy concentrating on their evil work to notice anything odd elsewhere.'

As men filed out, following Harry, Tweed turned to Beaurain. He kept his voice low.

'Jules, I would appreciate it if you were by my side on the embankment. To start with we shall probably be perched on a statue's plinth to get a good view.'

'My pleasure . . .'

As they were speaking, and before anyone had left the office, Buchanan called out in his clear voice.

'Two more things and then I'll shut up. One, you will all be in radio contact with each other. Equipment waiting in the basement. Two, the BBC, all TV and radio stations, have been told not to broadcast any news bulletins after midday. They will play music, explaining this is due to a technical fault. Al-Qa'eda may well have small TV sets and radio on board the barges. I have sent policemen everywhere to make sure these instuctions are carried out. Now I really will shut up . . .'

Soon the only people left in the office were Tweed, Beaurain, Monica and Paula. Paula went close to Tweed, whispered.

'You must be tired. You must get sleep here before the SAS contact arrives back at noon.'

'Never felt more alert.'

43

At Dick's wharf Ali had checked the control rooms at the stern of each of the six barges twice. When the convoy sailed on its last voyage he would be on barge number five, the barge which would destroy Chelsea Bridge. He would be in constant radio communication with all the other barges. He also had a small TV set in the control room of that barge. He would see the BBC broadcast the frightful destruction he would wreak.

Bridges smashed, the Thames full of cars and other traffic which had fallen into the river, crammed with people – either already dead or the few who would drown. It would be high tide. For years north London would be severed from the south. But it was the thousands of casualties he looked forward most to seeing.

He descended to the interior where all his cell was assembled. They were kneeling on their prayer-mats, facing east. They rose up slowly as Ali stood on a crate to address them in Arabic.

'Allah is great,' he began. 'Allah is looking down on us to see our work on his behalf. You will all carry explosives strapped to your bodies. The enemy will also be driving along both sides of the river bank, on their way home. Their last drive. You know what to do? To those who survive?'

'We know,' one huge Saudi called out. 'We get into the craft and speed to the shores . . .'

Ali had been meticulous in checking motor-powered

dinghies were arranged along the roll-over decks. His cell had forty men and he felt sure a large number would survive long enough to arrive on the embankments. Once there they would use their sub-machine guns to spray the slow-moving traffic.

'Then,' the Saudi continued, 'we slaughter as many infidels as we can before we rush at crowds of pedestrians, clasp them and detonate our bombs. The embankment will flow with their blood.'

There were shouts of praise from the packed cell, standing in rows behind each other. Ali raised a hand and the shouts ceased. It was not that he didn't approve of their reaction. Ever cautious, he didn't think there was any risk of their shouts being heard in the nearby hospital, not with the main hatch being still closed, but he couldn't risk it. Below the closed hatch was a roped-off area. Inside it perched the first of six torpedo shells, cramed with explosive, aimed to pass easily through the main hatch and then strike the central span. Beside it stood two men – one to press the button to activate the bomb, the second man to press the button which would send it winging its way upwards.

Ali, very athletic, shinned up the ladder (soon to be removed) and ran along the deck to the bows. Here they had placed a smaller bomb, the barrel of the launcher angled. This would be fired as soon as Nebuchadnezzar, the name of the main bomb, had been sent on its terrible way.

The smaller bomb at the bows would be aimed at the support struts of the bridge, to ensure the entire bridge collapsed. It was a refinement aboard all six barges – and something the defenders on the river banks were unaware of.

44

Dawn was a placid series of pink streaks in the east. The weather forecast was for a brilliant sunny day, the first for weeks, with temperatures still very low. Newman was behind the wheel of the four-wheel-drive taking his passengers – Paula by his side with Tweed and Beaurain in the rear seats – down to the embankment.

'Which route are you taking?' Paula asked, by now completely lost.

'Any which way,' he replied. 'To avoid early morning traffic already building up. Buchanan has already closed the bridges and both sides of the embankment.'

They wended their way down side streets Paula had never known existed. Behind them followed three more four-wheel-drives. One contained Harry, driving, with all the murderous equipment piled into the vehicle, covered with canvas.

Behind him Nield drove with Sarge, well-muffled, beside him. The rear of the vehicle was packed with more weaponry, also concealed under canvas. This consignment was for the SAS and Sarge had put it aboard himself. All that Nield could see of Sarge was his eyes and his mouth, above and below a scarf.

Characteristically, the fourth vehicle was driven by Marler, who was by himself. His four-wheel-drive was also transporting more SAS equipment. Again the equipment was concealed by a canvas sheet. On the seat by his side rested an

Armalite rifle, Marler's favourite weapon. He still held the legend of being the finest marksman in Western Europe.

Suddenly they were on the embankment. Paula sucked in her breath. She had never seen the embankment look like this before. She reflected she'd never see this sight again.

No traffic. No pedestrians. Westminster Bridge had been deserted. Dawn shed its spectacular light on the fast-moving Thames heading upriver. It was like something out of of a dream. The peace, the silence, only broken by the swish of the incoming tide splashing against the walls.

'It's high tide,' she said.

'Not yet,' Newman corrected. 'That's at 5.30 p.m.'

'So al-Qa'eda has chosen its attack time well.'

'It has,' he agreed. 'Tweed is convinced the same man planned September 11 in New York, the Trade Center tragedy. He's also convinced the mastermind is not an Arab. He's American or an Englishman.'

'Or a woman,' she said again.

She studied the map of the river Tweed had handed to her just before the vehicles left Park Crescent. At the head it was marked TOP SECRET. He told her Sarge had handed him this map on his first visit to Park Crescent.

'The blue circles show where we will be stationed at our firing points,' she remarked. 'The red ones are SAS firing points. Sarge must have recced this area in the middle of the night.'

'He did.'

Newman was driving at a moderate speed. He glanced in his rear-view mirror. The other three vehicles were strung out at intervals behind him. Paula stared across the river at the opposite bank. No sign of Buchanan's anti-terrorist squad, but she knew they would be there.

'We're about to pass an SAS firing-point,' she warned.

Newman glanced to his left. Beyond the pavement reared up a wall, a viewing platform almost invisible, surrounded by massed trees without foliage. Sarge had chosen well, but he would. Thirty yards past it he parked, leaving his engine running.

'Look back,' he said.

Vehicle No. 3, driven by Nield with Sarge by his side, had stopped. Four masked men with black caps and clothes had appeared from nowhere. They unloaded Nield's vehicle while Sarge supervised. Some of the equipment looked very heavy. Tweed spoke for the first time as he gazed back.

'Superbly well organized.'

Beaurain had also turned in his seat to look. His gaze was critical. Suddenly the vehicle was emptied. The masked men, some disguised for night with blackened faces, had vanished. So had all the equipment, some of it clearly very heavy.

'Incredibly professional,' Beaurain remarked. 'And they have camouflaged the jeeps brilliantly.'

'The jeeps?' Paula queried.

'Well,' Beaurain explained, 'they will start being positioned at that point to protect Waterloo Bridge. Once their work is done there they have to drive back like mad along the deserted embankment to reinforce the unit stationed further upriver. You'll find in a minute we also have jeeps.'

Harry, in vehicle No. 2, had paused while this part of the preparations took place. As Newman drove on so did Harry. Paula stared once more at the growing dawn, a spectrum of pink and blue and green. She wished she'd brought a camera to record the glorious sight.

Newman seemed to read her mind. Using one hand to drive, he delved under his windcheater with the other. When it emerged it was holding a small camera. He handed it to Paula.

'In case you need it.'

'Bless you.'

She took six shots of the dawn just before day came

361

and the spectacle was replaced by a clear blue sky. She purred.

'I could kiss you.'

'Not now. Keep your eye on the map.'

'Sorry. Slow down. I think we're almost there.'

Newman pulled up alongside a location where a statue of a man on a horse was perched on a huge plinth well back from the pavement, shrouded by a mass of leafless trees. Tweed jumped out first, clambered up to the plinth, took out a pair of field-glasses and scanned the river. Paula had hauled herself up behind him, followed by Beaurain and Newman. To their surprise vehicle No. 3 had arrived and Sarge leapt up to join them on the plinth.

'From here,' said Tweed, 'we can disable the first barge and protect not only Waterloo Bridge but Hungerford Bridge, which carries all the trains from Charing Cross.'

'If we succeed,' said Nield, who had joined them.

'*When* we succeed,' growled Sarge.

Vehicle No. 2, driven by Harry, had parked below them. His voice expressed frustration.

'You lazy lot up there. Get down here and help me bring up the weaponry. Now!'

Sarge took control. He lay down on the edge of the plinth and issued the order.

'All of you go down, fetch equipment, hand it to me. It will save time clambering up the plinth. We must keep moving.'

Paula was the first to reach the vehicle. Harry handed her a sub-machine gun, a satchel of ammo. She insisted she could take two guns. Scrambling with her burden up to the base of the plinth, she handed one weapon, then another, then the ammo satchel to Sarge, who grasped them in his hands, laid them behind him on the plinth. She was surprised at his great strength.

When all the weapons were delivered they were covered with heavy canvas to conceal them. All except Sarge were perspiring when they had completed the job. Paula stood on the plinth as she asked the question.

'Where are our jeeps?'

Sarge made a sound which could have been a chuckle. He pointed down to the side of the pavement.

'You've walked past them several times. They're under all those branches piled against the embankment wall. Now, we must start work.'

'What was that we have been doing?' Paula asked.

'Initial preparation.'

A semaphore light began flashing from the other side of the river. Sarge stared intently. Then he produced from a satchel over his shoulder a signalling lamp, flashed back a reply.

'What was that?' Tweed asked.

'Buchanan. Asking if all goes well. I replied all is going well, all will go well . . .'

The convoy of four-wheel drives reversed, except that Newman raced past them to take the lead, knowing the route. Now they had four more bridges, some way upriver, to locate and furnish firing-points already mapped out by Sarge.

He must have spent most of the night deciding on the best location, thought Paula. Yet he's moving round like a man who has had eight hours' sleep.

Again and again the SAS units appeared from nowhere when they reached a fresh firing-point. More and more weapons were stockpiled for both groups. At one point Newman approached Sarge to ask him a question he had forgotten.

'At the plinth between Waterloo and Westminster bridges I noticed we were overlooked by office buildings. Surely we would be seen by people inside?'

'No.' It was Beaurain who answered. 'Buchanan had every building evacuated. Reason given, danger of major

363

gas explosion. They were gone – if any tried to enter – long before we arrived. Including security and cleaning people.'

Paula found herself acting like an automaton. Carrying a load of weaponry, running back to Marler's vehicle which seemed stuffed with endless weapons. She was surprised at the rate Tweed kept up, showing no signs of fatigue. Then she remembered that these days he took to walking the two miles to and from his flat to Park Crescent. He looked remarkably fit.

They did not proceed with the vehicle convoy to Albert Bridge. As on the journey out, early in the morning only one vehicle made its way there. Newman again drove with Paula by his side. In the rear seats Tweed sat next to Beaurain.

As they approached the area Paula was once more struck by the eerie atmosphere. No traffic. No people. Nothing moving on the river. As though London had been frozen into a strange ice age. She pointed to the apartment buildings and houses close to the river.

'Anyone at home?'

'No one,' Tweed told her. 'Buchanan has evacuated everyone who might be within range of what is going to happen. A few argued but he didn't take any notice. Same explanation. A huge gas explosion feared.'

Newman stopped the car when they were close to the bridge. Paula stared in puzzlement. She was tired and couldn't grasp what might have happened.

'There are cars all along the far side of the bridge. Why?'

'It's wrecks obtained from a car crusher firm. Brought out on huge transporters. So the first bridge al-Qa'eda see will look normal.'

'I'd like to take a few photos. It's a beautiful bridge . . .'

They waited while she got out, aimed her camera. Lighting was perfect. She took twelve pictures. Then stood gazing at what wouldn't be there in a few hours. She felt

364

sad. Returning to the car she smiled, thanked them. They headed back for Park Crescent, Newman trying to find a way through alley-like streets.

During the complex drive back to Park Crescent Paula sat with a serious expression. She was unusually silent. Before getting back into the car she had glanced at the serene view downriver. Supposing al-Qa'eda succeeded? Destroyed all the target bridges? London would be severed in two. As in the time long ago of Roman occupation. Worse – the Romans had spanned the river efficiently. Behind her Beaurain leaned forward, as though sensing her fears. He squeezed her shoulder.

    'Stop worrying, Paula. We shall pull it off.'

45

At Carpford Margesson, wearing a suit, drove the four-wheel-drive he had kept concealed in a shed. The suit was necessary. Dressed in his robes, it would have been dangerous driving.

Skilfully, after leaving the village, he sped down the curving road. There was a wind, which rustled his beard. Above, the sun shone down out of a duck-egg-blue sky. His extraordinary face had a determined expression.

Anxious to reach his destination, he spun round curves at speed. He roared up the sunken tunnel with Black Wood above him on either side. Reaching the triangle he swung down towards the main road leading to London.

Inside a holster strapped under his jacket he carried a pistol, fully loaded. He had no illusions as to the jungle the world had become. At one deserted point he raised his voice, called out.

'Allah be praised.'

His tone of voice had a peculiar inflection.

Peregrine Palfry, faultlessly dressed, walked down White-hall. He wondered why it was so deserted. No traffic. No people. He had even had to identify himself at a police checkpoint before he could enter Whitehall.

He was mystified and very worried. In one hand he carried the obligatory briefcase, part of the uniform. The other hand grasped a tightly rolled umbrella. Ridiculous considering the clear blue sky, the sun shining down on him.

He checked his watch. It was all a matter of timing. He ran up the steps to the Ministry, jammed his thumb into the bell. He was taken aback when, instead of the usual guard, a uniformed policeman opened the door. Furious, he had to show identification before the policeman would let him enter. This really was too much. He was personal assistant to the Minister. He glared.

'What on earth is going on?'

'Danger of major gas explosion, sir. Could bring down whole buildings.'

Palfry hurried up to the Minister's office. He wouldn't be there. A full meeting of the Cabinet was in session. He had to find out what was really going on.

Drew Franklin, wearing a white polo-necked sweater and white, perfectly creased slacks, left his office at the *Daily Nation*. Erect as a military officer, he walked into the editor's office without bothering to knock.

The editor looked up, frowning, then saw who it was. He smiled. Drew was one of their major assets, a reason why their daily sales kept climbing. Drew was also prickly and had to be handled with care. He opened his mouth, but Drew spoke first in his upper-crust, barking voice.

'You have to hold the front page for tomorrow,' he ordered. 'It will be fully occupied by a major story I shall be writing. Do make sure those clots downstairs understand.'

Saying which, he left the room before the editor could reply. The editor rubbed his eyes, picked up the phone and passed the news downstairs. He refused to explain the reason for this unprecedented decision. He felt better when he'd put down the phone. Had to be careful. Drew could be back asking if he had carried out the instruction.

★   ★   ★

The Cabinet meeting was coming to an end. Victor Warner was looking pleased, self-satisfied. They had approved the new mandate the PM had personally composed. No option really. The PM was presiding at the meeting. A copy of the mandate was already on its way to Park Crescent by motor-cycle courier.

A spanner in the works at a critical moment. He only wished he could be present when Tweed received his copy.

Inside the Minister's penthouse, Mrs Carson was irritated beyond endurance. Eva Brand, seated at her desk in Warner's study, was checking her watch yet again. She must have checked the time five times in the last hour.

'Mrs Carson,' Eva snapped. 'First, you have no right in here without permission. Second, if you had to deal with this heap of papers by a deadline you would worry about time.'

'But you keep on checking your watch,' Mrs Carson complained, repeating what she had said when she'd entered.

'The needle has got stuck in the crack,' Eva retorted. 'You have said that once already. Now, tomorrow morning the Minister is holding a special meeting at Carpford. I have a lot to accomplish. May I, therefore, suggest you leave this room?'

'I am the housekeeper,' Mrs Carson replied, drawing herself up.

'Then go and keep house in the kitchen. Or the toilet for all I care. But get out of this study and stay out.' Her voice was hard. So was her expression. 'And close the door behind you. Quietly, please.'

'Well, I never . . .'

'No, you probably never did. Just go. *Now!*'

At this stage in her life the last thing Eva was prepared to put up with was impertinence from a housekeeper. As the door closed quietly she checked her watch once more.

★   ★   ★

It was a blockbuster. Tweed, together with Paula, Beaurain and Newman, had just settled in the office when Howard walked in. Moving slowly, he looked very unhappy. In his right hand he held a sheet of paper. Paula stared. Never before had she seen the Director look embarrassed.

'Sorry to intrude,' Howard began. 'I thought you ought to know right away, Tweed. The PM has revoked his previous order placing you in supreme command of the operation. This has just arrived by courier.'

For a short time there was silence. Then there were groans. Someone, under their breath, but clear enough for all to hear, questioned the legitimacy of the PM's birth.

Only Tweed remained undisturbed, his face without expression. He held out his hand to Howard who handed him the document. Tweed scanned it swiftly, then read it out aloud.

From now on I would appreciate close collaboration between the SIS and the Ministry of Security. Whenever this may be necessary to facilitate the success of the operation. As and when Mr Tweed may consider it will ensure success.

Tweed looked up. It was signed by the PM himself. Below it detailed copies to the Home Secretary, the Deputy Commissioner of Scotland Yard, Chief Superintendent Buchanan of Scotland Yard. Nothing more.

'It will be a disaster,' Newman burst out. 'A complete and terrible disaster.'

'I don't think so at all,' Tweed told him. 'You haven't noticed something is missing.'

'What is that?' Howard asked.

'No copy to me, listed at the foot of the document. This is a photocopy, doubtless sent by Victor Warner. The PM is simply soothing fevered brows. In no way does it change my original status.'

'Thank God,' said Howard. 'Sorry, I missed that omission.'

The phone rang. Monica called over to Tweed.

'Victor Warner is on the line to speak to you.'

Tweed switched on the new speak-box Monica had installed. He disliked it but had thanked her fulsomely. Now everyone would hear the ensuing conversation. He also pressed the record button.

'Yes, Minister.'

'That's Tweed, isn't it? I recognize the dulcet tones,' the voice sneered.

'What is it?'

'I have heard rumours – which I believe to be accurate – that a meeting was held in your office to which I was not invited.'

'That's right. You were not invited,' Tweed replied.

'Do you realize the Prime Minister has ordered the closest collaboration between all security services on the dreadful situation facing us?'

'Read the communication again, Warner. It does say, "As and when Mr Tweed may consider it will ensure success." So any decision is for me to take, as in the original mandate. You really should read communications from the PM more carefully.'

'*Tweed!* I consider you are exceeding your powers . . .'

'Then go on considering it. I am fully occupied dealing with the crisis . . .'

He switched off. Hand-clapping and cheers broke out. Tweed glared.

'That will be enough of that. We have wasted four minutes over nothing at all.' He turned to Howard. 'Thank you for keeping me up to date. I fear Warner is losing his nerve.'

'Thank you, Tweed.' Howard came forward and gripped him on the shoulder. 'You know I have the fullest confidence in you.' He turned to the others. 'In all of you.' Then he left.

371

Paula had often admired the way Tweed in a crisis never forgot a detail. He demonstrated this quality now. Handing the photocopy of the PM's latest communication to Monica, he spoke quickly.

'Better keep that. File it under junk mail. Now I'd like to know what has happened to Billy Hogarth. I imagine Harry and Pete brought him back here before we left for the embankment.'

'Yes, they did. He's downstairs.'

'Not in the basement, I hope?'

'Of course not. He's in the visitors' room. The door locked and George just outside.'

'Not a very comfortable place for him to be.'

'It is now!' Monica was indignant. 'I got some of the men in the basement to carry up the bed. I made it up with new sheets and blankets and pillows. I covered that bleak table with a thick tablecloth so he can eat there. He has a whole crop of paperback thrillers. I popped in to see him after I'd given him breakfast just before you got back. He was in bed, perched up against a pillow. He had a paperback in his lap and had fallen asleep. I think he needs a lot of sleep. Satisfied?'

'Bless you!' Tweed threw up his hands in aplology. 'You are an angel. I should have guessed.'

'Yes, you should have,' she retorted, still irked.

'I'll go down and see him when I can. When he's awake. He can use the shower upstairs when he wants to.'

'I should hope so,' she replied, staring at her word-processor.

'What happened to Pete and Harry when we got back?' Tweed wondered.

'Went down to the basement to get some kip on camp beds,' Marler told him.

'Anyone else who needs sleep?' Tweed enquired quietly. He pointed to Newman who had sagged in the armchair, eyes shut.

'Not me,' Beaurain said also quietly when Tweed looked at him. 'I can go a long time without it. If I close my eyes now it will just fog my brain.'

'Give me something to do,' Marler suggested.

'What you did before. Track down Eva Brand anonymously as you did last time. Then watch her and track her if she goes somewhere. I need to know who, if anyone, she contacts.'

'I'm on my way . . .'

When he had left, Paula came across to Tweed's desk, sat in the armchair opposite Newman. She began whispering when Newman opened his eyes.

'You can talk normally. A few minutes' kip and I'm a new man.'

'You do seem interested in keeping an eye on Eva,' Paula said. 'Could I see that photo Nield took when he went to the Finsbury Park mosque. Seems a year ago.'

She studied the photo inside a plastic evidence envelope Tweed handed her. She turned the photo this way and that, examining the picture of a tallish figure tilted sideways as it walked. Wearing Arab clothes.

'I do know who this is.' She pursed her lips in annoyance. I just can't put my finger on it. Maddening.'

She gave him back the envelope as the phone rang again. Monica said a visitor alleging Tweed knew him was waiting. Tweed checked his watch. Midday. As usual Sarge was on time. Tweed asked Monica and Paula if they would mind leaving them alone. Newman could stay, along with Beaurain.

46

The meeting with Sarge did not take long. Neither Tweed nor the SAS man believed in wasting words or time. Sarge listened while Tweed outlined the defence plan as he understood it. He had only one comment to make when Tweed concluded.

'I think we both know that no battle ever goes according to plan.'

'I anticipate the unexpected,' Tweed agreed.

As Tweed stood up, escorted him to the door, Sarge turned and shook hands. His grip was firm and above the scarf his eyes stared into his host's. Tweed knew what he was doing. He was shaking hands for what might be the last time – in case either one or both did not survive.

'Now,' remarked Tweed when Sarge had gone, 'I wish I knew the identity of the leader. Who really is Abdullah?'

'Abdullah?' Paula queried.

'I had a brief phone call a while ago. Informing me the head of al-Qa'eda was Abdullah. The voice of the caller was using a distorter so I couldn't tell whether it was a man or a woman.'

'And you believed the caller?'

'Yes. Now I must go down and see how Billy Hogarth is getting on. Later we all leave here on motor-bikes. Harry has hired several extra. We must take up our first firing position at dusk, being in place by dark.'

'One more sad aspect.' He turned before opening the

door. 'I took up the fate of Proctor, the guard at Dick's wharf, held prisoner. As you heard me do so. Sarge was emphatic, was he not, that we cannot risk alerting the al-Qa'eda cell before they attack. I had already come to the same decision.'

'That really is awful,' Paula said. 'His wife has been saved but he will die.'

'Finally,' Tweed told them before leaving, 'the Minister has invited me to meet him at his house in Carpford tomorrow morning at ten o'clock for what he ghoulishly describes as an inquest.' He extracted an envelope from his pocket. 'This, sent by courier, is what Monica handed me before she left the office. I shall accept and be there.'

'By yourself, you mean?' Paula asked.

'No. The invitation names only myself, but I'm sure others will be there. Palfry for one. Also Superintendent Buchanan. So my whole team will come with me, whether they are welcome or not. You'd better get dressed hadn't you, for what is to come . . .'

The phone rang. Tweed paused, then picked it up. He listened, ended the call, look at Paula and Beaurain.

'Something unexpected. A Mr Margesson has arrived downstairs. From the description it is our Margesson from Carpford . . .'

He gave them a little salute and went downstairs. Paula stared at Newman.

'What on earth is going on?'

Marler, Harry and Pete arrived in the office, loaded down with clothing. Black outfits with the large white "S" on the backs. Marler had even found an outfit which perfectly fitted the tall Beaurain.

Paula had donned hers before the others. She stood in front of a tall mirror attached to the wall, pulled down the jacket, studied the result quickly. The outfit was black leather. It had a psychological effect on her. Now she couldn't wait to reach the embankment. She then slipped on one of the green oilcloths which concealed what she wore underneath.

'You looked very come-hitherish in black leather,' Newman teased her.

'More than I can say for you.'

'Well, you'll be travelling on my motor-cycle, riding pillion, so you'll just have to put up with it. Mind you clasp me firmly round the waist.'

'The things I do for England.'

It had taken them a while for everyone to put on the kit. Pete Nield had trouble getting himself comfortable. They were all completely dressed when Tweed walked in. He immediately began to put on his own outfit without saying a word. Paula thought he looked exceptionally grim.

'It was our Margesson,' he announced when he had dressed. 'He is staying here the night. Monica is making the room Howard's secretary works in comfortable. With George downstairs, like Billy Hogarth he will be safe.'

'You really are looking very grim,' Paula remarked.

'Time to go,' he replied. 'Look out of the window. It will soon be dusk. We will soon know the outcome.'

47

Paula knew she would never forget the motor-cycle caval-
cade ride which took them down on to the embankment. It
was still daylight, on the edge of dusk. Newman led the way
after being given the exact route to follow by Buchanan on
the phone.

Each machine carried a yellow flag fluttering in the wind
which had sprung up. The moment a police checkpoint in
the distance saw them coming they cleared the way, forcing
irate motorists to drive up on to pavements.

All the motor-cyclists had their lights full on. In the
beams she saw a chaos of traffic worse then any she'd
ever seen before. Insults were shouted at them by some
motorists, while others made rude gestures. If only you lot
knew what we're trying to save you from, Paula thought.

Suddenly they were close to Westminster Bridge. It then
became a strange dream – nightmare? No street lights
along the embankment. Dusk had fallen and she realized
a moon was rising. Had they allowed for this unwanted
illumination?

Newman sped along the dark escarpment which was the
embankment. Even though she knew the firing-points,
Paula could see no sign anywhere of the SAS. They had
to be in position but were invisible. The wind ruffled
the surface of the swift-moving river. Had they taken
into account the effect a wind like this might have, she
wondered? It had not been forecast.

Arriving at the elevated plinth with the statue, Newman parked his machine against the inner kerb, jumped off as Harry arrived behind him. Normally so nimble, Paula was beaten to the top of the plinth by Harry. He immediately pulled back the protective canvas, handed her a sub-machine gun and extra ammo. He also gave her a radio headset to put on.

'We have total communication with the SAS and Buchanan's anti-terrorist mob on the other shore,' he told her. 'Get that microphone closer to your mouth.'

Tweed had arrived on the plinth. Like Paula, he threw off his oilcloth so his leather clothes were exposed. He attached a headset. He was followed by Newman and Marler, carrying his Armalite rifle. Nield joined them. He had thrown off his oilcloth on the pavement and accepted a sub-machine gun from Harry.

'Is this radio system completely safe, secure?' asked Paula.

She had a shock. Not realizing her words had passed into her microphne. A voice she recognised as Sarge's replied, as calm as if this were an exercise.

'Completely secure, Paula. We have a genius who produced it.'

'Thank you . . .'

'One more warning,' Sarge continued, 'when a transport goes down or is disabled, we may face motorized dinghies – or even small speedboats – heading for the shore. Assume all the men inside them will be suicide bombers – because they will be. Over and out . . .'

Only then did it occur to Paula that Sarge's words would be heard by several score men waiting on both sides of the river. And anything she said. She decided to do it.

'There's a very strong wind. Not forecast. It may affect the steering of the transports.'

'Good point,' Sarge replied. 'I was just going to make it myself. Assume it will be a circus. Those who can throw a good distance – and accurately – may wish to use grenades on any hostile craft approaching.'

'Here you are,' said Harry, one hand over his mike so what he was saying wouldn't fog up communications. With his other hand he gave Paula a heavy satchel. When she looked inside inside she saw a collection of grenades. She slung the satchel over her shoulder, checked her sub-machine gun by light of the moon.

'We overlooked the strength of the moon,' Sarge warned. 'It may be a help or a hindrance. We'll find out, won't we?'

Sarge was clever, Paula thought. He used 'transports' as opposed to 'barges'. It suggested to her he was not one hundred per cent convinced about the security of their communications.

'Pete and myself,' said Harry, one hand still blocking his mike, 'are going down to the edge of the embankment. If any try to come ashore we'll be closer to them . . .'

Saying which, he leapt off the plinth, a satchel of grenades over his shoulder, sub-machine gun in one hand, followed by Pete. Crossing the embankment, they crouched behind the wall.

'I think we're ready for anything,' said Beaurain, who spoke only rarely.

'Famous last words,' back came the comment from Sarge.

Beaurain was crouched behind the statue, which loomed above them. For the first time Paula wondered who had merited the honour of the stone figure on horseback. Some general who had commanded in some long-ago war. Now he was hardly noticed. Pass beyond your time and you became a footnote in history. Such was the juggernaut passage of life.

'Exbar is now leaving station,' a strange voice came over her headset.

Exbar? Must be the code-word for the six barges. They

were on the move. She felt Tweed, standing close to her, stiffen. He was wondering whether they had the sequence right. Paula checked the illuminated face of her watch. 4.35 p.m. Al-Qa'eda had started their attack early.

'Get ready.' Sarge's voice. 'Up here it should be a while yet. If we are right,' he added ominously.

Paula's nerves had earlier rattled her, a normal experience. Now she was cold. Her eyes were fixed on Westminster bridge, the first place their barge would appear. *If we are right.* She extracted a water-bottle from her new shoulder-bag which she always carried, containing the Browning. She sipped cold water, swilled it round her mouth, then swallowed. Might be the last chance for a drink.

Inside the managing director's room at Dick's wharf, Proctor was still tied hand and foot to the heavy chair. Earlier the ropes round his arms had been unfastened so he could exercise them. The same method had been used so he could exercise his legs later.

They had also fed their captive and provided him with water and tea. No humanitarian reasons prompted Ali to arrange these measures. It was important to keep Proctor fresh and alert. Then if Dixon phoned him he would be able to reply in a normal way.

Ali now came into the room and went over to Proctor. He had decided he *would* command barge No. 5, the barge which would bring down Chelsea Bridge. By then, destroying Albert Bridge would be a walkover. He bent down close to his prisoner, waved away the large ugly-looking guard.

'Mr Proctor, when we have completed what we must do we will leave you here. Then, when we are well away from this area, we will phone your wife and ask her to arrange for the police to come here at once. To release you . . .'

Proctor simply looked at him. By now he hated all these Arabs, would gladly have killed every single one, given the chance.

Ali beckoned to the huge guard, spoke to him in Arabic, well away from Proctor.

'When you see the last barge about to leave, men casting off the ropes, you will shoot your captive. A bullet in the head to make sure. A rope ladder will hang over the hull of the barge, waiting to haul you aboard before it sails. But for the moment we must keep him calm . . .'

Had Paula been able to witness the appalling cruelty of Ali's tactic and had a knife in her hand, she would not have hesitated to plunge it up to the hilt into Ali's chest.

5.05 p.m. The tide was turning. Paula had taken a pair of very small powerful binoculars from her shoulder-bag. They were adapted for night use, so everything came up green. She had them focused on Westminster Bridge.

Sarge had earlier confirmed that the 'transports' were moving downriver. That so far no bridge had been attacked, that they were spread apart at a greater distance than expected. So it was looking as though they had the sequence right.

'Here it comes,' said Tweed quietly.

'Red alert,' Sarge ordered.

In the lenses of her glasses Paula saw the huge bows of the barge slowly passing under Westminster Bridge. It seemed larger than the barges she had once seen proceeding upriver. A massive beast.

She frowned, adjusted the focus, pressed her eyes closer to the lenses. She was focused on the bows as the vessel was caught by a large wave, whipped up by the strong wind. She frowned.

'Main hatch open,' she reported. 'But there's some kind of machine or weapon in the bows. It appears to be angled at the main struts holding up the bridges. On deck. At the bows. Looks like a small cannon or missile launcher.'

'Thank you,' said Sarge. 'Thank you very much.'

Perched on the wall of his firing-point, camouflaged with branches, was a large weapon which looked like a mortar.

383

Below the barrel was a projection which emitted a laser beam on the pressing of a lever. It was brand new, an advanced version the Army did not possess, didn't even know existed.

Close to it was a smaller version with an even longer barrel, narrower than the large mortar. It too was equipped with another muzzle beneath the main one, the barrel of which also emitted a laser beam.

Closing down his radio set, Sarge walked over to the second operator, in charge of the smaller weapon. He bent down, talking quietly.

'There's a second weapon aboard the barge. On deck, at the bows. When Charlie fires his bomb you shoot a missile at the second target, equally dangerous.' He handed the operator his night-glasses. 'See if you can spot it. On deck. At the bows.'

'I see it,' the operator replied.

'You have to synchronize the firings.' He looked up at the operator's partner. 'Up to you, Ned – drop in the missile at the same moment.'

'We can manage that,' said the senior operator, who would adjust the aim of his weapon. 'Reckon so, Ed?'

Ed, the man who would drop the main bomb into the mortar, had been leaning over, listening. He just nodded. They would cope.

Paula couldn't take her eyes off the huge barge, now fully in view, riding the waves on its way to Waterloo Bridge. 'It would have been so much easier if the river were smooth,' she said, then remembered she was speaking into the mike.

'It would,' Sarge's voice agreed. 'But we'll still make it. Thanks to you . . .'

Tweed put a reassuring hand on Paula's shoulder. Beaurain crouched lower, as the barge would soon be opposite the SAS firing-point. Not knowing about the special equipment at the SAS's disposal, he had his doubts.

Marler came alongside her, holding his Armalite. He was

384

expecting trouble. She could tell from his expression. He glanced at her.

'Don't forget the grenades . . .'

He was still speaking when the full length of the barge arrived opposite the SAS firing-point. She raised her night-glasses, pressed them to her eyes just in time. A large shell-like object streaked in an arc over the water, dropped down the hatch. At the same moment a missile hit the weapon stationed in the bows. She wasn't ready. Wasn't ready for the titanic explosions. The barge shuddered under the impact. The shockwave thumped against the plinth. She jumped, steadied herself.

The bows dipped into the river, stayed dipped. The roll-over deck was hurled into the air in three large pieces, fell back into the river with a large splash. The barge was now moving sluggishly, the half-sunk bows slowing it so that it was almost stationary. It was going nowhere.

'Watch out!' Sarge's warning voice. 'They're coming.'

Motorized dinghies were being slung over the side of the hull, attached to ropes. Black turbaned men were sliding down the ropes into the dinghies. Motors roared, then they were heading direct towards the plinth. At least a dozen dinghies and one small speedboat, churning up water as it tore towards them.

All hell was heading for the embankment.

Paula hadn't seen Harry carrying a rocket launcher down to the wall. He rammed it into his shoulder. The speedboat had four men aboard, some waving savage-looking knives. Harry took careful aim, fired the rocket. It curved, dropped, bull's-eye on the speedboat.

The craft exploded. Everything became fragments. Fragments of speedboat, fragments of the men who had been aboard. Paula jumped off the plinth, ran down to support Harry and Pete. Beaurain was beside her. Dinghies were racing to where Harry and Pete crouched.

Something bloody and fleshy landed on the embankment near Paula. She glanced at it. Beaurain stared, frowned.

'Most of a man's stomach,' she told him.

'You know that?' he shouted.

'I've attended autopsies.'

'So have I.'

Beaurain was impressed with the steeliness and calmness Paula was displaying under fire.

Three dinghies, spread well apart, were racing to the embankment. Nield, moving his sub-machine gun in an arc, sprayed two of them. As his bullets hit, the explosives strapped round the Arabs exploded. There was a deafening roar. Arabs and dinghies vanished. Something small and white landed on the wall in front of Paula. A fragment of one of the devastated dinghies.

More dinghies raced towards the embankment. Again well spaced out. Harry let loose a burst. Nield was firing at the same time. More deafening explosions. Paula aimed her sub-machine gun at a dinghy which had pulled ahead of the others. For a moment she could see their savage faces illuminated by moonlight. She pressed the trigger. The faces, the heads, were no longer there. Another explosion. No dinghy. The stretch of river sweeping past had a reddish colour.

To their left a dinghy had reached the embankment wall. Two men scrambled over the wall. They had seen the group below the plinth. They elevated their Kalashnikovs. Beaurain had seen them. He aimed his sub-machine gun, was startled to see one man throw up his Kalashnikov, collapsing backwards. He pressed the trigger. A storm of bullets hit the second man like a hurricane.

'First chap was mine,' Marler's voice said behind Beaurain. He had shot him with his Armalite.

Further along to their right there had been continuous gunfire from the SAS, eliminating more dinghies with armed men aboard. Suddenly the inferno of sound –

386

exploding Arabs in their dinghies, the rattle of weapons keeping up a non-stop bombardment from the embankment – had stopped.

The silence Paula had experienced while they'd driven to the plinth returned. It was almost a shock. She wiped her sweating hands on her uniform, poked a finger gently in her right ear. The silence was more apparent. Her eyes were fixed on the barge in the middle of the river.

It was an awesome spectacle. The combination of the huge bomb waiting to be launched through the main hatch together with – perfect timing – Sarge's counter-bomb plunging down before the Arabs had detonated their bomb, had caused an explosion of terrible power. Plus the fact that the explosion took place in the confined space of the interior hull.

Amidships, the barge was splitting open. The river poured in, adding to the pressure. Paula stared in wonderment as the barge separated into two parts. The forward area where the bows were already diving below the surface. The stern area wallowing.

'You stupid sightseers, get back here into the jeeps,' Tweed's commanding voice echoed in the silence. 'Our friends are already on their way.'

'Coming,' Paula shouted back.

'We have to save Westminster Bridge,' Tweed thundered back.

She dived into the first jeep, where Tweed was already behind the wheel. Newman had cleared the camouflage branches from three jeeps. Tweed had started the vehicle moving when she looked back in time to see Beaurain jumping into a rear seat.

Behind them Newman was driving another jeep. She saw Harry scrambling over the back into a rear seat while the jeep was in motion.

The third jeep was being driven by Marler, shouting something she couldn't hear. Just as well, his language was salty. Nield just managed to climb over into a rear seat as Marler began moving. The fact that everyone was encumbered with heavy satchels, were clutching sub-machine guns, hadn't helped them.

Paula looked ahead, just in time to see the last of the SAS jeeps disappearing. They had to be in position before barge No. 2 arrived. At this stage Paula said to herself, 'No casualties so far.' Not aloud. Tempting fate.

Nor had she any reason to realize that the assault on Westminster Bridge would be a near-disaster.

48

Aboard Barge No. 4, Ali also had radio communication with the skippers of the other barges. Not as sophisticated as Sarge's, it still gave him warning of what was happening.

'We are being killed by gunmen ashore,' Mohammed, skipper of the first barge, reported as his control station at the rear began to sink.

'Stay calm. Be precise,' Ali ordered.

'All the men in dinghies who headed for the left bank have been killed. That is where the enemy is . . .'

'What weapons are they using?' Ali demanded.

'Automatic weapons. Many of them . . .'

'Where are the gunmen stationed?'

'Somewhere on the river bank. We didn't see them . . .'

Mohammed adjusted his headset. He voice was becoming hysterical. The deckhouse was now close to the water. Soon it would be under the river.

'What about the bridge? Your objective?' snapped Ali.

'Waterloo is standing. We are sinking. The whole barge . . .'

'You should have told me that first. What caused it to sink?'

'I'm leaving. I'm going to drown . . .'

The voice ended in a gurgle as the river flooded into the deckhouse with terrifying speed. Mohammed was drowned before he could make his way out.

Ali had heard the first gurgle, had guessed what had happened. The trouble was all the skippers of the other barges would have heard the calamitous news. Different tactics were called for as they approached Westminster. He took a quick decision.

Europeans always repeated their tactics. Especially when they were successful. He had to surprise them. His voice was calm as he spoke again.

'The plan will proceed. Mohammed was exaggerating. He became hysterical. I am now coming aboard Barge No. 2. Have a rope ladder at the stern I can use to come aboard.'

He turned to his deputy, saw that he had anticipated what Ali would need. He was lowering a small, powerful speedboat at the stern. He then shinned down the rope to take over the controls.

Ali was beside him before he had expected the commander's arrival. Ali spoke quietly, firmly.

'Top speed. Remember to *zig-zag* – the way you did once on the Nile. We will trick them.'

49

The SIS and SAS units were in position roughly midway between Westminster and Lambeth bridges. They were well-concealed. Paula wore her night-glasses as the menacing snout of the next barge appeared under Lambeth Bridge.

Once again she spotted the second weapon stationed on deck to take down the main struts of the next target. She reported to Sarge. The barge was clear of the bridge swiftly, helped by the turn of the tide now flowing downriver, by the wind which was gaining in strength . . .

She pressed the lenses closer to her eyes, puzzled. Could not believe was she was seeing. It was important to tell Sarge what she was seeing.

'Barge changing direction. Appears to be heading towards this bank, towards us.'

'I have seen,' Sarge replied. 'Thanks for confirmation.'

'That's not all. Wait a minute. I must be sure . . .'

She was scanning the deck from stern to prow. Large numbers of the enemy were crouched down on the port side. *Their* side. Why? Then she saw the barrels of many weapons perched on the gunwale. She made herself speak calmly.

'Arabs in force stationed along deck. Almost hidden by gunwale. A huge quantity of weapons ready to fire.'

'Thank you . . .'

Sarge raised his own glasses, swept them along the

deck. She was right. He grasped at once the new tactic. Diabolically clever. He issued a new order.

'No one, repeat *no one* is to open fire whatever happens. They are waiting for us to do that – so they can locate our positions. We may come under fire. Do *not* reply.'

The barge, looking immense the closer it came, was sailing on an almost diagonal course across the river. Sarge could not fire his bomb and missile at this angle. But soon they would have to change course or hit the embankment.

'No dinghies came our way. They will later,' Buchanan reported.

It was the first time the Superintendent had communicated with them. It told Tweed, Beaurain – and Sarge – that the police anti-terrorist force stationed on the opposite bank was in the closest touch with the situation.

'Turn, damn you,' Paula said to herself.

As though hearing her, the barge changed course to avoid collision with the embankment. Then it began. A storm of bullets raked the embankment and the area beyond. Once started, it never seemed to stop. Not knowing where their opponents were, the al-Qa'eda were doing everything possible to tempt return fire – so their enemy's locations would be revealed.

Paula crouched lower, pushed down by Beaurain. It took incredible will-power to stay still under the barrage of gunfire without returning fire. Paula gritted her teeth, hating this situation. She glanced at Tweed, was surprised at his clinical expression. Typical, she thought. In a crisis he freezes.

The murderous barrage continued. She heard a gulp from her left, saw Harry clutching his shoulder. He had been hit. Moving very carefully, she reached him, removed his hand – covered with blood. She felt inside her shoulder-bag, took out her medical kit.

Using scissors, she gently cut away a portion of his uniform from the top of his shoulder. She risked using her torch, shielding the beam with one hand. The bullet had grazed his shoulder, scooping out a shallow channel. She squirted antiseptic water on it, removed the blood. Harry was looking at her, smiling. He shook his head. *This is nothing*, his shrug told her.

When she had cleaned the wound she used an antiseptic pad to cover it. Fixed it in place with tape. No blood oozed from underneath the pad. She put her mouth close to his ear. It was the only way he'd hear her with the infernal gunfire continuing.

'Don't use your left arm. Not before we get back.'

'It's OK. I heard you. Thanks.'

A blasting explosion shook the ground under their feet. Now greandes were being hurled from the barge at random. Then the explosions ceased. She looked up.

The barge had turned away from the embankment, was heading towards midriver. All around them the cluster of trees they had sheltered under were shattered. Paula, knowing she'd not be seen now, stood up. The barge was heading straight for Westminster Bridge, the prize target.

The SAS unit was stationed nearer the target, to the left of where the SIS sheltered. Sarge was now able to adjust his large mortar, using its laser beam to aim the bomb. He looked at his subordinate, saw he was rapidly adjusting the angle of the missile launcher. He nodded.

The huge shell sailed towards its target, dropped neatly down the main hatch. At the same moment the missile whipped out of its muzzle, landed on the smaller weapon at the bows.

Paula felt sure the massive explosion was greater than she had witnessed with the first barge. The vessel shook from stem to stern. Flames lit up the river, then dense clouds of black smoke drifted above the flames. The barge began to heel over to starboard.

In the deckhouse Ali was badly shaken, but nothing in his

expression showed. He realized the entire barge would be going down. He turned to the skipper he had taken over from.

'I have to leave to check the other barges. You are now in command . . .'

He shinned down the rope ladder still attached to the stern. The small speedboat had been moored above the rudder. His assistant was already inside the speedboat, ready to operate the controls. Ali lost his calm for a brief moment. He shouted at his assistant.

'Get us the hell out of here. Back to Barge No. 4, my original command post.'

'Immediately,' said the assistant, who had cut the mooring rope. He started up the engine, swung the speedboat away from the huge vessel which was turning turtle. Ali pushed him aside, grabbed the wheel.

'You forgot. For the sake of Allah we *zig-zag*.'

50

'Everybody into the jeeps. Move if you value your lives.'

There was an urgency in Sarge's communication Paula had never heard before. Our on the river the barge was still wallowing above the surface. She tried to help Harry as they rushed to the jeeps. He smiled, pushed her away.

'I can get there. Shoulder just aches a bit. I can use both hands to operate a sub-machine gun . . .'

Everyone was inside a jeep in record time, even carrying their satchels and weapons. The SAS unit had already swept past under Lambeth Bridge. She looked back as Tweed rammed down his foot on the accelerator. She then realized the foresight Sarge had shown, the reason for his urgency.

The full length of the barge suddenly sank swiftly deep down into the river. Its descent, so swift, added to its weight, divided the river briefly. She felt sure she had a glimpse of the river bed. Then two monster waves swept towards each bank, struck them like a cyclone, hurling unknown tons of water across the embankment and up the sides beyond the pavement. They would have been inundated. She sighed with relief as they sped under the bridge and the river became normal.

There would have been no time for the crowds of men aboard to leave. They were now entombed in the sunken barge lying on the river bed.

The Arab commander of the three remaining barges, proceeding upriver, Sarge correctly guessed, would not try the same trick again. Sarge simply moved his three firing points closer to the target bridges, but far enough away so they would not be touched by his own bombs exploding.

Two barges were sunk by his bombs. They sank slowly, giving al-Qa'eda time to lower men in dinghies. But this time, on Ali's orders, they headed towards the right bank. None of them reached the shore alive. Buchanan's anti-terrorist squad killed them all while they were still on the river.

Barge No. 5, with Ali now aboard, assigned to destroy Chelsea Bridge, received its bomb and missile as soon as it was well clear of the bridge, earlier than Ali had expected.

The vessel burst into flames along its whole length. The Arabs in dinghies, who had fled the barge, again headed for the right bank. Again, Buchanan's men, some using flame-throwers for the first time, killed all the Arabs before any came near the river bank.

The barge, which must have carried a large reserve of ammo, suddenly blew up. The deckhouse was hurled into the sky, fell back into the river, disappearing with a sinister hiss. Other sections flew skywards, descended, to be swallowed up by the fast-flowing river. Buchanan later congratulated his men on doing a great job.

Despite all his other responsibilities, Buchanan had not forgotten the captive guard at Dick's wharf. He disagreed with the decision that they should not risk rescuing Proctor.

After all it was his city, his side of the river. Therefore he gave careful instructions to Sergeant Mackie, marksman. Marler was recognized as being the top marksman in Europe, but Mackie was number two.

Earlier, Mackie, his rifle strapped over his shoulder, had cycled to Dick's wharf. Marler would have admired how silently Mackie moved when he reached his objective. He had descended to the main building where lights shone in a large office. Peering through a window, he saw Proctor tied to a chair. He also saw the brute of a guard armed with an automatic.

The last barge, destined to target Albert Bridge, was still moored to the wharf. As Mackie watched he saw the guard go to a window, peer down at the barge where men were removing mooring ropes. It was about to sail.

Mackie tested the window, was surprised to find it was not locked. Al-Qa'eda's security was not perfect. The guard had his back towards him, watching the crew below, as Mackie slowly pushed the window open, inch by inch. Hinges well oiled.

One of the crew on the wharf beckoned to the guard, pointed to a rope ladder slung over the side of the hull, the escape route. The guard came back into the room, checked his automatic. He then walked behind Proctor, raised the gun to lay it alongside Proctor's head.

Mackie coughed. The guard swung round, removing his weapon from Proctor's head. Mackie shot him twice – once in the head just in case he was wearing a bullet-proof jacket – then in the back below the left shoulder-blade. The guard toppled down forward, hitting the wooden floor with a thud.

Mackie climbed inside, ran to the prone guard, kicked away the automatic close to his hand. Bending down, he checked the carotid artery. Nothing. Dead as a dodo. He turned to Proctor, who had a dazed expression.

'Don't worry. I'm British anti-terrorist squad. Let's get these ropes off you. Expect you'll want to call your wife.'

51

'No sign of the SAS jeeps,' Harry called out.

Paula had helped him up into the rear of the jeep driven by Tweed. She looked back. Harry was right. There were three jeeps behind them but they carried the rest of Tweed's team. Beyond that there was empty embankment as they headed for Albert Bridge. Driving with one hand, Tweed reached for his radio-telephone, hoping it had not been disconnected.

'Sarge, any hope of saving Albert?'

'Sorry. None. We have used up our special equipment. Only just come into service. I raided the store. Keep well clear of Albert. I leave it to you and Buchanan to deal with any enemy who might survive. My unit has been proud to cooperate with yours. Until next time . . .'

Then the connection was broken. The SAS had gone, as invisibly as they had arrived. Paula caught a glimpse of police cars racing along the opposite bank, keeping pace with Tweed's unit.

'I at least want to see Albert,' she said.

'But not too close,' Tweed warned.

'At least we've saved five out of six major bridges,' Newman commented over the phone, which was independent, had earlier been linked with Sarge's communication system.

Tweed parked close to the Chelsea Royal Hospital area. The other three jeeps pulled up behind him. He jumped out, went back to them.

'I am now giving you a direct order. You will stay here and go no closer to the bridge. You probably heard Sarge's warning. We can do nothing to save Albert. But, as Newman said, five out of six major bridges saved is a good score.'

'We may be able to take a few more of them,' said Harry, now standing beside Tweed, his sub-machine gun tucked under his right arm.

'It's coming now,' Paula shouted.

On the opposite shore Buchanan stood outside the lead police car. Many vehicles were parked behind him. The dreadful silence had returned, the silence Paula found so eerie. She was standing on the embankment, holding her camera. She knew the pictures she would take would be horrific but she felt she needed a record. She took two quickly.

The sixth barge, which had, according to plan, left Dick's wharf so late, was hardly moving as its bows thrust under Albert Bridge, reminding Paula of the snout of some monstrous shark.

In the deckhouse Ali was controlling the barge's momentum with great care. He had fled in his speedboat back to the last barge when he realized his operation had ended in disaster. And Abdullah had promised it would make the Trade Center operation in New York look like child's play.

He reversed the engines briefly, to halt the barge with the main hatch under the centre of the bridge. Then he ran out, along the deck, dropped down the ladder into the main hatch. He threw away the ladder.

He was going to press the two buttons for detonation himself. Ali would die with his remaining men. He stared round at the men with him on the base of the hull. They were kneeling on their prayer-mats, facing east.

Ali took a deep breath. Then pressed the first button, then the second. The huge shell-like bomb streaked upwards, aimed at the the centre of the bridge. He clasped his hands in prayer, his last movement.

Gazing through the viewfinder of her camera, Paula saw a huge object hurtling upwards. A brief vision. Then the world exploded. Deafening thunder rolled down the river. A swift blinding flash.

The entire centre of the bridge shattered, great sections of it hurtling into the sky, taking for ever to descend and disappear under the water. Waves rolled towards both shores. Fragments of white-painted railing hurtled up even higher to greater altitudes. Chunks of masonry the size of huge boulders flew across the embankment, crashed into the houses in the Cheyne Walk area. The initial ear-splitting crash when the bomb hit had died down. Now they could hear the masonry fragments hitting buildings like a bombardment. On both sides of the river. A lot of black smoke obscured the wreckage which had once been a bridge. The a breeze blowing downriver cleared the smoke, revealing the ghastly spectacle of the remnants of the bridge which had spanned the Thames for so many years.

Paula could take no more photos. She stood staring, camera held in hand by her side. The barge had gone as if it had never existed. Confined under the bridge, it had taken the full force of the devastating explosion. Later its entire savaged hull was found on the river bed.

Only one section of the bridge still seemed intact. On the left bank side a third of the span perched over nothing. Tweed pressed his binoculars to his eyes. Just in time to see the span wobble, give way, plunge down into the river. Albert Bridge was no more than a memory.

'Well,' Newman said, 'now we can see what we saved the other major five bridges. London would have been bisected for years.'

Paula turned away. She no longer wished to look. As she did so she heard on her headset Buchanan's firm voice.

'I think everyone might like to know Proctor, the hostage

401

guard at Dick's wharf, was rescued. Alive and well, he's on his way home to meet his wife.'

'Thank God,' Paula whispered.

52

During the long, slow, circuitous drive back to Park Crescent Newman sat next to Harry, behind Paula. He explained he'd handed over the wheel of his jeep to Beaurain. After this remark no one spoke for a long time. Tweed broke the silence when they were close to Park Crescent.

'Tomorrow we all have to keep our appointment with Warner at Carpford. It is only polite to do so.'

'So we can all come with you?' checked Paula.

'Yes, everyone. I don't think he's expecting anyone except me, but he'll have to put up with that. We were all part of what happened.'

'Forecast is for a clear sunny day tomorrow,' Newman said cheerfully, then shut up.

He didn't think Paula would appreciate the remark. From the way she was sitting, motionless, he guessed her mind was on what they had seen during the last moments of Albert Bridge. He thought of something else.

'Interesting that this time no dinghies were lowered. None of al-Qa'eda survived.'

'No they didn't.' Paula's tone of voice was a mix of cynicism and contempt. 'They thought they were on their way to heaven – where seventy-two beautiful young girls would be waiting, available. They've got a hope.'

'Just before everything blew up,' Newman began, 'through my binoculars I saw a slim, intelligent-looking man run from the deckhouse to the main hatch. Struck me he

403

could well have been the mastermind behind the whole operation.'

'Maybe,' said Tweed. 'While I remember, travelling with us to Warner's meeting tomorrow we shall be taking Billy Hogarth and Margesson with us. So you know, Bob, how many four-wheel-drives we'll need.'

'Billy Hogarth and Margesson?' queried Paula. 'Why?'

'Because they live in Carpford.'

'Oh, I see,' she said. But in fact she didn't.

'Well, at least,' Newman said, 'there won't be any more of those disappearances. I wonder what did happen to those people. Such a strange mixture.'

'One other thing,' Tweed said as they reached Baker Street, a stone's throw from Park Crescent. 'I've invited Buchanan to join our party tomorrow. He played a great part in what was achieved. So add him to your list, Bob.'

'Quite a party then.'

Approaching Park Crescent, Tweed eased the jeep on to the pavement. It was the only way to get there. The road was solid with traffic bumper to bumper, and nothing moving. A uniformed policeman rushed up to him, furiously indignant.

'You can't do that. The pavement is for pedestrians. I'm going to have to . . .'

He stopped in mid-sentence. He had just noticed the yellow flag waving on Tweed's bonnet. He swallowed, saluted.

'Sorry, sir. We've been told to watch out for you. Hold on just a tick . . .'

He turned round, began ushering pedestrians to move back. He was not popular but he was firm. He gradually cleared the pavement back to the entrance to the Crescent. Tweed thanked him. The policeman saluted again.

'Who's that?' a Cockney voice called out. 'I don't think . . .'

'He's probably the most important man in Great Britain at the moment,' the policeman shouted.

'Come through on the grapevine,' Newman suggested.

'From Buchanan,' Tweed corrected.

'Anyone else except Warner expected to be at Carpford?' Paula enquired.

'Yes,' he told her. 'The apparently clownish Palfry. Also Eva Brand.'

'I predict I'm going to be bored stiff,' she replied.

'Odd you should say that. Your predictions are normally so accurate.'

53

It was a brilliantly sunny morning when they reached
Carpford. An icy nip in the air. No fog. Not a trace of mist.
Carp Lake was a blue still sheet, like glass. Paula sat beside
Tweed, driving the four-wheel-drive. In the back Newman
sat beside Billy Hogarth, as though guarding him.

In the vehicle close behind them Nield was driving
with Harry next to him. In the back sat Buchanan with
Margesson next to him. Again like a guard.

The rear vehicle was driven by Marler. Travelling alone.
A characteristic arrangement. Paula experienced a pang as
Tweed drove round the curve with a rock outcrop. This was
where Linda Warner had mysteriously disappeared, never
to be seen again.

Tweed alighted as they reached Garda. He walked up
to the heavy studded door, was about to press the bell
when the door was opened. Eva Brand, clad in black
trousers and a long loose black jacket, smiled, gave a
small bow.

'Please come in. He is waiting for you. I see you have
company. Maybe everyone would like to join you. Hello,
Paula. You are looking very serious.'

'I suppose it's after what happened yesterday.'

'Yesterday. Of course . . .'

She waited by the door as everyone followed Tweed and
Paula, like a crocodile. She smiled at Beaurain, closed the
door when they were all inside. Paula was struck by the

407

luxury of the interior – the furnishing, the gilt-framed portraits on the wall. She recognized Wellington.

Arriving at the door to Warner's spacious study, Eva gave him a warning. 'Your guests have arrived.'

'Guests?'

The Minister was seated behind a large Georgian desk in an imposing throne-like chair covered with tapestry. He sat close to the panelled wall behind him. Clad in a formal dark business suit, he stared as everyone entered. Peering over his pince-nez, he gazed at two of his visitors.

'I fail to see why Mr Hogarth and Mr Margesson have come with you.'

'They are your neighbours,' Tweed said easily. 'I have brought them back from London.' He looked across at Palfry, standing a distance away from the desk, also formally clad. 'You did not tell me your assistant would be here. So we have both taken liberties. Can we proceed with the – was it inquest you called this?'

'It was.'

Buchanan had taken up a position, standing, near the leaded light windows. From here he could see everyone. Beaurain stood alongside him. Eva had positioned herself in a far corner, hands in the pockets of her jacket. She had guided Hogarth and Margesson close to her. Everyone was standing. They had not been asked to sit down. Paula was perched against the back of a couch which faced the windows, so she also could see most of the occupants.

The large study was cheerful with the sun shining outside. So Paula wondered why she sensed a sinister atmosphere. Her right hand was close to her shoulder-bag, within inches of her Browning.

'You lost Albert Bridge,' Warner said acidly.

'True,' agreed Tweed. 'But we saved five other bridges, key bridges. With support from the SAS.'

'Why wasn't I informed of their presence?'

408

'Presumably their commander thought it unnecessary. The SAS work in great secrecy.'

'The Cabinet won't like that, won't like it at all.'

'So why did I receive a note of congratulations and thanks sent by courier this morning from the PM himself?'

'That would be purely a political communication,' sneered Palfry.

'I don't recall asking your opinion,' Tweed said quietly, staring hard at the speaker.

Palfry looked uncertain how to reply. He turned to look at Warner for help. At that moment the door opened and a servant appeared. She was looking nervous.

'Sir, we have another visitor. Mr Drew Franklin.'

She had hardly finished speaking before Franklin practically pushed her aside. He told her she could go now, that this was a private meeting. As she left he walked further in, looked round, went over to stand near Eva.

'I knew you'd not want to discuss this without me,' he told Warner in his most arrogant voice.

'Of course not.' Warner was obviously taken aback by this new arrival. He recovered quickly. 'You know, Drew, you are always welcome.'

'Very diplomatic of you, Victor. You can think fast on your feet, I'll give you that. You can even do it sitting down. What is the purpose of this meeting?' Drew demanded.

'From my point of view it is to identify the mastermind who planned this damnable al-Qa'eda attack,' Tweed plunged in. He glanced at Palfry and Eva. 'Master criminal might be a better description. That person is in this room now.'

'What the devil do you mean?' rasped Warner, looking at Palfry and Eva, where he had noticed Tweed staring.

'At an early stage,' Tweed explained, 'I developed the suspicion that Carpford was the original base for a number of al-Qa'eda killers. So strategic. They would be landed

409

from small ships at a remote beach where transport would be waiting for them. Then along the A268 passing close to Northiam and across a series of country roads which eventually brought them here to Carpford. These movements always at night. But where could they install each group in comfort and secrecy – prior to their moving on to Oldhurst Farm near Milton Keynes? Why – in Mr Palfry's very large house which has many bedrooms on the upper floor. Where in one room we found twenty sleeping-bags piled up . . .'

'This is outrageous!' Palfry burst out. 'I do not see why I should listen to any more of this nonsense . . .'

'Those sleeping-bags will be examined by forensic experts,' Tweed continued remorselessly, 'and I have little doubt they will find fibres, hairs which never came from a European.'

'I'm leaving . . .' Palfry began, his faced twisted in fury.

'I don't think so,' said Buchanan.

He grasped Palfry, who had started to walk, twisted his arms behind him, produced a pair of handcuffs. In the silence Paula clearly heard of the click of the handcuffs locking.

'You don't have to say a word . . .' Buchanan began, continuing to read him his rights and informing him he could make one phone call for a lawyer.

'I don't want a friggin' lawyer,' Palfry screamed.

'I think a period of calm would help this situation no end,' Warner suggested, staring at Palfry. 'From what I gather, Superintendent, you have no actual proof yet for this extraordinary accusation. I was a lawyer before I entered politics.'

'We have probable cause to treat Mr Palfry as a suspect in a crime almost without precedent,' Buchanan retorted.

'Don't you need a warrant?' Warner enquired.

'It does help,' Buchanan agreed. He produced a document from his pocket. 'So I obtained one. It gives me

410

permission to search Peregrine Palfry's house. I can understand your reluctance, Minister, to accept your assistant would be involved with al-Qa'eda, but he certainly provided accommodation for at least twenty of them, maybe more over a period. He acted as halfway house from the coast to Oldhurst Farm.'

'And where, may I ask,' Warner demanded caustically, 'is this place?'

'I told you,' Buchanan continued, 'it is near Milton Keynes. It is where five stolen milk wagons were used to transport the shell-like bombs destined to destroy six major bridges over the Thames. At the farm the bombs were transferred inside small white vans which would take them to the banks of the Thames.'

'Sounds a most ingenious plan,' Warner commented, staring over his pince-nez with cold eyes at Palfry.

'But then,' Tweed broke in, standing with his hands in his overcoat pockets, 'there is the mysterious flight which Drew took to Cairo quite a while ago. And on that flight he had a companion – Miss Brand. They flew on to Tel Aviv before returning via Cairo. Who, I wonder, were they going to meet?'

As he spoke, Tweed swung round. His grim gaze swept over Franklin and Eva. Drew, compact and neatly dressed as always, stared back at him with a hostile expression. By his side Eva stood very erect, her beautiful face showing nothing of her reaction.

'Now this is getting interesting,' remarked Warner.

'Very interesting indeed,' Tweed agreed. He now held the attention of everyone in the room. He turned round again. 'Mr Margesson, I think it is time we gave you the opportunity to tell us what you know.'

Margesson, looking very different wearing a business suit, stepped forward. When he spoke his voice was no longer that of a lofty preacher. He looked alternately at Tweed and Warner as he began.

411

'Victor Warner paid frequent visits to my house at night. We have had many long conversations. When I use the word "conversations" I mean he talked, I listened. He has a most forceful manner. I realize now, after my night in London away from here, that living alone I was susceptible to what he said. So much so I came to believe him.'

'So what did he say?' Tweed asked, encouraging him.

'He felt Western society had collapsed, that it no longer had any moral structure. That the so-called liberation of women was to blame. Morals had been thrown out of the window, the divorce rate was soaring, everyone behaved as they felt urges. Married men went with other women, women were worse, going with other men when the mood took them. Married women. He thought the only salvation lay in the East. Muslim women kept their place, would walk three paces behind their husbands, covered themselves with clothing and veils, so avoiding the attentions of men. Discipline was a word he often used. He wished to impose the Muslim system on the West.'

'Fundamentalist Muslimism?' Tweed suggested.

'Oh, he used that first word frequently,' Margesson replied. 'I found myself absorbing his views, his language, believing in it. Now I know I was used.'

'Used how?' Tweed enquired.

'He needed someone he could bounce his ideas off. I feel he is a lonely man, under permanent pressure.'

'You do realize this man is as mad as a hatter,' Warner said quietly. 'He should be in an asylum,' he went on as he polished his pince-nez, then perched them back on the bridge of his hooked nose.

'It's a thought,' Tweed agreed. 'The trouble is we have another witness with damning evidence. Billy Hogarth.' He turned to Hogarth. 'Would you describe to us what you saw on the night Paula Grey was attacked and imprisoned?'

'I saw it clearly.'

Billy was a less confident speaker than Margesson. He

hesitated. Tweed made no effort to prod him to continue.

'A friend who visited Israel gave me a pair of night glasses,' Billy went on. 'Being on my own I often used them to scan the village. I was doing so on the night you are talking about. I didn't know what to do, so I did nothing.'

'After you have witnessed what?' Tweed prompted.

'I saw Miss Grey call at Drew Franklin's house after dark. Drew came to the door. I had the impression their conversation was short.'

'Gerald,' Tweed said suddenly. 'Enjoy the Bahamas?'

'Beautiful . . .' Warner stopped suddenly, his expression panicky.

'Meet Gerald Hanover, financier and master planner for al-Qa'eda. Please go on,' Tweed urged Billy Hogarth.

'She was leaving Drew's house,' Billy explained. 'I think she had decided to return to her car parked in Mrs Gobble's shed.'

Billy paused, as though recalling something which had scared him. Taking a deep breath he continued.

'As she started to walk off, the front door of this house opened. A huge man wearing a black turban appeared, crept up behind her, hit her on the back of her head. He carried her unconscious body back inside this house.'

'He's potty,' Warner burst out. 'Pecksniff chose some strange people to occupy rented houses. And you've lost *your* mind, Tweed. Gerald Hanover indeed. Who the hell is he?'

'You are. Master planner and financier of al-Qa'eda. We have witnesses in the Bahamas who identified you from photos airmailed to the Bahamas,' he fibbed. 'Better still, we have the evidence of Billy Hogarth about Paula's kidnapping. Billy, you are sure it was *this* house Paula was carried into?'

'Quite sure,' Billy replied emphatically. 'Garda is set

413

apart from Drew's house. So the brute walked a short distance to get here, carrying Miss Grey's limp body to this house. Saw it clearly.'

'He's simple-minded,' Warner raved. 'A fairy-tale.'

'There is one way to prove it,' Buchanan said in a stern voice. 'You may have heard two cars pull up outside. Police cars with trained searchers and forensic experts. Miss Grey gave us a detailed description of the cellar where she was held before, showing great courage, she escaped. We will soon find that cellar if it is under our feet.'

'No, you won't!' Warner had jumped up behind his desk. 'You cannot search this property which is owned by a Minister of the Crown.'

'But we can,' Buchanan informed him. 'I have warrants in my pocket to search every property in this village. Including this one.'

He walked forward, dropped a long folded document on Warner's desk. Then he retreated to his original position at the back of the room. Warner opened the document, read it very swiftly. He looked up with a self-important smile.

'This is signed by a judge everyone knows is senile.'

'It is still a valid search warrant.'

'What the devil do you expect to find?' snapped Warner.

'Possibly the horrible cellar where Miss Grey was held. We are also interested in discovering the bodies of five people who have disappeared. Including that of your wife.'

'Then I have something here which will make you change your mind.'

He unlocked a drawer, ferreted among a collection of files. He then stood up. In his right hand he held a .455 Colt automatic. He aimed it at Paula's chest. Newman withdrew his hand, empty, from inside his jacket where his Smith & Wesson was holstered.

'You will all leave this house immediately,' Warner ordered. 'All except Miss Paula Grey.'

414

'No, we won't,' am icy voice spoke.

Eva Brand was walking forward towards the desk, a Beretta automatic gripped in her right hand, steady as a rock, Paula observed. Eva paused within ten feet of the Minister.

The tone of her voice, her expression, were almost frightening.

'Attempt to shoot Paula,' she continued, 'and I'll put a bullet into that evil head of yours.'

54

A stand-off, Newman thought. Two guns, each aimed point-blank at a different target. Dangerous. Eva's 6.35mm Beretta. It was a light weapon, but fired at close range it would crush Warner's skull, kill him.

'Eva,' Warner said with the hint of a tremble. 'Why?'

As he spoke he was careful to keep his Colt aimed at Paula, a clever move to freeze everyone else in the room. With her left hand Eva reached inside her jacket, took out a newspaper cutting, dropped it on his desk. Tweed recognized it as the strange, much delayed obituary notice Newman had extracted from the *Daily Nation*.

'What is this?' Warner asked, his voice weaker.

He made no attempt to look down. He was too concerned with keeping Paula under his gun.

'An obituary of a man who died two years ago in Yemen,' Eva told him. 'Captain Charles Hobart. Remember him? Don't say you don't. I'll pull the trigger.'

'Vaguely.' He hastened to amplify. 'It's coming back to me. A . . . casualty. A . . . Special Forces . . . officer.'

'Yemen,' Eva repeated in the same disturbing monotone. 'A mission to kill an al-Qa'eda unit in the desert. One man volunteered to wipe it out. He could have done. Except he was betrayed. You were there when it happened. You'd just been appointed Minister of Security. You out-ranked the unit's commander. You secretly sent a message warning al-Qa'eda he was coming. Alone. So they killed him. An ambush. Killed my father . . .'

'Hobart . . . you are . . . Eva Brand.'

'No, I am Eva Hobart. Before leaving Medfords to get a job close to you I changed my name by deed poll. The Director of Medfords, a friend, agreed to keep quiet. I know you were the mastermind controlling the attack on London. I can prove it.'

'Im . . . poss . . . ible.'

Again Eva used her left hand to reach inside her jacket. She produced a folded sheet of paper, dropped it on his desk. Once more Warner dare not look down. Had to keep his eye on Paula, his Colt still aimed at her chest.

'That,' Eva told him, 'is the first coded message which I told you I had never received. So another was sent to you. It's in Arabic, but not from the Embassy – instead from an address in Cairo. I decoded it, then told you it had never arrived. Want to know what it says? Top Secret.'

'You had no right . . .'

'Shut your treacherous trap. It reads, "Happy to hear attack on London is imminent. That it will be greater than September 11."'

'There must . . . be a . . . mistake.'

'No mistake. It was addressed to you. "For your eyes only."'

'You decoded it . . . wrongly.'

'Victor, I was very fond of my father. He meant everything to me. When I flew with Drew to Cairo I talked to Sergeant Langford, retired now, but a key NCO with the unit in Yemen. He overheard you talking in Arabic in a tent on a phone – Langford is fluent in Arabic. He heard you say that one man only, a Captain Hobart, was coming to eliminate them the next day. Langford decided he couldn't report it because who would believe him? He's now flying to London to report to Drew, under oath, what he heard. Drew will publish. You are going down.'

418

'You bitch . . .'

'Superintendent Buchanan, could you come alongside me? But don't attempt to grab my pistol. I can fire instantly.' She used her left hand to extract something from a pocket. 'Mr Tweed, I would sooner you came to me.'

Tweed approached slowly, stood beside her while Warner kept his Colt aimed at Paula. She asked Tweed to hold out his hand, dropped a small key into it. Tweed went back to where he had been standing.

'Victor Warner is a master planner,' Eva went on. 'I will give him that. He also was the planner behind September 11. That key opens a secret drawer in the *side* of his desk. I managed to open it while Warner was in Cabinet. Medford training. In that drawer you will find a mass of material – a big airline timetable, American, listing all major flights. All those long distance, carrying a huge petrol load, are marked in blue. In red are marked the flights used from Boston and Newark on September 11. Al-Qa'eda trained the killers. Warner planned the routes . . .'

'I should kill you,' screamed Warner.

'You want a bullet in the head now?'

Warner, still aiming the Colt at Paula, began backing away from his desk. He soon reached the panelled wall. He used his left elbow to press against it. A section slid back like a secret door. Beyond was a tunnel. As he dived into it, Eva fired. The bullet hit the panelling.

'Missed,' Newman said to himself.

Eva, like a panther stalking its prey, slipped over to the door, disappeared into the tunnel. Paula ran forward, was thrust aside by Tweed, then by Newman. The tunnel, wide and tall, the floor stone-paved, sloped down. Warner was running when Eva fired again.

'Missed,' Newman repeated to himself.

At the end of the tunnel was an opening, daylight. Pressing the hidden button on the panelling in the study opened doors at both ends. Warner's tall figure was leaping down

419

the tunnel, Eva not far behind. She fired again. 'Missed,' Newman repeated.

It was Paula who caught on to what was happening. She caught up with Newman, spoke in a quiet voice.

'She's missing deliberately, driving him into something.'

Warner reached the opening, was diving through it, when Eva fired again. The bullet hit the top of the opening. Newman grunted. The fourth shot. Three more bullets left in her Beretta. Both Tweed and Newman had guns in their hands but dare not use them for fear of hitting Eva. Suddenly they emerged into the open. It was misty at this level. Eva fired her fifth shot. It landed close enough to chip the edge of Warner's right shoe.

He panicked, tearing down the slope into the mist, followed by the others. Eva stopped, fired carefully. The bullet chipped the edge of Warner's other shoe. The mist thinned so they saw what happened.

Warner suddenly realized he had reached the brink of the lime pit. Too late. He lost his balance. He screamed as he plunged into the pit. His pursuers stood stock still, frozen by the sight. Warner managed to heave the upper part of his body upwards, smeared with lime. He waved his arms desperately, screamed again. His body was sucked down into the pit. With only his head above the whiteness, he opened his mouth to scream again. He swallowed lime. The scream came out as '*Goo . . . ch*! Then the head went under and where he had gone down the surface of the lime swirled for a few seconds, then settled.

Epilogue

It was three weeks later.

Tweed was holding a meeting in his office. Present were Paula, Beaurain and Newman. The end of February was going out in a blaze of sunlight, a clear blue sky. In front of him Tweed had a sheaf of several reports. Airsight had provided several photos of Carpford. Paula's comment on their belated arrival was caustic.

'These reports are from Professor Saafeld, the pathologist,' Tweed began. 'As you know, Buchanan dropped the idea of searching for the missing bodies under the quarry, accepted my suggestion that it was the lime pit which should be cleared. This he achieved quickly, with the help of experts and specialist equipment. It can't have been pleasant.'

'Did he find everyone?' Paula asked quietly.

'He did. Six corpses. Some of them, to quote Saafeld, "little more than skeletons". But the brilliant Saafeld, with help from Paula, has identified them all. The first one, not surprisingly, was Victor Warner's – in good condition. He even had that pince-nez jammed to his nose.'

'A bit late, I've realized that photo of someone in Arab dress taken at Finsbury mosque is Victor Warner,' Paula remarked. 'Any trace of Linda Warner?' she enquired anxiously.

'Yes. Almost decomposed. He identified her by the two rings on the finger of her left hand – by the descriptions I gave him. Jasper Buller was in a bad state but amazingly enough his leather wallet, crammed with identification, was preserved.'

'And Mrs Gobble?' Paula asked. 'That dear old lady?'

'She was the second victim, so I was out of sequence. What remained of her corpse was identified by a string of blue beads she wore. Still attached to what, I fear, was little more than a skeleton. Again Paula helped Saafeld, since she'd described the blue beads she'd seen on Mrs Gobble when she visited her shop. Then there was Pecksniff, the crooked lawyer. Paula's description of him helped, plus the fact that his large watch-chain was still hanging loose from what was left of him. The last corpse to be hurled in was Martin Hogarth's after he committed suicide. Easily identified.'

'What a gruesome business,' Paula commented.

'Well,' said Tweed, reviewing the case, 'I did suspect Victor Warner early on. I knew his wife, Linda, and she was both intelligent, patriotic and had her wits about her. I tried to think of who she would stop for in her car on that isolated road. For no one, knowing her. Then it struck me the only person she would have stopped for was her husband, parked in a car coming the other way, blocking the road. But that was only a theory – not evidence. Then Victor Warner began throwing road blocks in my way on several occasions.'

'Jules,' said Paula. '*Decoy.*'

'I must admit,' agreed Beaurain, 'that the Minister seemed to hinder rather than help Tweed's investigation.'

'Victor Warner was a fanatic,' Tweed said grimly. 'Converted to Muslim Fundamentalism, he was ruthless, without pity. He murdered continually to close any loopholes which might give away his plan. I can only guess, but I'm sure that was why he murdered his wife. Linda discovered what he was up to and was going to expose him. His

422

solution? Kill her. And the method of disposing of the bodies was diabolical.'

'The trolley on a rail line inside the tunnel I escaped on,' said Paula.

'Exactly. The victims were first shot by a bullet in the back of the head. Saafeld discovered the fracture it made on several corpses. He even found a bullet lodged inside Jasper Buller's brain. The body was then placed on the trolley, accompanied by one of his thugs who used the brake. Once it reached the end of the tunnel it was not far to carry the corpse and hurl it into the lime pit.'

'Which is what would have happened to me had I not escaped,' Paula said quietly. 'And strange how it was Eva Brand who detonated the climax. She had her justified revenge. So ironic that Warner perished in the same way as his victims.' She checked her watch. 'If you'll excuse me, I'm having lunch with Eva, so I'd better go . . .'

'The government was crazy to try and hush this up,' Newman remarked. 'A spin operation which left them dizzy. What crushed them was the discovery of the bodies in the lime pit.'

'Plus,' Tweed added, 'the fact that Palfry committed suicide while being held, pending trial, in Belmarsh prison. He must have been easy for Warner to manipulate. Then there was the secret drawer in Warner's desk Eva gave me the key to. I spent a whole night going through the material at my flat.'

'What did you find?' asked Beaurain.

'The plan to destroy the six bridges over the Thames. Different suggestions as to the base to be used, ending up with choosing Dick's wharf. But there was more. Complete detailed plans for how to carry out the September 11 atrocity in New York. Warner planned that. Significant that he flew to New York, then to Boston, just before and after the frightful attack on the World Trade Center. After photocopying everything myself, I sent all the originals to the States, to Cord Dillon, recently appointed from Deputy Director to Director of the CIA.' He paused. 'In addition the details of a second new attack planned on certain targets in the States. Also sent to Dillon.'

'With the PM's permission, I imagine?'

'Exactly. Now the rumours are growing that the government is about to fall. Strictly between us, the PM said he'd be glad to go.'

'I did hear,' Newman said tentatively, 'that Eva Brand might be joining us.'

'I'm seriously considering it. She has the experience, the brains, the character.'

'Won't that possibly put Paula in a hostile mood? With your having Eva also by your side?'

'If I decide to take her on she'll spend time down the Crescent in Communications.'

'But,' Newman persisted, 'she'll be coming round here a lot.'

'So I'm considering it,' Tweed replied.

'Don't fool me.' Newman chuckled. 'You've already made up your damned mind.'